1

How do we know?

2

ISBN: 9781926820118

Printed and retailed: Lulu.com

Wholesale: Ingram books

Webzines of Vancouver

2901 – 969 Richards Street

Vancouver B.C. Canada

V6B 1A8

.anthropologising.ca/webzines/webzines

By the Same Author

Island Administration in the South West Pacific

Changing Melanesia: The social economics of culture change

In Search of Wealth: A study of the emergence of commercial operations in the Melanesian society of South Eastern Papua

The Great Village: The economic and social welfare of Hanuabada an urban community in Papua

With H. Hawthorn and S. Jamieson: The Indians of British Columbia

Under the Ivi Tree[1]: Society and economic growth in rural Fiji.

The Conditions of Social Performance: An exploratory theory.

From Traditional Exchange to Modern Markets (also in Portuguese, Spanish and Indonesian)

Towers Besieged: The dilemma of the creative university

The Sorcerer's Apprentice: An anthropology of public policy.

The Complete Good Dining Guide to Vancouver Restaurants

From Youth Maturity to Global Government

Choosing our Destiny

Remuera: Memories of a New Zealand boy between the wars

Bumps on a Long Road: Essays from an Anthropologist's Memory – 2 vols

---

[1] Pronounced "eevee"

Fixing the World: An anthropologist considers our future: Anthropology, holism and innovation theory provide answers.

Publisher's note.

The contents of this volume have been scanned and adapted from a variety of originals.

How do we Know?

Applying theories and methods for Anthropology.

Cyril Belshaw

Webzines

Vancouver 2011

7

Contents

<u>Why?</u>

As I look back over the past years from the vantage point of advanced age I realize that many of my favourite papers have been published in locations which mainstream anthropologists, and particularly graduate students, seldom consult. My ego tells me that they have something to say to some of those graduate students as they grapple with the strategies of their own ideas. So here I put together a collection and to round out the volume add a few papers which may be somewhat better known but may have some historical interest.

The papers deal with aspects of theory. In some instances they use data to arrive at a theoretical proposition. In others they apply theory to inform the data. In my conception of theory some colleagues may find me idiosyncratic, but I stick to my position.

Considering the vast amount of anthropology writing there is remarkably little of what I call theory. Most ethnographies are *interpretations* of the data, and discussions frequently centre on whether those interpretations are persuasive or whether some other interpretation is more acceptable. The insights provided significantly influence the directions of anthropological thought and are taken up by scholars in other disciplines and often by the general public. Some of the concepts used are influential and essential elements in the anthropological toolbox – "culture", "endogamy", "cross cousin marriage" are among the many examples.

Yet to me, the interpretations themselves are matters of individual choice. I cannot find a clear cut methodology which would enable me to determine, objectively rather than subjectively, which interpretation should win the competition, irrespective my personal values.

I personally like the Popperian view which requires theory to consist of propositions which are written in a way which opens them to falsification, rebuttal, whether or not those rebuttals are in fact successful. In one of my ethnographies[2] I deliberately cast some of my chapters to arrive at perspectives which were indeed open to challenge.

---

[2] *Under the Ivi Tree*

And much to my pleasure a human geographer did just that with respect to one point, although I did not know of it for some time. Much of the book, however, was interpretation rather than theory.

Ideally the theoretical propositions should be combined in such a way as to constitute a coherent logical argument in which each proposition can be applied individually and challenged and as a result possibly amended. There is very little of this in anthropology. Indeed the only comprehensive attempt of which I know was that of S.F. Nadel[3]. I did make an exploratory attempt to produce a theory which addressed a significant practical issue – what do we need to know when we judge the success or otherwise of a political system?[4] Ironically, and without my sayso this was published in a sociological series and to some extent missed its intended anthropology audience.

Comparative data are one of the most useful tools, other than logic from basic assumptions, for the formation of theory. Using time comparisons for a given culture is one of the most used. Once upon a long time ago, well before the advent of functionalism and structuralism (which are methodological perspectives rather than theories)

[3] *The Theory of Social Structure*
[4] *The Conditions of Social Performance*

the issues of culture change were first and foremost in argument. Sat that time too, and for the same intellectual preoccupations, comparison *between* cultures was much in vogue. In both instances the methodologies used became scorned – they certainly had huge flaws. Nevertheless contemporary scholars of changes in culture should revisit them and draw out an array of theoretical propositions which, with today's methods, could be stimulating, tested, revised or scrapped, and offer possible ways to make sense of the subject.

Another approach to the advancement of theory consists in the deliberate attempt to make use of the rich harvest of ethnographical data to establish a theoretical position. Perhaps the most famous is that of Marcel Mauss[5] (not an anthropologist *per se* but with a huge influence on anthropological analysis). Then there is the acerbic work, in my view thoroughly justified, of Rodney Needham[6]. At much the same time Fred Eggan was advocating his method of controlled comparison.

There have of course been many other such comparative works. They are, however, seldom produced at the doctoral level. I suggest that a

---

[5] *Essai sur le don*
[6] *Structure and Sentiment, Rethinking Kinship and Marriage and much more*

revolution in graduate expectations is long overdue. Luckily for me, Raymond Firth allowed me to write a library doctoral thesis, which gave me the opportunity to coalesce some of my theoretical ideas. But even then he did so on the grounds that I had already been in touch with Melanesian society and had written about it, and when the thesis was done he announced "Now you must go and earn your spurs in the field." And later we have had the prolific examples of Mary Douglas and Maurice Godelier making use both of their field knowledge and comparative data..

This convention in my view is quite wrong. Doctoral students and their supervisors should be totally free to mine the immense body of anthropological data to produce comparative studies which advance theory. Otherwise the main value of anthropological field work and its resultant data is lost.

So to return to my question, Why? I hope that some of these essays at least will tempt some colleagues and graduate students to do a great deal better. Perhaps some will take up a theme, show it to be lacking in precision or reality, and carry on into new dimensions. My one regret is that I did not do more to develop these perspectives. But that is another story.

The Identification of Values in Anthropology

First published in the *American Journal of Sociology* volume 64, 1959

This paper sets out to examine some of the notions of "value" which are current in anthropology, to relate them, and to con☐sider the problems they set for the empirical identification of values in historical cultures. The treatment aims not at an exhaustive presentation but at highlighting a number of issues somewhat neglected in anthropol☐ogy. I shall use some economic concepts which, while useful to clarify thought, sug☐gest that the field is scattered with traps which we are unable, at the moment, to avoid.

The most systematic and influential ex☐ponent of a theory of value in anthropology today is undoubtedly Kluckhohn[7], who has gone so far as to state that values constitute systems which should be a subject of in☐quiry just as are cultures and social struc☐tures.[8] In most cases, however, this degree of

---

[7] C. K. M. Kluckhohn, "Value and ValueOrien☐tations in the Theory of Action," in *Toward a Gen☐eral*

systematic abstraction is not achieved, and values are thought of as elements of culture or of social structure.

In Kluckhohn's thought two separable ideas are brought together. In this presenta tion they are distinguished, and a third is added which, however, Kluckhohn re jects.

The essence of the first, the Type A approach, as expressed with great clarity by Nadel[9], is that values are *ideas about* worth whileness. As Nadel states, the conceptual index may vary (using scales such as "good —bad," "desired—not desired"). Such values are significant because of a relation ship to action or potential action. Kluck hohn holds that a value is a *conception* re lating to a code or standard. It implies the desirable—but just any kind of desire will not do: it must be justified morally, by rea soning, by aesthetic judgment, or by some combination of these.[3] Kluckhohn's Type A notion of value is thus more restricted than Nadel's; it covers a narrower range of judg ments and preferences. But Kluckhohn does explicitly recognize that value implies choice ("selection").

Now Type A values are largely, as Firth [10]p uts it concerned with *ideals or expressions* about the

[8] *Theory of Action,* ed. Talcott Parsons and E. A. Shils (Cambridge, Mass.: Harvard Univer sity Press, 1951), p. 395.

[9] S. F. Nadel, *Foundations of Social Anthropol ogy* (London: Cohen & West, 1951), p. 264.

dictates of moral obligation. The expressive feature is often uppermost in Kluckhohn's thinking, and he is quite ex☐plicit about the means available for identify☐ing them. It must, he says, be possible to conceptualize the value and express it ver☐bally. The expression will be made either by the actor himself or by the anthropologist *who gains the actor's acceptance or rejec☐tion of the formulation.* In other words, values are abstract qualities attaching to verbal statements.

Although Type A values may range widely (including aesthetic judgment, for example), they specifically include, and are sometimes considered to centre upon, ethical or moral judgment. Despite this, it is inter☐esting to note that the two most exhaustive recent accounts of the ethical systems and moral codes of a preliterate people make only passing reference to values, and, if reference to values were removed from their argument, the argument would not suffer. (This suggests at least the possibility that we could do without the Type A notion of value, since its reference is covered by other terms.) Brandt holds that common usage demands that values should be related to standards of permanence and goodness or desirability. Dictionary definitions do not support his idea of ordinary usage, and it is not at all clear as to how desirability, worthwhileness, and goodness are to be dis☐tinguished and related. Ladd, following

[10] Raymond Firth, *The Study of Values by Social Anthropologists* ("The Marett Lecture" [London, 1953]). Cf. *Man,* CCXXXI (1953), 18.

Kluckhohn, regards moral values as a part of values in general.' Both Brandt[11] and Ladd[12] are interested in systems of ideas.

Common usage, however, as found in the *Shorter Oxford English Dictionary,* speaks of ethical value in terms of "esteem for its own sake and intrinsic worth." Here at least the social scientist must reject common usage, since ethical judgment involves preferences and the relegation of some alter natives to an inferior position of esteem. So that even ethical values, as all values of Type A, must relate to judgments about degree and scale.

The Type B approach to values is nor mally present in the same argument that uses Type A. Firth draws attention to Type B values as "social imperatives . . . the basic assumptions of a society. Brandt talks of relative permanence,[9] and Ladd quotes with approval statements about value in terests as "wider and more perduring." ° Kluckhohn, writing primarily of Type A values in relation to a theory of action, points out their relevance for a Type B analysis. He conceives of Type A values or ganizing "a system of action," shows that individual values must adjust to goals, the

[11] R. B. Brandt, *Hopi Ethics: A Theoretical Anal ysis* (Chicago: University of Chicago Press, 1954), pp. 3839

[12] John Ladd, *The Structure of a Moral Code: A Philosophical Analysis of Ethical Discourse Applied to the Ethics of the Navaho Indians* (Cambridge, Mass.: Harvard University Press, 1957), pp. 6263.

maintenance requirement, and the interests of the actor, of other individuals, and of the sociocultural system, and adds that "values add an element of predictability to social life.

Nadel puts the Type B method in a nut shell: "When we take the respective forms of behaviour to be instances of a 'value,' we understand that here suchandsuch an idea of worthwhileness is *consistently applied* to the various occasions of acting."12 If we include ideal statements or reaction to pro jective tests as behaviour, Kluckhohn's application of his analysis to social systems falls within this category. For he is con cerned with finding consistencies in behaviour, relating them to ideas about worth whileness, and deducing valuational themes which apply to whole cultures or subcul tures. (There is of course an obvious danger of circularity here. If values are identified as persistent themes of worthwhileness, one cannot *explain* persistent themes by refer ence to them, since they are the same thing.)

The method, with its emphasis upon ideas and concepts, and upon the anthropologist's interpretations of consistency, is a sophisti cated and highly technical advance upon the older approaches to themes in culture, to ethos, and to cultural patterns. A few minutes spent with Mead and Metraux[13], Bateson[14], Honigmann[15], and Benedict[16] reveal that, although

---

[13] Margaret Mead and Rhoda Metraux, *Themes in French Culture* (Stanford, Calif.: Stanford Uni versity Press, 1954).

[14] Gregory Bateson, *Naven* (Cambridge: Cam bridge University Press, 1936).

[15] John J. Honigmann, *Culture and Ethos of Kaska Society* ("Yale University Publications in Anthropology," No. 40 [New Haven, Conn.: Yale University Press, 19491).

[16] Ruth Benedict, *Patterns of Culture* (Boston: Houghton Mifflin

there are many im□portant and subtle differences of emphasis, their gross concepts can be translated into Kluckhohn's framework. A major character□istic common to all these investigators is their search for unifying or organizing gross cultural categories built upon psychocultural premises. Sometimes the new phrasing of the Type B approach seems to move very far indeed from the Type A requirement of verbalization recognizable to the actor. Kluck□hohn's themes, such as "determinate—inde□terminate," "unitary—pluralistic," and "au□tonomy—dependence," are highly abstract and seem to be interpreted directly from behaviour without the intermediation of Type A values or indirectly from behaviour through Type A values[17].

In short, Type B is recognizably related to values when, as Firth[s] says of Ruth Benedict, there is "an explanation of domi□nant traits of civilization in terms of cultural choice." But when choice and scale are left out, and we have dominant theme alone, we have left values far behind, and the reader must perform extra acts of interpretation to think of them. Theme implies values, but the act of thematic modelbuilding removes the variable of choice from the anthropolo□gist's purview. This is an important way of contributing to theory, but it should not be allowed to conceal the fact that the identi□fication of value should be related to evi□dence about choice and

---

Co., 1934).

[17] C. K. M. Kluckhohn, "Toward a Comparison of ValueEmphases in Different Cultures," in *The State of the Social Sciences,* ed. L. D. White (Chi□cago: University of Chicago Press, 1956).

scale. If this were not so, and we had theme alone, we would not need the concept of value but could rely solely on concepts such as ethos or theme.

The third, or Type C, approach begins with the analysis of individual preferences as expressed through behaviour (whether or not verbalized by the actor). Firth's review of values in anthropology suggests its impor□tance alongside the others." Kluckhohn re□jects it and, in rejecting it, describes some of its elements very well:

A cathexis is ordinarily a shortterm and nar□row response, whereas value implies a broader and longterm view. A cathexis is an impulse; a value or values restrain or canalize impulses in terms of wider and more perduring goals. A football player wants desperately to get drunk after his first big game, but this impulse con□flicts with his values of personal achievement and loyalty to teammates, coach and univer□sity.

The Type C approach would regard this as a conflict of possible objectives, reflecting the presence of inconsistent values, each with a different valence and potentiality for being translated into action. The actual choice in the light of behaviour would be a reflection of the dominant value subscribed to by the actor, given the specific circum□stances surrounding the action. The ap□proach is neutral between "more perduring and less perduring," since the emphasis upon more or less in this matter is itself a matter of valuation. If the football player gets drunk despite the opposition of coach, team□mates, and university, this would, according to Type C, represent the valuation at that time and place and would show that, in spite of the importance the player may attach to these others, there are elements in the situ ation which cause him to pay the price, such as it might be.

These three approaches to values have been set out to emphasize the importance of scale and degree, on the one hand, and the relationship between worthwhileness and preference, on the other. The concept here advanced is close to common usage and to technical usage in fields such as music, painting, and economics. Value implies worth, and worth cannot be thought of intransitively; we ask, "Worth what?" In its simple form this implies a conception of equivalence, which in turn implies measure ment. Measurement by direct equivalence is impossible in many contexts• where this is so, rank order takes its place. [11] This point of view is essential to the legitimate use of the concept in such a way that it does not conflict with other concepts already estab lished in technical anthropological usage.

We may now turn from this threefold classification to examine the conventional materials available for anthropologists in their attempts to identify the values of indi viduals or cultures, to place the values in the scale of preferences, and thus to assign an importance and a weight to them.

One set of data which Kluckhohn would emphasize consists of individual statements about worthwhileness of conduct and goals, related to a conception of the world around the speaker cast in a moral frame of refer ence. In the first place, the field worker can elicit statements of theory (e.g., descriptions of ideal conduct), and he can record com ments which imply judgments of worth whileness in response to normal situations.

An example would be a mother scolding her child, or an old man commenting on the behaviour of a neighbour's son. He can also use projective tests and like techniques to imply a basis of personality, and therefore a frame work of moral judgment, without the subject being aware of what he is revealing about himself.

This approach is necessary in the search for values, but by itself it does not identify them. Verbal statements can be interpreted as rationalizations justifying one's course of action despite knowledge that the action runs counter to the mores. They may be used to discredit or approve of another per son's conduct, not on the moral grounds stated in the text, but for some social reason not stated in the text. Nevertheless, pre cisely because they are rationalizations, they are so formulated as to be likely to appeal to the moral views of at least some of the hearers. This implies that the speaker is re flecting to some extent what he believes to be the current mores of the community (or, in carelessly set up field situations, of the anthropologist). Does this mean that the rationalizations describe values? Certainly, with appropriate interpretation, they reflect something which may roughly be described as the "value tone" of the community; but this is only one side of the medal.

Projective tests circumvent objections based upon rationalization but do not avoid others. Quite apart from the effectiveness or otherwise of the tests in obtaining defined psychological information (a question which I am not competent to discuss), projective tests and verbal statements have certain common merits and disadvantages. They do reveal some potential goals, principles of conceptualization, and ideal ordering among ends. They do not put the actor to the test of his actions, making him responsible for actual choice, with all its consequences vis□ited upon him. Although there may be a connection between ideal values and psycho□logical characteristics, on the one hand, and the valuations of living persons in historical context, on the other, it is not a simple cor□respondence. Prediction of human choice on the basis of ideal statement or psychological characteristic is, for several reasons, likely only under very limited circumstances. First, each situation being complex and unique, the analyst cannot foresee the effective vari□ables; this observation affects social time prediction in general but cannot be allowed to prevent the formulation of theory. More serious is the second reason: both ideal state□ment and analysis of projective test are abstractions which do not take into account such matters as discounting the pain of fu□ture situations and, for this reason, do not with certainty anticipate the likely concrete judgment from the point of view of the actor himself. There is a very close similarity here to parties of political opposition (including those in colonial territories), which, when faced with responsibility in government, may develop markedly different corporate personalities.

A second analysis, which can build upon the former and which is particularly related to Type B values, is to construct a "system of values" for a culture. The statistically or morally normal values of the culture are here based on statements about individuals. Pre□cisely the same reservations need to be made as for the first type of analysis, but there are other difficulties.

In societies with few authoritarian, theo□logical, or theoretical devices, what weight is to be given to differences in ideas and viewpoints? Sometimes it is possible to state that authority leans to one view and that there are sanctions against others. Again, it is possible to introduce deliberate impre☐cision, indicating that variation of certain degrees is tolerated. Sometimes, as with Gluckman[18] , conflict and disagreement are shown to have functional implications. But sometimes the concepts of national charac☐ter, basic personality, and world view—all of which concepts imply systems of values for cultures—push the exploration much further, seeking dominant principles, even in complex societies. Such examinations are worthwhile, particularly as theoretical mod☐els to be argued about, but they are clearly oversimplifications if they are meant to refer to historical societies. The trend toward the concept of modal personality, permitting a spread of characteristics, has not been suffi☐ciently used as an analogy for the treatment of national character, world view, ethos, values, and like concepts which may be dis☐tributed throughout culture according to structural, idiosyncratic, or other principles.

A third approach is concerned with an abstraction of the working principles of a culture or the relation of cultural processes to an ideal model. On the one hand, verbal statements or observed behavior are treated abstractly to provide, for example, a struc☐tural frame of reference. On the other, verbal statements or observed behaviour are related to an a priori frame of reference which de☐scribes the normal operation of a society or culture in relation to assumed goals of main☐tenance, equilibrium, mental health, and the like. In either case an external standard of value may be applied (just as when "more perduring" was used in a

---

[18] Max Gluckman, *Custom and Conflict in Africa* (Oxford: Basil Blackwell, 1955).

different context as a criterion of value) . We can speak of an institution as "important" because not only do people adhere to it but it fits in with a social purpose. This teleological functional approach has had its significance for our society. It has countered the thoughtless re□former by providing a basis for the analysis of a presumed purpose in apparently irra□tional custom and conduct. But it has also led to an arid relativism which seems to assume that all behaviour gives evidence of equal value. But the aridity is more apparent than real. It is based on a weak handling of social l_i models. Merton's[19] concept of dysfunc□tion and Leach's[20] of a normal disequilib□rium, though they are by no means ideal correctives, offer promise of new models which at least put the question: When does value exist, and how much? It is necessary to ask this question, for now in social theory (as distinct from points of view about social work) we have to ask ourselves whether this or that institution has a negative function in the workings of society or whether it rep□resents a force opposed to others. But even this approach does not offer a technique for assessing the raw material upon which it is based or for identifying particular values to place them in the operational context of the model in use.

A fourth scheme is possible. It focuses primarily upon the identification of particu□lar values (rather than value in general), so that their significance for social and cul□tural processes may be deduced on a firm base of data. This will be a disappointing scheme, since there are probably as

[19] Robert Merton, *Social Theory and Social Struc□ture* (Glencoe, Ill.: Free Press, 1949).

[20] E R. Leach, *Political Systems of Highland Burma* (London: Bell, 1954).

many pitfalls as in any other. It offers one advan tage over others, and one only: it endeavors to trace the steps needed in order to state categorically that a specific cultural group places a known value upon a given item If my conclusion must be that in strict terms we cannot provide the evidence in an oper ational form, we may nevertheless endeavour to approximate it and improve both analysis and technique. Above all, the statement of complexities may do something to reduce a sometimes overconfident optimism

The approaches so far considered have centred upon characteristics of individuals or cultures. Sometimes they are expressed verbally, sometimes they are inferred from casual or manipulated behavior, and some times they are inferred from or stimulated by custom. One cannot conceive of a value without an expression of the goal envisaged. Thus a moral precept, for example, is impor tant because it expresses a goal; if it did not relate to behaviour in this way, it would have no significance as a value. Thus a significant element in the anthropological treatment of value so far is that it purports to elucidate goals. Whether an author sets out to present a "value system" or to analyze the customs, culture, or social structure of a particular people, the end result is a statement of goals. In the case of a value system, more weight, it is true, may be given to the description of an ethical or philosophical set of ideas to which people relate their goals; but, unless the ethics or philosophy do come down to earth in this fashion, we have ideas only and not values.

Insofar as goals are verbalized or inferred from nonsituational data (e.g., by projective tests or from dreams, myths, or statements of ethical theory), they are only potentially achievable. The costs of achievement, and the bearing of competitive goals, weighted for value, cannot be assessed accurately from such data. There is therefore one set of goals which are not achieved by means of current behaviour. For these one may adopt the standard economic term, "potential de mand," implying that what persons say or think they want, or what the outsider infers they want from unconscious motivation, represents a potentiality of action only which might, in fact, never be achieved. Potential demand is largely represented by hopes, de sires, moral judgments, and unconscious motivations.

It is clear that forecasting the manner in which potential demand is or is not trans lated into reality is an extremely tricky business and is not likely to be accurate or possible save in smallscale units of shortterm analysis, in cultures known to be static (and seldom do we really know this), or in parts of culture for which reward and cost are readily quantifiable and are known and relevant to the actors as well as the observ ers. Cost is of the utmost importance to the analysis, just as is the competition of values for prepotence, and most treatments of value in anthropology completely fail to take cost into account as a variable of significance.

The role played by cost can be seen even more if we examine the bearing of descrip☐tive fieldwork studies upon the identifica☐tion of value. It might be assumed that, since such studies describe what people actually do, that is, the *effective* demand of a culture, they would reflect current wants and preferences and hence the operation of valuation in a specific cost situation. In other words, fieldwork studies should de☐scribe values for a given place and time.

Whether fieldwork studies can do this precisely is doubtful, but some progress can be made by recognizing limitations in the current approach. The first requirement in empirical value study is weighting by quan☐tity; it would be tempting to say "measure☐ment." Clearly, we cannot measure such matters as religious satisfaction directly, but sometimes we can determine how fre☐quently persons are involved in initiations or in magical rites, and it may be possible from that to make suitable, though limited, deductions. Fortunately, such detail is be☐coming more and more a criterion of good field work; but, unfortunately, many writers who deal in values or in cultural themes turn their backs on this kind of weighting as if it were unimportant. The idea, the prin☐ciple, is the datum to be obtained by the most direct approach, counting smacks of statistics, economics, and materialism.

I do not contend that counting or meas☐urement implies objectivity or that counting and measurement are the essential methods of science. Some problems are beyond our reach; for other problems an undue stress on counting and measurement may be un☐necessary or dangerously misleading. And the study of values is the study of some quantitative aspects of cultural qualities. Value implies worthwhileness which implies degree, which implies scale, which is com□pounded of quantity and measurement. Furthermore, statements about the charac□teristics of a population are essentially quan□titative, for they imply that the appropriate proportion of the population shares the characteristics. Such quantitative judg□ments to the required degree of precision may be achieved without *actual* counting or measurement; but, unless we know and state our margins of error, we are left with subjective inference. Again, this may be useful; however, there is always the danger that subjectivity creeps upon authors un□awares.

But measurement, whether exact or in□exact, is only another step toward assessing valuation. It involves primary difficulties which would have to be removed before the objective could be achieved. The first is to construct a scale. When economists speak of market value, they indicate measurement according to price (which may be manipu□lated or constructed in such a way as to cor□rect for inflation and similar cultural aspects as a whole, such a scale is hardly possible. Physical measurement in□volves using an artificial device on which the symbols of the criterion are marked; the cri□terion may be a parallel characteristic (say, length) which applies equally to the artificial device and to the object measured, or it may be responsive to forces resulting from a proc□ess set in motion (say, as measured in a voltammeter or balance). Economic measure□ment is in a sense responsive, for it occurs as a result of processes; where value is con□cerned, it is indirect. It is assumed that, the more worthwhile an object (to the market), the more people are prepared to meet the cost per unit. This is precisely the element of analysis which is lacking in anthropology.

In point of fact, this extension of analysis does not go far enough. Market value is a particular subvariant of our genus: it re□flects certain valuations, but it does not represent the whole range of valuations, nor is it valuation *per se*. And we cannot accept money or any other tangible good as the relevant element in price if we are to compare values throughout a culture. There is only one resource which is given up every time an action is undertaken, that is which can be regarded as a universal cost element in valuation. – *time*. And, paradoxically enough, although economists accept the notion that time is a resource, it enters infrequently into anthropological discussions of resources.

But it is not possible, without a great deal of difficult calculation, to convert every ele ment in cost into a time equivalent. Such a computation which has been rejected by most economic theorists; but the analogy is superficial, since the labour theory of value is con cerned with the explanation of prices, sup ply, and demand, whereas our cultural theory of value is an attempt to state what things and modes of behaviour are regarded as worthwhile in a culture as a whole and not merely in the market.

There is an obvious objection to the argu ment so far: no onetoone relationship exists between the quantity of time given to achieve a goal and its value. The criticism applies to any other form of assessing cost as well and is the reason why market value cannot be taken as equivalent to cultural value. A possible way around this difficulty is suggested by the proposition that an index of value, or worthwhileness, is the degree to which persons are prepared to give up an objective, or to consume more of it, because cost conditions (translated into timeprice) have changed This proposition leads to the notion of *elasticity of demand*, which draws attention to the responsiveness of demand, or goal achievement, to variations in costs. When translated into cultural terms, it sug gests that for every goal there is a ratio be tween a movement in the quantity of the end product achieved and a movement in the total balance of advantagedisadvantage appropriate in the relevant situations. If an actor wants something desperately, he will be prepared to achieve it in at least the same quantity as before, even though the costs of achievement rise, and this is a reflection of the value of the goal to him; he does this by reducing the actual achievement of other objectives, even though their cost of achieve□ment may have fallen. By following through ratios in these kinds of ways, the anthropol□ogist would lay bare the ramifications of choice and would assess value by showing how much persons are prepared to hold onto the goals they want or to give them up in response to changing conditions. An empiri□cal exercise of this kind would be difficult and would of necessity involve diachronic studies.

Clearly, the practical difficulties of using the tool to provide neatly measured quanti□ties are insuperable. We simply do not have available the techniques which would enable us to measure units of cost and consumption in such fields as religion and aesthetics, let alone responsiveness to changes in timeprice.

Since this is so, what are the conclusions? In straightforward conventional fieldwork analysis we imply values but do not describe them. Normally, two related but quite sepa□rable things are described: effective demand across the total range of institutions and the ideational content of potential demand. This does not mean to say that we are unable to approach the objective a little further. With a slightly different orientation of field work, we could present new data bearing upon the problems mentioned above, though still without the precision of agreed measurement. In the future, field work should pay much more attention than hither□to to costs of achievement of existing goals and to responsiveness on the part of groups to alterations in costs, for these are essential elements in a concept of value[21].

---

[21]   C. S. Belshaw, "Revaluation of Time in a Papuan Community," *South Pacific* (Sydney), VI (1952), 46672.

Culture and Holism in Ethnography and Exogenous Factors in Economics.

An Approach to the Meaning of Ethnography in relation to Economic Theory

First published in *Archivo per l'Anthropologia e la Etnologua* Volume CXXII – 1992 (Firenze) pp.129144.

In 1986 Prof. Ulf Himmelstrand, the Swedish sociologist, organized a symposium, on behalf of the International Social Science Council and Unesco, to explore an interdisciplinary approach to the treatment of what economists call "exogenous variables" The meeting consisted fifty per cent of economists and fifty per cent of representatives of other disciplines. The results have not been published.

The present paper consists of a slightly amended version of my contri□bution. In writing it I came to realize that, for the most part, we as anthro□pologists take for granted the economists' image of where our discipline lies, and often accept that as truth, without questioning the fundamental theoretical concepts. Although my task was to talk to economists, I found myself reaffirming and rethinking the consequences of a postulate I have held throughout my academic career, namely that there is a philosophical and theoretical unity between the core ideas of economics (as distinct from some of the contemporary elaborations and compromises with that core) and the operations of ethnography (as distinct from its contemporary theo☐retical apparatus). Thus I found myself writing about matters that I feel need rethinking in anthropology as much as they do in economics. And it is for this reason that I hope the 'arguments I now present will have some future value to colleagues in my own discipline, as well perhaps as in economics.

Ulf Himmelstrand, in his summing up of the meeting, inferred that I was accepting a great deal of what has come to be known as the « imperi☐alisb> position of economics. This is not the case. What I do accept is the desirability of using some of the earlier theoretical ideas of economics. But then I depart from conventional economics almost completely, and most certainly do not accept its version of the world around it — or even within it. And in accepting the *earlier* versions of these concepts I argue for their transformation in a way that is not usual within economics itself — or, I may say, anthropology. There have been some brave attempts by a very few economists to extend their concepts into areas covered by other social sciences in a nonimperial manner, but, at least insofar as anthropologyethnography are concerned, without making use of what we have to offer in a positive way. That is partly our fault, since we ourselves have done little to show what our observations have to say in a framework that permits theoretical dialogue.

The present essay is an attempt to hint at possibilities.

In a background paper contained in a Newsletter to the participants, Ulf Himmelstrand grappled with the meaning of «exogenous variables» in economics. In essence they are those variables which lie *outside* the basic selfcontained formal model. Since such models, though basically similar in contemporary economics, are not completely unified, there is room for differences of opinion as to what is exogenous and what is not. In practice, as Himmelstrand points out, the term frequently refers to fac☐tors which must be considered as *given* (my italics) in a certain context of economic decisionmaking, regardless of whether it is an economic or noneconomic factor, though in this context we are referring mainly to socalled ononeconomic» factors. We could think of family structure, ethos, religion, power, class structure, propensity to innovate, the environment — indeed almost everything that has cultural and environmental reality in determining choices and decisions. In economic modelbuilding it is so easy when all that is regarded as external to the model.

So I set out to try to give one answer, among many possible ones, to the question, what can anthropology contribute that will cast light on the nature of exogenous variables, as conceived in economics?

To take the question literally would mean accepting the validity of the analysis which posits the usefulness of systems which can logically func□tion only if there are exogenous factors = not merely as a temporary ac□commodation to the limits of observation, but as an affirmation that such systems may be seen to work well.

From the perspective of anthropology, such a position has to be fun□damentally flawed with respect to adequate models of reality, and, I would argue, is inconsistent with the classical axioms of economics, which are still fundamental to it.

Hence I partially transform the question by asking the question, can the models be increased in explanatory power if the notion of exogenous variables is *discarded,* or at least substantially modified?

First, some background explanation. Within social and cultural an☐thropology and even more within conservative ethnography, abstract model building of the kind economists perform is extremely rare. It is overdue, even with the branch known as economic anthropology. Although we deal with social relations and social structure and organization, anthropology derives its basic concerns from the overriding importance of cultural sys☐tems which permeate all thought and decisions, and are essential to the definition of cultures and peoples who create variations of economic be☐haviour.

I believe that this is, or can be, done in a manner which can be related rather precisely to at least the earlier axioms of microeconomics. And despite some field work choices, we are concerned with humanity in all its expres☐sions, not limiting ourselves, in the popular and economists' view of us, to the apparently exotic. (The economists present at the meeting were totally surprised to find that anthropologists had anything to say about modern health delivery systems, industrial workers' attitudes and cultures, modern urban systems, city planning, or anything of that ilk. Fortunately I believe this perception is changing amongst some.)

Most anthropologists, without thinking about it, subscribe to the idea that the discipline is holistic (sometimes spelling the term owholistic 0). Major theorists have suggested that beyond any macroculture there is a level of principle which can be used to explain a cultural system in terms which go beyond its parts (cf. the «superorganic» of A.L. Kroeber (1917), some versions of the I value systems» of Clyde Kluckhohn (1953), and now the structuralism of Claude LeviStrauss (1963).

Such constructions are far from commanding total acceptance. The bulk of anthropology is not holistic in that sense, but deals rather with the functioning of parts of the system *within* the systemic whole. While constructs such as society, culture, polity, institution, even economy, are not in fact organic as are biological organisms — there is for humans only one selfcontained system, namely the global society, and even that can be debated — yet it sometimes suits our purposes to use an organic analo□gy, and to think of the parts as necessary to the total system. Although our language is very different, this is not far removed in principle from the mechanical systems of economists.

Also, holism as used in anthropology perhaps unthinkingly implies a different dimension, namely that the only real system embraces global society in all its aspects, which ultimately must be understood through the use of massive data (including «thick », or highly detailed and evoca□tive, ethnography) and insights drawn from all disciplines. Since such a task is in reality clearly impossible, abstracting minisystems out of the maximum, and the selection of a few interdisciplinary themes out of the infinity, is justified — and there are as many ways of doing this as there are anthropologists.

Anthropology differs from mainstream economics in that we do not concentrate on one limited way of doing this, and (although we have much dogma) it is usually evident to us that such partial systems cannot give complete results, even within their terms of reference. What is left out can be as significant as what is put in, and, contrary to much of economics, we welcome the additional perspectives and linkages provided by those who are working with an adjacent dimension.

It is with such attitudes that anthropologists approach the kinds of issues that are embodied in the idea of exogenous variables. The idea im plies that there is more at stake than heuristic expediency; the core of the model has a special primacy, a key significance, for enlightenment and additions to knowledge. It would be extremely difficult for anthropol□ogy to accept this, since it appears that the conclusions drawn from the model, whether explanatory or practical, are *bound to be false*. The only chance of correcting them appears to be to *incorporate* the exogenous vari□ables *into* the core model (leaving aside the question as to whether the model itself should be replaced, a question to be determined by results and criticisms).

Granted, this would reduce such mathematical power as the models seem to hold, would reduce some of the elegance, and make the life of analysis much more complicated. But who can pretend that social life is not complicated? And is it not out of complications that the overriding themes and principles and theories emerge, as we search for the ultimate simplicities? And if mathematically inclined economists were to take the anthropological perspectives more seriously, treating them as challenges to the improvement of the models rather than as curious nuisances, it might well be that the game of mathematicization would not be as hope□less as at first sight it seems to be (cf. , for

41

example, Becker, 1981; Belshaw, 1959, 1969, 1978; Blau, 1964). Anthropologists could certainly learn from the attempt.

I should give some grounds for making such brash assertions.

The notion of choice is central to neoclassical economics. As I have mentioned, a few anthropologists, and the now somewhat discredited na tional character school (e.g. Gofer and Rickman, 1949), have attempted to seek supercultural principles which would constitute what the sociolo gist Talcott Parsons (1935, 1937) called normative orientations which govern the way preferences are chosen and means are used to satisfy them. If such a search were successful, and most anthropologists believe that it is some thing more than an intellectual game producing stimulating insights, it would alter the whole paradigm. All exogenous factors, translated into behaviour, could then be predicted on the basis of their immediately preced ing state and their linkage to known superior forces. Nothing like this has happened, or is likely, even with the intrusion of biological and genet ic knowledge into the considerations. Man and his variations are too com plex, there is strong evidence that any posited principles change in given cultures over time in such significant ways that, while continuity may be there, it is less than mechanistic.

On the other hand we do, at a lower level of abstraction, speak of cultural systems and social structures, and make sense of their dynamic forms. Depending on analytical circumstances, these can be presented as constraints on choice, in that, through various processes such as socializa☐tion, limitations of perceptions, strong moral valuation, and many more, thay put boundaries around the supposed infinity of wants and around the definition of resources and means. The latter are not so much techno☐logically given, but are defined as perceptions within the culture. What is a resource to one people is unknown or irrelevant to another, whether or not it is physically present.

Within such boundaries, choice is wide open: society is free to change or not to change, to create new religions or stay with the old. And by the exercise of individual choice within society and culture, aggregated and ramified, social systems and cultures themselves change and adapt, sometimes through external, i.e. foreign or environmental, pressures and influences, which are interpreted through the *same* processes, and just as much through their internal activities, tensions, resolutions.

Although many ethnographic descriptions read statically, all contain the data which anthropologists and economists can tease out to reveal the exercise of choice.

The fact of choice is even more central to anthropology than to eco☐nomics, since the totality of the subject deals with its empirical manifesta☐tions. The major stream of analysis originating with the work of Marcel Mauss (1925) on the gift and its prestatory status, would derive social struc ture in any society at any given time from the cumulation of individual choices. (There is an echo here of the perspective of RadcliffeBrown, that social structure is a statistical phenomenon). This has led to a grouping of theoretical stances variously labelled «social exchange theory». «Trans actional analysis» and «social network theory (e.g. Bailey, 1969; Barth, 1966, Blau, 1964; Kapferer, 1976; Orans, 1968; Ortiz and Howard, 1971).

Individual choice extends to the choice of persons with whom to in teract, perhaps within defined categories (but you can always choose *not* to interact if you are willing to pay the price of noninteraction). The interaction includes the flow of symbolic messages, material things, emo tions, and what we would call services. Of course choices are influenced by culturally emphasized preferences, including many the conventional economist leaves out of consideration, such as salvation, prestige (Veblen should be reread), love of family, beauty, aggression, habit versus innova tion, and all the others you can think of. In turn, the choices result in a reaffirmation or a change in the culture.

Such analysis, despite limited manpower directed to its extension, has been used for such diverse subjects as kinship and family patterns (Homans and Schneider, 1955), ceremony and the social order (numerous deriv ing from Mauss), political parties in Britain (Bailey, 1969), leadership and power (most abstractly by Blau, 1964; Bailey, 1971), the social organiza tion of the Swat Pathan (Barth, 1959 a and b), fishing entrepreneurs (Barth, 1963 and his followers), regularities in peasant markets (Mintz, 1959, 1961), premonetary exchange systems (Belshaw, 1965), Mediterranean feuding (Bailey, 1971), to name but a few.

How analytically, can this situation be tied into the problem before us? I shall take, one by one, a selection of theoretical concepts presented for discussion by Kenneth Hartley, an economist at the Universi ty of York.

He states that «Utility or preference functions are central [to econom ic analysis]... and are assumed to be given». That is, there is no discussion in the central model of how individuals or groups choose preferences or determine utility (in the special economists' sense of that word). There then follows what, to an anthropologist, Would be an offhand sketch of what in fact is a limited range of influences upon those givens, which we need not go into.

To explore the genesis and dynamics of such givens, which surely must be essential to a knowledge of the dynamics of an economy, is, as we know, extremely complex and fundamental to any dynamic interpreta tion of social systems. Even ethnologists often abjure digging into the dy namics, preferring a static description. But to assume the functions to « be given» is to relegate the act of choice to the administration of resources only — how choices, given, are satisfied — whereas the overwhelming characteristic of human culture is choice between each of the ends, objec☐tives, goals, wants and ambitions.

This of course is not overlooked in economics, though there is a ten☐dency, except in fields such as welfare economics, to subsume linked goals under a broader classification. Thus the goal of maximized profitability can accommodate the consideration of competition between the goal of making automobiles and that of making snowmobiles. But it is more difficult to include in the consideration that an individual, an entrepreneur, a firm (large or small), a civil servant, may have alongside of strict profit a concern for an optimal mix of return embracing such matters as profit, prestige and social status, expansion for its own sake, successful gamesmanship, environmental protection (not simply as a conservation of means but as a goal in itself), aesthetics of work and product, philanthropy, family sup☐port, worker support.

Apart from providing a false simplicity of argument, the notion that preferences are given enables the economist to avoid what he may see as the trap of cultural relativism Relativistic explanations are indeed insuffi☐cient, but nonrelativistic explanations of cultural difference, and of the articulation of differences of culture within a system, must be sought deliber☐ately. It is highly significant that no attention whatsoever was paid to such issues in the economists' contributions to this particular symposium, even when considering exogenous factors. It is as if history and culture do not exist.

Yet surely it is very clear (as some economists do indeed recognize) that Japanese, French, Russian and British, to say nothing of Indian or Uzbek, preference functions differ enormously between each other and change significantly; and also that with each of these societies there are ethnic, class, professional, cultural, religious and other significant groups who choose differently from other citizens. Production, trading, market□ing, consumption, yes and working and organization, are reflections of such differences, and of the articulative interaction between them.

Most economists I am sure would concede this, the point at issue being whether they are, or should be, *exogenous* in their thinking. The hold up, as I see it, is not in the potential mathematical technique, but in the relative vagueness of some of the concepts, in problems in getting agreement on operational definitions, and in lack of attention to modes of measurement, particularly when the link to monetary price is not there or not apparent.

Alternatives to monetary price have been suggested (e.g. Belshaw 1959, 1965, 1969, 1980), and are legion in studies of nonmonetary societies. Whatever the practical difficulties — and there are many — it appears there are few difficulties of theoretical *principle*. Every economics fresh□man student is told that maximization in relation to consumption be□haviour is not to be thought of in terms of a single commodity, but of optimal mixes in a preference schedule. Thereafter, in the handling of such institutions as the firm, the principle gets thrown away, profit being, usually, the single determinant. But if the principle of optimal mix were applied to all behaviour, an understanding of the work place, of contracts, of exchange relationships, or interactive dynamics would be more reveal□ing, if not as <precise» as that provided in econometric models.

To some extent the raw data are there.

In anthropology, in the beginning is ethnography. Despite holistic principles, no ethnography can be culturally complete. In all such studies the data are selected in accordance with theoretical or interpretive canons of significance, which vary according to problem. Yet *an ethnography, with or without quantification, is a statement of an effective demand schedule for the people concerned,* that is a broad statement of what individuals actually consume at the moment of observation. The effective demand schedule is an essential tool in economic thinking, which the conventional tools of economics simply cannot approach with the same richness and directness as is achieved in ethnography. Nor can conventional economics take into account an enormous range of /satisfactions» which are routinely handled in ethnography — the demand for religious ritual, storytelling, recreation, even sleep, sport, work as a value in itself, learning, and on and on. How, one may ask, can economists have a realistic view of the competition and linkages that exist between elements in a demand sched□ule without knowing about such things?

Ethnographies — though here, customarily, they are not as strong as they might be — also have things to say about the *potential* demand schedule, that is those things people would *like to* have, do, experiencethose things they would direct their actions and energies towards obtaining by way of satisfaction, *if the costs were right.* This ethnographies do by reference to enduring values, ideologies, structures, ambitions, frustrations and so forth.

Few economists have the patience to read ethnographies, and few ethnographic studies revealing the cultural behavior of entrepreneurs and wheelerdealers of the kind responsible for economists' data have been made. They should be and will be.

Ethnographic data are far too diffuse, even when quantified, to per☐mit of immediate incorporation into models which make major use of national statistics. Yet the effort is immensely important. I would like to see economists and anthropologists, both, working on the translation of such types of data into models which would avoid the concept of the exogenous in its current forms.

Similar arguments apply to the consideration of costs, where non☐material issues are, for example, often behind the socalled / conservatism» of populations confronted with the possibilities of technical innovation, or with choices between immediate maximal exploitation of a resource or its husbanding for the future (Belshaw, 1976).

The work of the economist Gary S. Becker (1976, 1981) suggests that, to some degree, the extensions I have advocated are feasible within the terms of economists' forms of reasoning. The work is far too little read among anthropologists, who would benefit their own discipline by respond☐ing to its stimulus. How can it be carried forward? Where is it wrong? What can be done about incorporating «soft » ethnography? Nevertheless, it is but a brave beginning, and needs development and extension in two directions.

In *The Economic Approach to Human Behaviour* (1976) Becker re☐jects the Robbinsian approach to o the economic» — that which represents the application of scarce means to infinite ends — as being embarassingly broad, without sufficient focus, and holds that o the economic» should be that which relates to the market. He mostly maintains this perspective in his essays, though it is pretty well abandoned, as it has to be, for some of his papers in A *Treatise on the Family* (1981).

The socalled o substantive» school of economic anthropology would tend to agree, classifying oeconomies» into those based on reciprocity, redis☐tribution, and market forces (Polanyi, 1957). (But if «the economio> is that which is connected to markets, how then can reciprocal systems be « economic.

Others, including myself, criticize such a distinction in its purist form, since it overemphasizes the differences rather than the similarities and continuities in the social and historical process. Scarcity, supply and de☐mand, exchange transactions, and similar processes are present in *all* socie☐ties: so is the operation of choice.

To consider transactions and choices together is, for example, to rev☐eal interactions between behaviour in a monetary market and behaviour outside that market, which is fundamental to the understanding of the market itself (Mintz, 1959). Further, the significance of Marcel Mauss' work in *Essai sur le don* lies not in his treatment of gifts *qua* gifts, but in laying the groundwork for contemporary social exchange theory, in which *all* human interactions can be seen as exchange transactions, with atten☐dant costs, benefits and real, if not monetary, prices. (The principle has even been extended, with advantage, into animal and insect biology). To make the most of social exchange theory, we ethnographers would do well to adapt Becker's models, and ask ourselves how we can make ethnography useful in that adaptation (not necessarily retaining all the logical formal☐ism of the models).

The second direction of extension and development is to wrestle with the ethnographic real. Becker realizes he must do this when be treats of institutions such as polygyny, which are mostly (not by any means entirely) foreign to Western culture, but it has to be (and I do not fault him) entire☐ly superficial at this stage. He uses appropriate noneconomists' literature when dealing with primates. But he does not refer to or incorporate either ethnographic or theoretical work in anthropology on such areas as altru☐ism, social interactions, divorce or family evolution. On other matters such as division of labour the references are unsystematic and less than minimal. The problem is not with Becker's brilliant pioneering work (some have suggested worthy of the Nobel Prize in Economics), but with the failure of anthropologists to take up the challenge in a form that forces economists to take their work seriously — without abandoning its integrity.

It has frequently been said that the basic classical model of choice and rationality, which makes no moral judgements as to ends, and accepts that when people choose it represents their valuations *at that time and place and bearing the applicable costs, material or nonmaterial in mind, together with an evaluation, conscious or unconscious, of alternatives* is tautological. And hence of no value. Tautological it certainly is. But it shows the value of tautology, since indeed one can use it, if not to discover final causes, then to forecast future events And to predict logical extensions of theory. Hartley states that Becker's approach is «often guilty of *ad hoc* and of failing to provide distinctive hypotheses capable of being refuted». Not so.

Such charges are also levelled against the extension of the model. It appears to be a sin to embrace an enormous range of data into a basically simple, single, model, although in other sciences the canons of preferred explanation call for such abstraction and simplicity. Yet the power the model gives to explanatory elucidation of empirical material is considera□ble, and general, testable (provided some form of quantitative judgement is possible) hypotheses abound.

Some examples. In applied or developmental work, or work analyzing social change empirically, it more often than not turns out that forecasts can be made on the basis of cost benefit analysis, or something similar, taking into account the wider and nonmaterial factors I have indicated as significant. The forecast fails. The model then enjoins the search for « the missing factors», or the factors that were not appropriately weighted in the original scheme. The awareness of the need to adjust the schedule of preferences accordingly is surely fundamental to subsequent forecasts, and if used properly adds to our knowledge of the interplay between ele ments of culture which affect choices.

Second example. The assumption of rationality in the existing model is frequently challenged (e.g. Godelier, 1966). But such challenges ignore the special meaning of rationality in economics, which has nothing to do *with psychologically rational processes* or otherwise in the selection of goals. Usually, with such challenges, nonrationality» can be broken down into component parts, such as search for prestige, altruism, antisocial behaviour, asceticism, fanaticism. But in fact all we are doing here is to add elements to the preference schedule, saying that people *want these things,* that they are different perhaps from the norms of Western society (perhaps...) and in so doing we add distinctive, sometimes curious, production functions for their satisfaction.

Third example. From anthropology one can pull out numerous gener al hypotheses, dealing with the way cultural elements dynamically articu late. That is, in them, we account for adjustments in preference schedules over time and in response to new conditions. Some are at the level of deductions close to the basic model (Belshaw, 1969), as «Where actors *perceive* that ends are incompatible, conflict, synthesis and adjustment will occur with a view to making them compatible». Surely this sets the stage of the possibility of disproof (i.e. the search for contrary cultural examples) and refinement, that is defining the conditions under which the various alternative empirical paths will be followed.

Other hypotheses derive from the independent examination of social phenomena. Thus the study of millenarian movements posits specific con ditions under which, among other things, populations will engage in the immediate destruction of resources in anticipation of special kinds of gain (Jarvie, 1964). (Ethnocentric observers call this «irrational», but in the eco nomic model it is highly rational, in that the people are behaving in accor dance with perceptions that state that destruction is the means to the desired salvation). Such generalizations about millenarian movements can be ex tended, with appropriate modification, to embrace wider phenomena such as more conventional social movements, and other kinds of social protest, into one overriding formula, though this has not yet been completely done. And it has been used, albeit clumsily, for an attempt at historical forecasting, which was in fact partially falsified (Belshaw, 1969, 1976). (I used the model to forecast the outburst of millenial movements in the Palestinian diaspora, whereas in modified form it burst out in Iran —possibly in accordance with the model, but not as I stated it).

Many such hypotheses, since they deal with the articulation of aspects of society and culture, institutions, social and natural environmental fac☐tors, cultural categories, and so forth, speak directly to regularities of inter action which the symposium papers identified as linkages (where anthro☐pology and economics have much to say to one another). (Linkages = articulation in Belshaw, 1969).

A final issue. Economists are busy trying to find effective ways of handling variations in the state of knowledge, to which the crucial concept of innovation is closely related. From its very beginning, though in dis☐guised language, anthropology and ethnology, through the study of social and cultural change, even of evolution, have been preoccupied with simi☐lar questions. «The state of knowledge» is of course nothing more nor less than the state of culture, including symbols, perceptions, ideologies and moral codes.

Anthropologists are now chary of jumping to conclusions that given societies or groups are inherently more innovative than others, though de☐velopment economists sometimes cling to the despair of such an idea. Our empirical materials do concede that innovations may be concentrated in varying areas of culture at any given time (religion as against agricultural technology, for example). Our theories include general statements about the probability of innovations behind produced and/or accepted or reject☐ed, and the ways in which they are necessarily adapted when adopted. There are also general statements about what causes innovation and what factors are relevant to the prediction of a rate of innovation (Belshaw, 1969). If economists are to include knowledge and/or innovation as factors of production, anthropologists have much to say, both theoretically and empirically.

Economists continue to ask, what relevance does ethnology have to modern society? I need not belabour the point to this readership, since so many of our colleagues are directly involved in such societies. But there is of course a different relevance also.

It was the study of the potlatch among North American Indians and of the kula of the Trobriand Islands which enabled Marcel Mauss to de☐velop ideas which are now being applied to Western political parties, per☐sonal and subjective relations in the behaviour of entrepreneurs, and the enormous effect that ceremonial exchange has within the confines of the capitalist economy. Ways of thinking about small bounded groups enables analogies to be used in the analysis of boundaries and articulations be☐tween ethnic groups and social classes, between subcultures (including those of professionals, entrepreneurs and bureaucrats) and the nation state. Studies of small scale entrepreneurs carried out in Fijian villages contain points entirely compatible, historically, with considerations affecting OPEC oil ministers, and the Swat Pathan were not irrelevant for classic studies of Norwegian fishermen.

To conclude, the enormous material now present in the theory and practice of anthropology is essential to the consideration of economists' exogenous variables. It would ultimately be more effective if variables could be incorporated directly into the basic models. Nevertheless, even if con☐servatism prevents this, each exogenous variable, whenever defined, is open to ethnographic data and anthropological hypotheses, and can be refined into many traceable parts. To achieve this is a programmatic matter, an issue of scientific strategy and priorities, rather than one of insuperable intellectual obstacles.

I wish to acknowledge the support of Unesco and the International Social Science Council for participation in the symposium, and of the Wenner Gren Foundation for Anthropological Research for a general writing grant that enabled me to proceed with these matters.

REFERENCES

Acheson, James M. (1981) Anthropology of Fishing. Annual Review of Anthropology, 275316. Bailey, E.G. (1969) Stratagems and Spoils. Oxford.

—ed. (1971) Gifts and Poisons, the Politics of Reputation. Oxford.
Banton, M., ed. (1965) The Relevance of Models for Social Anthropology. London. Barnett, H.G. (1983) Qualitative Science. New York.

Barth, F. (1959a) Political Leadership Among the Swat Pathans. London.

- (1959b) Segmentary opposition and the theory of games: a study of Pathan organiza

tion. Journal of the Royal Anthropological Institute, 89: 521.

—(1963) The Role of the Entrepreneur in Social Change in Northern Norway. Bergen.
— (1966) Models of Social Organization. London.

— (1980) The data base in economic anthropology, in Robert Hinshaw, ed., Currents in Anthropology. New York, Berlin
— (1987) Some limitations of classification in comparative studies exemplified by the anal ysis of parallel economies, with implications for development theory. L'Uomo, xi, n. 2: 295317.

Benedict, Ruth (1934) Patterns of Culture. Boston.

— (1946a) The Chrysanthemum and the Sword: Patterns of Japanese Culture. Boston.
— (1946b) The study of cultural patterns in European nations. Transactions of the New York Academy of Sciences, ser. 2 8: 274279.

Bennet, John (1968) Reciprocal economic exchanges among North American agricultural operators. Southwestern Journal of Anthropology, 24: 276309.

Blau, Peter (1964) Exchange and Power in Social Life. New York.

Brown, R. (1963) Explanation in Social Science. London.

Burling, Robbins (1962) Maximization theories and the study of economic anthropology. American Anthropologist, 64: 802821.

Burridge, K.O.L. (1969) New Heaven, New Earth: A Study of Millenarian Activities. Oxford. Cancian, Frank (1965) Economics and Prestige in a Maya Community. Stanford.

Cook, Scott (1969) The obsolete antimarket mentality: a critique of the substantivist ap

proach to economic anthropology. American Anthropologist, 68: 323345.

— (1969) The u antimarket y> mentality reexamined: a further critique of the substantivist approach to economic anthropology. Southwestern Journal of Anthropology, 25: 378406. Davis, J. (1972) Gifts and the U.K. economy. Man, 7: 408429.

Edel, Matthew (1969) Economic analysis in an anthropological setting: some methodological considerations. American Anthropologist, 71: 421433.

Epstein, T.S. (1967) The data of economics in anthropological analysis, in A.L. Epstein, ed., The Craft of Social Anthropology. London.

Firth, Raymond (1951) Elements of Social Organization. London.

—(1953) The Study of Values by Social Anthropologists. The Marett Lecture. London.

—ed. (1967) Themes in Economic Anthropology.
London.
—and Yamey, B.S., eds. (1964) Capital, Savings and
Credit in Peasant Societies. Chicago. Geertz, C. (1957)
Ritual and social change. a Javanese example. American
Anthropologist, 59: 3254.

— (1959) Toward a comparison of valueemphases in
   different cultures, in L.D. White, ed., The State of the
   Social Sciences. Chicago. 116132.
          Kroeber, A.L. The supercharging. American
Anthropologist, 19: 163213.

—and Kluckhohn, Clyde, eds. (1952) Culture• a critical
review of concepts and definitions.
   Papers of the Peabody Museum of Archaeology and
Ethnology, 47, vol. 1. Cambridge LeClair, E.E. and
Schneider, H.K., eds. (1968) Economic Anthropology.
New York. LeviStrauss, Claude (1958) Anthropologie
Structurale. Paris (English translation 1963 New York).

          Mauss, M. (1925) Essai sur le don, forme
          archaique de l' echange, in Sociologic et
                      anthropologic,

   Paris. Reprinted 1950. English translation 1954 et
seq as The Gift, London. Mead, M., ed. (1955)
Cultural Patterns and Technical Change. New
York. Mead, M. and Metraux, R. (1953) The Study
of Culture at a Distance. Chicago.

          Mendelsohn, E. and Elmana, Y. (1981) Sciences
and Cultures: Anthropological and Histori

cal Studies of the Sciences. Dordrecht.

Mintz, Sidney (1959) Internal market systems as mechanisms of social articulation. Proceed☐ings of the American Ethnological Society, 2030.

— (1969) Pratik: Haitian personal economic relations. Proceedings of the American Ethno☐logical Society, 5463.
Nash, J. (1981) Ethnographic aspects of the world capitalist system. Annual Review of An☐thropology, 393424.

Orans, Martin (1968) Maximising in Jajmani Land: a model of caste relations. American Anthropologist, 70: 875897.

Ortiz, S., ed. (1983) Economic Anthropology: Topics and Theories. Landham, MD.

— and Howard, A. (1971) Decisionmaking and the study of social process. Acta Sociologi☐ca 14: 213226.
Parsons, T. (1935) The place of ultimate values in sociological theory. International Journal of Ethics, 45: 282316.

— (1937) The Structure of Social Action. New York.
Polanyi, Karl, et al. (1957) Trade and Market in Early Empires. New York. Ponsionen, J.A. (1962) The Analysis of Social Change Reconsidered. The Hague. Sahlins, M. (1972) Stone Age Economics. Chicago.

Schneider, Harold (1974) Economic Man: the Anthropology of Economics. New York.

StuddertKennedy, G. (1975) Evidence and Explanation in Social Science. London. Tax, Sol, ed. (1977) Horizons of Anthropology, 2nd revised edition. Chicago. Waltman, Sandra (1979) Social Anthropology of Work. London.

Worsley, Peter (1957 revised 1968) The Trumpet shall Sound. London.

—

62

63

On Scale, Organisation and Performance

First published in *Paideuma* 24 1978 pp 1123 a volume in honour of Vinigi Grotanelli. Two books cited at the end have been republished as *The Conditions of Social Performance: an exploratory theory.* London Routledge 1988 and *Towers Besieged: the dilemma of the creative university* Vancouver Webzines and Lulu Books 2010

Social and cultural anthropology, and ethnology, have during their history been agreed upon one thing: the foundation of the work has been the detailed recording of the facts of social and cultural life. From that point on, there have been divergences, which, by comparison with diver□gences in other disciplines, have been extraordinarily minor. We have argued over the place to be accorded to indirectly observed data (by comparison with participant observation), about the length of field studies required to give reliability.

Above all there has been argument about "theoretical" perspectives which, in the main, have a great deal to do with the philosophical po□sition of the anthropologist and the selection of questions asked, and almost nothing to do with "theory" as the word is understood in most other subjects.

Grottanelli is honoured as an ethnographer; one of a significant group of European scholars, but for many years almost alone in Italy, who "informed" his ethnography with insights, built upon international trends. Behind this position, and perhaps especially now, is a deep, passionate and *engaged* concern for civilized values, for the future of the world of which the ethnogra□phic reality is the foundation, for the interplay of ideas, forces, peoples, and social movements. Scholarship may be separated and controlled in writing, but not in the anxieties and aspirations of the person engaged in it. However one may agree or disagree with this position or that, one respects intensity, commitment, the continuing and troublesome search for the future, and the sense of values which guides it. The ethnography of other societies is joined to the ethnography of the scholar's own, and the interplay creates deeper understandings. This indeed is the objec□tive of anthropology as a humanistic discipline.

This paper is, in a way, a request, to Grottanelli, his disciples, and to others, to extend the manifestation of their insights by applying them in scholarly writing to questions which con□cern them about the future of world civilisation. A Festschrift is a rite de passage, a movement from the constraints of the past to the openness of the future. This one is particularly timely because the diversity some would say chaos of intellectual trends in the discipline now po ses questions about the future of anthropology; and because one of those questions is the manner in which anthropology can or cannot, should or should not, be involved with the future.

It would be true I think to say that in the last twentyfive years there has been a major shift in emphasis in the use of ethnographic data. While "informed" interpretation of data is still by far the predominant mode, the vast increase in the data base, the penchant for "hypothesizing" (particularly in North America), the structure of the most elegant essays directed toward the answering of a specifically stated question, the inroads made on the humanities by scientism, and the growth of statistical and computer applications, have enriched and confused our metho dologies. What can be distressing about this situation is not the fact of divergence, even of con fusion for with synthesis and dialectic that is likely to be productive in the long run. It is that the proponents of specific methodologies often present them as the only source of validity and the *only* true anthropology. That is messianic nonsense, and has to be.

My position is that even the battery I have listed is incomplete and insufficient. Here I pre sent an argument couched in a further alternative which, for reasons of time and space, is not nearly as tight as the method requires. I argue that interpretation of empirical data, leading to the further reflection upon and elaboration of general positions, can be usefully supplemented by the reverse process, namely by the elaboration of formal logical models which can be used for deductive prediction. Ideally, such models should at least be informed by stated ethnogra phic information, though again for reasons of space and time, this will not be attempted in the present paper. However, the inherent strengths and weakness of such models can often be exa□mined better, or rather with a different lens, when they are stated in pure abstraction, ultima□tely in symbolic logic. I hold that formalism of this kind is not to be separated from ethnography, since each informs the other, since neither has a monopoly on approaches to validity, and since in fact the formal model can often be more usefully linked to questions of policy, social purpose, and the options of the future, which are upon observation ethnographic in their mani□festation.

In this paper I intend to argue about scale and organisation in the abstract, and in doing so raise questions about the implications of scale and organisation for the performance' of socio□cultural units, and thus for human satisfaction. The subject is of concern for several reasons.

First, ethnographers, social and cultural anthropologists, social historians, to say nothing of scholars in other disciplines, have been interested in phenomena which they identify as contain□ing variables of scale, have been interested in comparing situations of differing scale, and have informed their interpretations by assumptions about the implications, or indeed effects, of vari□ation in scale. A catalogue is out of place here; one only has to think of the concept of social and historical evolution, of the work of Godfrey and Monica Wilson (1945) on social change which was one of the earliest attempts at a formal theory and the volume of work which has emerged from the initial idea of the folkurban continuum

Second, a concern with scale is an important part of what I call the ethnosocial science of at least European and North American culture. That is, there are assumptions about scale present in sections of the community, including political leaders, which imply propositions which could be stated in social science terms, and are hence theoretically subject to scientific or scholarly examination. Such propositions can coincide with or diverge from propositions which are pre□sent in social science formal thinking, and we as anthropologists should have data and theories of our own by which to examine them.

Third, other disciplines have formal theories relating scale and organisation. The theories are drawn from different data, and are congruent with a different wider range of formal statements, than would be the case with anthropology. We lack such a theory, but worse, we fail to bring our positions to bear upon the formal models used in other disciplines. Economics, for examp□le, has for decades been concerned with the optimal size and organisation of the firm, and with the dynamics of change in size and organisation. The statements are now even being cast in an "evolutionary" perspective (see, for example, S.J. Prais, *The Evolution of Giant Firms in Great Britain.* Cambridge, Cambridge, University Press, 1976.) There will be no impact of anthropolo□gy upon economic thinking until anthropology has its own models which can be compared with those of the economist, and which it tests by reference to the kind of data that is at our com□mand' .

1 The performance of a social system or unit is defined in such a way that an increase in performance may be said to occur when (a) the behavioural profile of culture expands, this value being modified by the capabi□lity of the system to move further in the future. (b) the costs of achieving the behavioural profile decline, and (c) the gap between the

behavioural profile of culture and the potential (Le. desired) profile of culture decreases, neglecting consequential redefinition of the potential profile. For elaboration, see Belshaw, 1970.

2 A recent example of interplay between ethnographic data and generalized statement on this topic is con☐tained in G. Berreman, Scale and Social Relations", to be published in *Current Anthropology*, June 1978.

> The present discussion, then, bears these issues in mind. It is an attempt to systematize some interconnected propositions in abstract form, rooted in the author's (unexpressed) reading and experience of the ethnographic data, including the ethnography of complex societies. It is also oriented toward issues about the evaluation of the existing social system as it moves into the fu☐ture, rooted in ethnosocial sience and of course in the author's own prejudices and perspectives. If successful, the abstract statements ought to be readily applied to the interpretation of ethnographic material, yielding the probability of reformulation and modification; and in a si☐milar way should be comparable with statements in the formal models of other disciplines, yield☐ing the fruits of a dialectic argument. Neither of these extensions will, however, be attempted here.

> The idea of scale is itself highly ambiguous, and it tends to become more so the more we try to pin it down. In anthropology there is a trend to the linkage of scale and complexity of social organisation, not by asserting that they are synonymous, but by holding that as the one in☐creases, so does the other. There are equivalent problems in economics, which might serve to guide and warn us. The most widely known concepts which can serve as analogies are those of growth and development. Although economics and sociology are still confused in the usage ac☐corded to these two terms, there is a sense in which growth can be reserved for increases in

per formance indicators such as output, and development for increases in the complexity of organisation. When such a distinction is made, it is easier to see that growth does *not* necessarily mean development, and does not always or necessarily produce development or correlate with develop ment. When such relationships do exist they are due to special circumstances which can be examined, and both may be traced to a third causative factor. An increase in grain supply may be traced to a change in fertilizer used, or to haphazard seasonal variation, and may have no thing to do with prior organisational development, nor be followed by a lagging development. The same remarks hold for decreases in scale or growth, phenomena which are insufficiently studied.

Scale is a quantitative phenomenon. The question quickly arises as to the tools available for its measurement, and that in turn depends upon what is to be measured. Our concern in an thropology for the qualitative and descriptive has hindered the ingenuity with which measure ment should be approached. We stop at certain critical affirmations of distrust about measure ment in other disciplines, and a certain scepticism, usually justified, about the bases of measure ment in our own. First we must come to terms with the probability that all measurement in the social sciences does violence to the phenomena measured by simplifying, that is by leaving something out. This is particularly true of indices, even or perhaps especially in economics, and of the use of comparative data divorced from context, as with the Human Relations Area Files. What is left out *can* turn out to be crucial to the relationships examined, but it can also be tri vial, or can faithfully follow the trends determined by the measurement. Judgement and criti cism provide the correctives and modifications; the wholesale rejection of measurement does not.

Measurement when properly carried out does two other things. It provides a controlled basis for comparison, and, what is really a variant, it provides for controlled observation over time. Most studies of scale in anthropology use the basic perspective of comparison of social units which represent different scale characteristics, for example village and town. The conclusions drawn from such studies may be compared with long term evolutionary studies of civilisations, or short term studies of the dynamics of social change. Such studies can hardly be carried out at all without statements about scale, whether or not measurement is in fact used. The measure ment may be incipient rather than openly stated..

To understand this, it is necessary to make the point that qualitative statements are them selves statements of scale. "The Kwakiutl demonstrated rich cultural and artistic achievements". Such a statement includes at least two statements of scale. "Rich" implies complexity and va riety *greater* than that present in cultures with "poor" cultural and artistic achievement. "Achievement" in this context implies that in the eyes of the observer there was *greater* quali ty manifested than was the case in some other cultures. "Greater" implies the possibility of "still greater", "equal" or "lesser". The person making the rough statement invented here may deny that such a comparison was intended, but if so he would have to find different words. If he were successful, which I would consider impossibility, he would have arrived at a mean ingless statement. He may, for example, try to escape by saying the cultural output of the Kwakiutl was "beautiful" in some absolute sense. But that implies more beauty than in an hypo thetical situation in which the output could be judged "ugly". The idea of scale is still present, thought it may be reduced to its utmost simplicity, namely the assertion of presence or absence of a specific criterion, that is positive or negative on a scale.

Clearly, too, the observer has his standards of judgement, which in a scholarly work would be revealed. Those standards of judgement constitute the method by which he arrives at his *index*. He may not use a formal statistical index as invented by the quantitative methodologists. But index he must have. The problems of indexation are with us, whether or not we use figures. In the statement made above, "rich" masks an index, and so does "achievement". It may also be argued that "cultural" and "artistic" mask indices of culture and art. A great deal of the debate in anthropology surrounds definitions of more or less operational concepts. A definition implies an index, because an index is the operationalisation of a definition. While many classical indices are single resultant figures of a number of complex variables, it is also possible to have profile indices in which the various parts are not summed, but are expressed separately so that they may be seen at work, and because the act of summation is either impossible, or because there are no adequate principles to allow for weighting. The profile welfare level of living index deve□loped by the United Nations Research Institute for Social Development is an example; my own concept of the behavioural profile of culture is another.

The literature in anthropology which refers to scale specifically is usually concerned with fairly gross comparisons in which the subtleties I have mentioned are not of great importance. Nevertheless, they should be kept in mind, because they may influence our perception of the nature of the data which can be brought into the discussion.

Furthermore, any discussion which focuses upon the implication of differences of scale is bound to be insufficient it the scale reference is unclear. For example, we may be concerned with the scale of productive units. We presumably mean size, and intend to compare big ones with small ones. Ethnographically, there is an immediate problem of the boundary assigned to the unit being examined. Here we have to use criteria which we impose on the data; we are arbi□trary, though not purposeless. For example, it is our tradition to identify the productive unit in Melanesian society, x, as a household containing a two or three generation family, segmented possibly at the time of marriage. In Canada, it is our tradition to identify the productive unit as the factory or its equivalent in related sectors. We compare the two, making judgements about scale. But it is important to note that the choice of the units has a strong arbitrary element. It would be just as justifiable to compare households in both societies at one level, and factory with village at another. If we did this we would find many nonliterate or peasant societies in which the scale of productive units, coordinated in some form, is the equivalent in scale of many types of productive enterprise in modern capitalist society. The problem does not entirely disappear when we use the polity as the unit of comparison, the polity being the largest coordinated organisation of power relevant to the society in question [3] . For such comparison involves the discussion of the constituent units which make it up.

One might have thought that this question had been resolved in economics, in view of the long history of theoretical formality. However, this is not so, and the concept of the size of a firm changes according to the topic being examined in ways which may be instructive to anthro□pology. Size can refer to scale according to the following criteria, among numerous others: numbers of persons employed, monetary value of capital, monetary value of market turnover, monetary value of production, proportion of GNP. represented by the monetary value of turn□over or by production. Furthermore, the typical unit of examination can be either the plant, that is the physical unit which is organized for production, or the firm, that is the largest com□merciallyoriented unit which responds to a single authority.

In anthropology we have all these choices and many more. The simplest thing to note is the number of persons contained in a given social unit, the boundaries defined by some principle of organisation, from household, to lineage, to geographicallydefined community, to church or firm, to linguistic group, to polity. We can also start with any given ego, and ask at least two questions. How many persons does ego interact with on a daytoday basis? How many persons are contained in ego's widest network of contact? The two answers may vary independently and in contradictory directions.

There is also a scaling dimension which involves intensity of interaction. There is movement from one extreme, in which the boundary encloses a rolecomplete group, to another, in which a person lives through a multitude of roles, each of which relates to a different corporate institu□tion, and often to a complex range of bounded groups (ethnic, political, religious, and so forth). The scale dimension linked to the number of persons will not take this variable directly into ac☐count. Similarly, one might argue that yet another scaling dimension often (though not always) decreases with increases in other aspects of scale. If there is a household of thirteen in a village of sixtyfive, the village constituting an inwardturning rolecomplete group, it may be that there is extremely intense level of daytoday personal interaction. On the other hand, two house☐holds of five and sixtyfive, but lacking a network of wider kin or friends, with a work setting based on online production and a hierarchical social division of labour, could have a very low level of personal interaction. Thus a dimension of scale based on numbers would be equal, but one based on the number of personal interactions taking place in a given period would be high in the first instance and low in the second.

On the other hand, rather than counting the mere number of social interactions, one may be interested in assessing the way in which the interactions relate to complexity. If this is the case, the larger the number of roles and the more clearly differentiated they are, the greater, other things being equal, the complexity of the system. Of course, everything depends on how you count the roles. A case could be made for saying that a Melanesian adult married male fulfils one role, which combines the social expectation that he will be a shifting cultivator, father, hus☐band, brother, son, fisherman, canoebuilder, magician, defender of the community, and a num☐ber of other things wrapped up into one package. But you don't have to count all those things together, particularly when closer inspection reveals that not all Melanesians do all these things, with the same skill and intensity, and that they often borrow skills from others. So then it may be that a Melanesian is involved with more roles than many Westerners, for example the post man who is father, husband and son, but nothing else. On the other hand, in typical Western so cieties one does add a range of roles to that limited list, and furthermore even when the num bers of roles in the two styles of society are similar, some of the Western roles are, intuitively, more separated from each other than are the Melanesian ones, and they may even be in conflict. To be realistic, any counting of roles needs to be weighted by attention to such variables.

The mention of conflict leads to the next important set of variables which anthropologists have to take into account. Scales are applied not only with reference to social relations as ab stractions but to goals and preferences, in short to values. As I have argued elsewhere *ad nau seam,* the treatment of values in anthropology is thoroughly confused because some of the most prestigious and influential accounts completely overlook the point that, at least in the English language, the concept of value *cannot* be divorced from the concept of scale. A value is not a piece of philosophical mystery floating around in a culture, as most anthropology would have us believe. A value is an measure attached to something; by extension values in a culture are (for example, but not exclusively) goals, objectives, or preferences which are emphasized *to vary ing degrees,* and according to scaling criteria; by further extension, one does not value some thing, one values it a great deal, moderately, a little, or not at all; one can even negatively value it.

Here of course we are talking of individual goals or preferences, presumably assessed by indi viduals, or by individuals expressing them on behalf Of institutions. This is the topic par excel lence of welfare economics, a subject which we anthropologists do not read, partly

because it is too difficult, and partly because it would raise
enormous questions for ethnography and ethno☐logical
interpretation which I suspect we know we cannot
handle. Yet welfare economics, con☐cerned as it is with
the ways in which individual preferences interact as a
result of their valua☐tion, and produce a cultural
resultant, is also anthropology, particularly as more of
us come to use the BarthBlau approach to choice and the
impact of action upon structure.

In most of anthropology, particularly when we are
concerned with culture and social organi☐sation, even
when the approach is particularistic, our focus tends to be
on some form of group. We study perhaps the village, as
representative of a wider unit, and have been criticized for
this. Some of us, more sociologically oriented, are
interested in varieties of corporate group, such as lineage,
credit association or age grade. Some of us put the units
together under the heading of culture, for which the
boundary is usually, though not always, defined by
language. In the So☐viet Union, the ethnographic object
can be the "ethnos", elsewhere the ethnic group. We
speak, it turns out very loosely, of society or social
system, which, so long as the participants are
inter☐acting, can be bounded according to a thousand
criteria, it seems, or even none at all. The most common
usage of "society" is a euphemism for a polity.
Inspection shows that quite often, particularly in
complex conditions, social relations are not at all
limited by the boundaries of the defined society, and that
the analyst, for good reason or unthinkingly, is imposing
the bound☐ary that by definition fits the polity, that is
the largest identifiable unit, short of global socie☐ty,
in which power can be seen to be organised and an
administration effected.

In the early postwar years, and before that following the influence of Malinowski and Boas, it became fashionable to downplay the significance of those anthropologists who were con□cerned with trait analysis, particularly because they were addressing themselves to the diffusionevolution controversy in a doubtful way. However, the Human Relations Area Files, the work of G.P. Murdock, S. Udy, and many others, and most recently the contribution of Lomax and Arensberg, indicated that the identification of traits for large statistical and modelrelated com□parison was in fact still a lively and debatable issue. It is going to become even more so as new theoretical questions are asked, and indeed the time has come for a reappraisal of the lessons, the achievements, methods, and failures of earlier scholarship or we will have to learn them all over again.

I raise this question because it is fundamental to any concept of scale which involves culture. It is even fundamental to the critique of participantobservation fieldwork. "Which units of cul□ture do you observe and record and put together in systemic analysis?" is a question which applies to *any* method of anthropological enquiry. In modern fieldwork we tend to follow the tra□dition of earlier ethnographies, with modifications suggested by refinements of philosophy or slight changes in question. (How tired one is becoming of the continuous onstream production of ethnographic treatises on New Guinea cultures, which do not have the modesty to admit that they are putting on record material for the ethnographic map, but rather insist that the treat□ment justifies a philosophical position.) We have seldom developed the resources which enable us to gather new types of data, except where teamwork becomes practicable. We are thus vul□nerable to the charge that the phenomena we record could be atypical, that the single instance we give of ritual cannot be assessed for its representative qualities that we are not in a position to judge the intensity of valuation. Of course, we have at least partial answers to such charges, but we deceive ourselves if we feel that we are superior in this respect of those naively frank about the manner in which they assembled traits. The loss of the word does not mean the loss of the problem.

The issue becomes more germane when we consider the type of question for which scale in culture becomes of theoretical significance. What is scale in culture? It has to do with such things as the volume and diversity of messages passed through the symbol system, or the volume and range of ideas and concepts which are present. It may have to do with the number of persons who are using the symbol system, who share the ideas and concepts within the other wisedetermined boundary. If this is the case, is the index of scale simply the number of persons within the boundary?

That could be the case, and I think it is in many possible treatments of cultural scale. If so, it is not very interesting, and does not answer very interesting questions. But I think there are inte resting questions which suggest that this approach is only a simple beginning.

The idea of scale in culture (in differing forms of words) has been implicit in some approa ches identifying qualities of civilisation. Most attempts in this direction have been treated with scepticism in anthropology, largely because we see dubious value premises in such attempts, or because we would wish to be more rigorous in criteria. Nevertheless, our scepticism cannot dis pose of the validity of certain kinds of questions. One such field of concern is the quality of in☐tellectual achievement in a culture. While we are going through a period in which the very no☐tion of quality is being barbarically attacked, we should reexamine the foundations of the is☐sue. There is one sense in which civilisation and intellectual quality can be linked to the range of ideas, concepts and propositions which are used and to the complexity of the concern which the mind is accustomed to tackling. Both dimensions require careful definition and modifica☐tion (for example, with reference to dynamics and intellectual utility) which cannot be expressed here.

The relevance of the point, however, is to show that both dimensions, that is range and complexity, are dimensions of scale. The preoccupation with quality inevitably involves a pre☐occupation with quantity.

Let me take up an example of a different kind of question, namely the examination of a pro☐position in the field of culture. Propositions state relationships, and any such statement involves the presence or absence of the variables, their growth or diminishment, in other words state☐ments of quantity. They can come in many different kinds. One such, which I consider to be crucial to anthropological theory, would assert that the rate of innovation is, to simplify, a func☐tion of the size of the pool of ideas modified by the rate of circulation of those ideas [4] All the terms in this equation are aspects of the scale of culture, and it is asserted that one of them is composed of relations between the other two. It is difficult to see how this proposition can in practice be tested or falsified without the development of an indexing and measuring technique. Part of that technique will have to be the identification of the units of culture in the form of ideas, and another part will have to be the identification of message conduits appropriate to the culture and the observation of the messages passed along them. Other disciplines, particularly economics, sociology, and political science are already using macro statistical and survey devices which purport to resolve into indices which bear upon aspects of the question. Yet the question, dealing with culture as it does, is surely at the heart of anthropology, and we will be most dissatisfied with the validity of the work attributed to our sister subjects.

The statements above have been concerned primarily with definition and clarification. I now with to propose some theoretical relationships which should be tested more deeply with ethno graphic material, even though in some instances I cannot be confident about the precision of even the direction in which the forces are working. However, to begin, it seems to me that, both in ethnosocial science and in anthropology there has been a tendency to think of scale as a single and sufficient variable in the process of explaining other variables, such as the impersona lity of relationships or secularisation or anomie. The central feature of scale in such arguments is the size of the population being considered. It will be my contention that the size of the po pulation is not the governing variable in itself, and that the resultants in question must be seen as the outcome of an interplay between several scale variables, and particularly between ele ments of scale and modes of organisation to which the scales relate.

For example, following Redfield, authors too numerous to mention have pointed to the city as an agent of secularisation and impersonalisation, contrasting it with the folk village. I do not recall that Redfield made the distinction on the basis of population size alone, or even serious ly; he was much more concerned with what we would now label life styles, and he saw the city being influenced by external, even global forces whereas the folk village was protected from these and inward turning. The universality of Redfield's model was limited to the existence of specific, though not theoretically elaborated conditions. It could not apply to the mediaeval ci□ty, the historical oriental city, the city of preColumbian Mesoamerica. It is very doubtful in□deed whether it applies in many large contemporary cities, and insofar as it does, the larger city is not necessarily more secular and impersonal than the smaller, even within the same culture.

What is at issue is the way in which the life and culture of the city is organized. A large city may be divided into neighbourhoods, ethnic components, guilds, workshops, and other groups which mobilize interest and loyalties so that it can retain intensities of personal rela□tions and of focussed cultural communication, and even cause these to grow in ways that are be□yond the capability of the small town or village. Without controlling the ethnographic facts, I cite the probability that this is the case in Florence and Siena today, that it is important to the understanding of Rio de Janeiro and Sao Paulo, and to the way of life of the much maligned shantytowns, bidonvilles, favellas of Africa and Latin America, and the new Toronto which is becoming ethnically dominated. On the other side of the coin, the social organisation of the vil□lage or rural populace is equally important. A small populace can be intensely interactive and inward looking, divisively organized with little internal interaction, geographically scattered, and so forth.

There is also an important element of timedynamics to be considered. From the thirties to the sixties numerous studies provided evidence that urbanisation brought breakdowns of family life, kinship organisation, and ritual. Perhaps. But urbanisation also meant population shift, and many of the phenomena were at an early historical stage, even then. A migrant family, isolated from kin by the move, naturally has to live with important modifications (although even here it has been noted from Africa and Oceania that where conditions are auspicious the urban kins☐man often retains strong ties with his rural relatives). This is particularly the case when the sea, or expensive transport, intervenes. But as time permits the growth of population, the cut off fa☐mily unit gains the potentiality to reinvent, as it were, kinship Furthermore, many of the stu☐dies were undertaken at a time of relatively low per capita income; the priorities for its expendi☐ture were survival, and also tapping in to the fascinating consumer world which is an important positive value of city life (however much intellectuals may endeavour to impose their negative judgement upon it). But with almost global increases of real income, the possibility has also in☐creased of diverting substantial percentages to ceremony, ritual, and the religious life. Hence large groups of modern city dwellers oriented towards redefinitions of religion, ceremony, and the folk life, are growing up in parallel with the detached impersonal apartment dweller or suburban family of the stereotype. Indeed it may be the case that in the United States there is more mo☐bility of residence than in other countries, particularly among university intellectuals, but by no means limited to them. Mobility of residence in a large country involves frequent changes of personal ties. I believe there has been a tendency for North American analysts to superimpose a model derived from their own society upon the phenomena of others, though this is not the whole explanation.

Similar remarks apply to the examination of politics. Differences between Switzerland, the Western Provinces of Canada, France, and the United States, have very little to do with the size of the population as such, although I must admit that there is a relationship between popula tion and geographical size which makes certain types of organisation very difficult to put into practice (and hence I would argue that in an ideal world it would be of great benefit if the U.S.S. R., the U.S.A., and China each consisted of half a dozen or more truly separated countries.) The differences in the ways in which the politics in question contribute to the satisfaction of the citizens, that is, in my jargon, contribute to social performance, is very largely an outcome of the nature of political and ethnic boundaries within the countries concerned, on the one hand, and the internal structure of communications on the other. Both of these things can be expressed in scale terms, but it is not population scale per se. For example, the question of Que bec in Canada, and the industrial and commercial structure of British Columbia, would have very different manifestations if (a) Canada had been organised on a cantonal basis with ethnic and linguistic overtones, and (b) the communications system of British Columbia had been orga nised and developed in a selfcontained Swiss style, rather than being dominated by federal geo graphical considerations.

The issues of scale also apply to corporate groups. At what size are they the most effective, in terms of costs of output, or the personal involvement of participants? Once again, the answer is that it all depends on the organisation, and, in the larger units, the ways in which the consti tuent parts of the organisation articulate with each other. It has been observed, for example, that the International Telephone and Telegraph Company is highly centralized, nationally con trolled despite its global operations, and yet the component parts operate as if the others do not exist. On the other hand, International Business Machines, Royal Dutch Shell, and Nestle though all large multinationals, have varying degrees of international participation, interaction between components, and plant control and size. In the decades of takeoff into modern industrialisation, very large scale Japanese enterprises operated by incorporating into their processes the output of small family workshops. The permutations and combinations are endless, and are open to anthropological comparison.

It is now fashionable to support the slogan "Small is Beautiful" as a critique of contempora☐ry society, particularly in production and technological matters. In July, 1977, for example, I attended the InterCongress of the Pacific Science Association in Bali, Indonesia, which was treating the theme of "Appropriate Technology". Margaret Mead was a participant, and I admired the restraint with which she refrained from pointing out that in 1955 she was responsible for the then influential volume *Cultural Patterns and Technological Change,* which at that date treated most of the issues which are now still current. The economists, engineers and bankers who were present in Bali, were making their points on the basis of selfdiscovery, as if there was no history in the literature. And they were making their points in extreme terms; either small was good and beautiful and effective or it could never meet the optimum effectiveness represented by large. Very little attention was given to the possibilities of combining small and large, or having both in parallel, or of deciding between the two on the basis of a combination of social objectives and the cultural content of activity.

I can give but one illustrative example. Electronic communication can be put together in technological packages of very high capital cost, and complexity and very low personal involve ment. A nationally centralized television system based on satellite technology would be an example, and one debate centres upon whether this. is the most suitable kind of system to be thought of for large population countries with large geographical areas, even though they may be poor on a per capita basis. Again, on a global scale poor commodityproducing countries which cannot connect with the satellite transmissions used to handle commodity market infor mation and transactions are at a disadvantage. Yet the idea of such systems is often criticized on account of the scale and cost implications.

But it might also be argued that, even given the huge networks involved, it is technically, ad ministratively, and socially possible to link them effectively with small scale units of interac tion to increase decentralisation and to enable ethnically disparate communities to communicate effectively and regain a selfrespect, a vitality and a viability which would otherwise be in jeopardy. A national satellite television network does not *have* to be organized centrally; that is a political and administrative decision not necessarily dictated by the technology. It can be used as a conduit from the parts to the other parts Similarly, given certain questions of economy and technology that cannot be gone into here, it is possible for sophisticated information to be made available to the smallest possible social unit by electronic means, whether that unit be house hold or village or office in town or countryside. It is no longer necessary to go to the expense of establishing largescale university libraries in numerous centres, or insist that users of infor mation travel to national data centres. In this kind of instance, largescale organisation is essen tial to smallscale use.

The debate about scale, in ethnosocial science terms, has been particularly vigorous with re ference to university organisation, and the structure of the research establishment. It is perhaps appropriate to use this as the final area of discourse in view of the intensity of the debate in Italian, as well as other, circles at this time. It might indeed be argued that Italian university troubles are largely attributable to the immense growth and huge size which some of them have attained. Parallels could be drawn with the University of California and Parisian universities in the sixties. Obviously, complaints are not focussed specifically on the issue of size, but the question remains, and has been put, is size itself the factor which leads to administrative atrophy, policy negation, teaching poverty, research confusion, political confrontation?

Many scholars, of course, refuse to consider universities as goaloriented institutions, largely because strong elements in the public think of the goals in unacceptable vocational manpower producing terms, and this kind of objective becomes highly inflammatory in times of crisis when students are resolving in their own persons the conflict of intellectual openended enqui ry and restrictive professional demands which can be related to the "mealticket" complex. While such confusion and negativism prevails in the scholarly community, that community has no means whereby it can judge the performance of a university; indeed many of its members deny that such a concept has any significance, and so we are led to a justification of anarchy.

It is, however, possible to affirm certain goals which, while not acceptable to all, provide a set of performance criteria which then enables us to consider questions of size. I have argued at length about this elsewhere, and arrived at the following summary:

> "The special characteristics of university quality are:
>
> a) the objective of generating enquiry and creativity,
>
> b) the objective of expanding cultural resources, including scientific knowledge and artistic works,
>
> c) the objective of developing powers of scientific, aesthetic and moral judgement, which is also essential as a means to the first two characteristics,
>
> d) the assumption that students are adults,
>
> e) the *derived* activity of education for the application of cultural resources, including knowledge, attitudes toward enquiry, and disciplined judgement." (Belshaw 1974.
> Emphases ad de d.)

Once performance objectives have been stated, whether one fully agrees with them or not, they can be used as a reference point for the evaluation of the effects of the social organisa tion, cultural values, communication of ideas, and scale, of specific organisations on the analo gy of any other social organisation with which anthropologists deal. Here, of course, I am con cerned with the general rather than the specific, and I must focus on scale, rather than all the other factors with which one could deal.

Small universities (let us say, under a thousand students) have often been lauded for the qua lity of intellectual education, especially in the humanities, which they can provide. They are, however, somewhat like culturally bound villages, in the sense that the student is limited in the types of ideas with which he deals. If the university has a clearly expressed philosophy of edu cation, which the student maturely and consciously chooses as his road to creative thinking, the clarity of method and the intensity of personal support can be formative in a disciplined and productive way. But this is not necessarily the case. If the student is philosophically misplaced, he will spend his time psychologically fighting the system, without escape, and if the university has no philosophy of education, (a) the likelihood of student misplacement will be high, and (b) the student may be subjected to a mishmash of wishywashy ideas, so that his ability to sur vive, in a creative sense, becomes a matter of accident and personality Small universities have virtues, then, only in special circumstances and for specific kinds of students.

The middle range university, say up to 10,000 students, is again in a variable position. Some such universities have established a very high tradition of creative scholarship, in both student and faculty member. They have tended to be somewhat purposive philosophically, e.g. by orien ting themselves to the creation of cultured leaders and gentlemen, and by reinforcing the tra dition of the scholar who is individual as a scholar but in his social life is a member of an intel lectual community Sometimes the philosophy has had a strong religious support, and although such universities may have been somewhat short on scientific hardware, they were strong on people and books. Most have used the concept of the college as an organising principle providing smallness of scale within the wider framework.

From a faculty perspective, such universities, once established with a long continuing tradi tion, have retained much of their creative appeal, but their appeal and effect on students is by no means as strong as it used to be. With their emphasis on books and people, such universities could often maintain and support highly esoteric branches of knowledge, with very few stu dents, who selected themselves with advanced scholarship in mind. But, even allowing for such outoftheway disciplines, the expansion of such universities could not keep pace with the ex plosion of knowledge and the diversification of its organisation, except in a few special fields. Furthermore, the close relation of faculty member to student, and particularly to the student advancing in a scholarly career, tended to be highly dependent, of clientpatron form. The emergence of schools, that is very restrictive approaches to disciplines with a high degree of ortho□doxy, turned the notion of discipline into its biblical rather than its intellectual meaning. This was helpful to some forms of faculty creativity, and was good for the students who under□stood it and accepted it.

In Europe, and in mediaeval times, the confinements of scale which we can see operating here were counterbalanced by a process which now seems to be declining in Europe, and to have little place elsewhere. The student searched beyond the confines of his own institution. This is particularly possible where universities are in close geographical connection, and where the stu□dent is not confined by the kind of high school class which is typical of North American under□graduate education. Students would know of lectures given elsewhere, would be able in cafes and in other ways to gain access to specialists and scholars of influence (though often the path to contact was strewn with difficulties) and would seek stimulus accordingly.

The giant university can contain elements of the small and medium, and the student can be caught in the same way. He finds himself in an urban setting rather than a village, and he can be isolated, alienated and destroyed by the impersonality and confusion of the system. He can al☐so learn to find his way through the maze, and if and when he knows what he wants, he can usual☐ly find it because it is likely to be there. It is now calculated that in most conventionally de☐fined disciplines it requires forty to fifty faculty members to cover the field with depth; only the massive university can hope to achieve this in a large number of fields, and to add the further depth of research institutes and programmes, and interdisciplinary combinations. Under☐graduate student preparation today consists in permitting students to explore within this range, and to start to make intellectual connections which could not otherwise have been imagined. Advanced student work may involve a choice of a narrow subtopic which could not be present in a smaller university except by chance, or a wideranging breadth of interest for which the small university is too restrictive, or even a combination.

Of course whether the large university does this or fails depends on the way it handles its size. Theoretically, and ideally, it could be constituted of small parts, each intellectually and phi☐losophically defined, among which the student was encouraged to roam. Unfortunately, in most university traditions the defamation of such parts is as departments or discipline faculties, which places unnecessary and sometimes damaging restraints on the organisation and presentation of knowledge. Also unfortunately, some university systems attempt to impose a structure defined in teaching terms upon the research process. While the two are interlinked, they require very dif ferent concepts of manpower, its distribution and concentration and even of hierarchy. Thus the large university fails to capitalize on the advantages of its size by, in most cases, failing to invent an internal organisation designed to optimize intellectual conditions.

It also is evident that, historically, many giant universities are simply cancerous growths upon the old smaller body, using patterns of organisation and material resources which were de signed for them when they were small, and when the nature of knowledge was relatively simple. They have, in other words, failed to adapt with growth, for reasons which are usually traced to governmental influence, but which are also rooted in the combination of academic inertia and radical unreality.

To sum up, scale in its various manifestations has complex interactions with organisation and performance, with numerous permutations and combinations of possible variables. The study of those manifestations, particularly through the use of anthropological and ethnological observa tion in contexts which may be unorthodox for those disciplines, is still in its infancy, and there is much to do before a theory can be productive. I hope that these remarks may encourage others to pursue some of the questions, and that some of the answers will come from the vigor☐ous Italian ethnology which Vigini Grottanelli and his colleagues have done so much to form.

Bibliography

Belshaw, Cyril S. *The Conditions of Social Performance: An Exploratory Theory..* London, Routledge and Kegal Paul, 1970 and 1995.

—, *Towers Besieged, The Dilemma of the Creative University.* Toronto, McClelland and Stewart, 1974. Also webzines of Vancouver and Lulu Press 2010. Berremann, G. Scale and Social Relations. *Current Anthropology,*

Mead, M. (ed.), *Cultural Patterns and Technical Change.* New York, Mentor Books, 1955.

Wilson, Godfrey and Monica. *The Analysis of Social Change.* Cambridge, Cambridge University Press, 1945.

Which Theory for Which Development?

First published in *L'Uomo* Universitá di Roma Vol. XI n.2 1987 pp.295 – 314 with summary in Italian.. This paper was completed under the terms of a Senior Research Stipend of the WennerGren Foundation for Anthropological Research, New York.

Without challenging the obvious need for classification as an instrument of anthropological thought, I have in the past drawn attention to the way uncritical methods can mask potentialities of examining the force of variables in comparative studies (Belshaw 1969). In this paper I return to the issue by examining another example of the limitations of classification. The example is the analysis of economies parallel to industrial and commercial monetary economies (whether "capitalist" or "socialist"). My in☐tent is to ask (a) whether clarity and accuracy are lost through present methods of classification, (b) whether there is an alternative method, and (c) whether such an alternative method might be useful in examining propositions relevant to development studies.

The stimulus for the paper is derived from an important study undertaken by Veechibala Das (1986) entitled *The urban informal sector: an alternative analysis* carried out for Ph. D. work in Community and Regional Planning. The study draws heavily on work in economic development, human geography and planning, and to some extent on anthropology, revealing a plethora of classifications, and attempting to resolve the confu□sions and inconsistencies in the literature, related to a dynamic of origins and functions of informal sectors, worldwide. It is the global implication that something called "an informal sector" al□ways exists in parallel with capitalist market or socialist centrally planned economies that provides the challenge. For this provides opportunities for comparative examination of forces which affect the total performance of economies, polities and societies, where□as discussion of the market or planned economy alone provides only part of the answer.

I choose the therm "parallel economies" only for heuristic purposes, to distance myself from the terms already established in the literature, and because a shorthand reference is needed (though I will abandon it by the end of the paper.) All cultures are now part of nation state systems. The examination of the eco□nomy of relationships has largely concentrated on the dominant ideological perspective of the system, that is market capitalism or state socialism, or some combination. Nevertheless, ever since the sunset of colonial rule, minority attention has suggested that activity lying "outside" the dominant systems is of very great im portance, even in the most advanced of capitalist and socialist countries. It is this activity which the Das thesis and major con temporary literature outside of anthropology dubs as "informal", and which I am calling "parallel", at least for the nonce.

I admit immediately that the term "parallel economies" has all the difficulties associated with the plethora of other terms that are favoured by this or that author. "Parallel" implies a social equivalence which may or may not be present, and begs the issue as to whether the activity in question is, for example, subordinate, dominant, intertwined with, or detached from, the capitalist or socialist activity. Much of the early literature suggests subordina tion, though more recent studies are more consistent with intert wining at various levels.

Further, the word "economy" suggests a closed system, again an issue that should be subject to empirical enquiry rather than being assumed. While few would doubt that one can normally abstract systemic and closed characteristics of capitalist and social ist polities, it must be admitted that such an abstraction defies reality. International forces have always been recognized, and now in the main body of economics the significance of exogenous variables and of parallel activities is getting considerable reinforce ment. If this is true of the orthodox economic systems, it is even more true of the parallel sector. It has to be determined empirical ly whether such a sector is or is not an economy in the systemic sense. That is, can an analyst armed with data determine a system of interacting relationships which he can consider closed, other things being equal? This can frequently be done, and is indeed a commonplace in anthropology; but it cannot be assumed. While the black market may evidence a system of its own, self help bricolage activities may influence supply and demand in the market☐place more than with each other.

With such cautions in mind I shall nevertheless retain the term for convenience, *pro tempore.*

The attention now being given to the role of parallel econo☐mies emerges from a gradual recognition that models limited to capitalist or socialist relationships are in fact ethnocentric or ideologically biased if they purport to deal with global phe☐nomena. The origins of such a correction in perspective lie with the dual economy of Boeke (1942, 1953) and the perhaps more accurate plural society of Furnivall (1939), who held the capitalist colonial model could only be applied to a restricted range of be☐haviour. Yet even here the ethnocentrism is now apparent. Capi☐talism represented such a unique cultural mode that there was a sharp boundary between that and other cultures. Non capitalism, or tradition, or the "Asian economy" was completely different in world view, in values, in social exchange relations, and particular☐ly in the absence of a dynamic (this was more strongly stated in Boeke). In making comparisons, capitalism was the starting point.

That perspective remains true today. Fundamentally, the pa☐rallel or informal sector is that which economists classically do not model ... Historically, it has been left out. Now that it is being discovered and rediscovered, it turns out that it seems to operate with different rules, not merely empirically but also theoretically. Some anthropology, derived from Polanyi (e.g. 1957) and the sub☐stantivists (e.g. Paul Bohannan and George Dalton) reinforces such a position, suggesting that there are few if any "universal" models of behaviour, each culture providing a firm boundary, often with stasis on one side and dynamism on the other. Usually, this is to confuse empirical cultural variation with a presumed abs☐ence of universal, or broader, process, a confusion which makes the study of change and development almost deniable.

Before entering into the question of the validity or otherwise of boundary statements, let us overview the range of concepts, and the ideas behind them, in the literature. It must first be said that the literature is immense, and that neither Das nor I, nor any earlier author attempting a review, has covered all possible refer☐ences. Computer searches (even if all references were in data banks) are necessarily limited because the full range of terms can☐not be predetermined, and do not necessarily show up in titles or keywords. My own selection here will be to follow the literature which Das accessed and examined, and then look for similar con cepts in anthropology. In anthropology it appears that reference to even the plethora of terms used in other disciplines is minimal. This is not to say, however, that we do not examine the issues. Indeed we do, with different terms, and very frequently arriving at a consensus which is opposed to perspectives in other disci☐plines, but not directly confronting them.

In fact Das' review reveals an immediate weakness of any classificatory system, where the terms are not agreed upon, name☐ly that it is difficult to be sure that all possible classifications have been taken into account in theoretical statements. A literature search must begin with what is known, and does not automatical☐ly lead into the discovery of what is not at first known.

I also impose a further restriction, following Das. I shall con☐centrate on that literature which deals with urban society. Das herself does not completely restrict the search to urban studies, taking into account, for example, wider national examinations; but it is the analysis of urban life that is her main goal. In a way this makes her task a little more difficult, at least on the surface, since it is perhaps easier to discern a certain kind of dualism based on the pair of concepts "city/town" and "rural/country". Indeed, talking about town also usually implies at least passing reference to country, as if country were an opposite, but interconnected, and Das of course does this. The dichotomy is one way or another inescapable in the anthropological studies. But within the city it☐self, the distinctions are not as superficially easy (I say "super☐ficially" easy because the town/country distinction is not at all easy when one probes in depth).

What does this kind of sampling do to reveal issues of clarity and accuracy? From the Das monograph we can *see* that there is no agreed terminology, arguments abound as to whether the real☐ity is one of dualism or pluralism, and what the criteria for deter☐mining separated systemic sectors should be. Here are some of the main classifications to which Das refers.

Most of the designations of sector I are, or can be, criteria used to determine whether an activity or a section of the popula□tion can be described by some such term as "informal" by contrast to the "formal" sector II. Each of the authors above uses the crite□rion or criteria as the primary determinant of classification, although he may elaborate by breaking up the criterion by means of lists of components, e.g. by listing appropriate occupations. It is quite evident that the method of arriving at the criteria is to determine on the basis of common sense, field experience, and the like, that there are at least two different kinds of lifestyles in a city or group of cities which correlate to differing methods of production and/or distribution. When authors have engaged in empirical investigation their research method frequently requires

Sector I

Representative author ex Das

Traditional eastern

limited needs

Production for use Nonevolutionary

Rural

Bazaar sector Peasant

Formal

Unstructured Unprotected

Lower circuit

Urban   poor/squat□ters/immigrants   in certain occupations

Petty traders lacking skill and capital Peasant using total family

Sector II

Changing "western" open needs

For gain

Dynamically changing

Industrial Firmcantered Capitalist Informal Structured Protected Upper circuit

Others

Skilled capitalized firms

Labour outside family

Individual and cor□porate entrepreneur

Government or trade

Union supervision

Enterprise state protected

Registered

Wage employed Regular workers

Wages at or over minimum

Representative author ex Das

Boeke (1953)

Furnivall (1939) Brookfield (1975) Chayanov

(trans. 1966) Higgins (1968) Geertz (1963) McGee (1971) Das (1986)

Emmerji (1974) Mazumdar (1979) Santos (1979) Moser (1978)

I.L.O. (1972) Franklin (1965)

Friedmann & Sullivan (1974) Mazumdar (1975)

Weeks (1975) Sethuraman (1976)

Sethuraman (1976) Schaefer (1976)

pluralist rather than dualist.

Some authors add an "intermediate sector" (Steel 1977) and others stress "petty commodity sector" (Forbes 1981, McGee 1979).

Again since the informal sector is sought in opposition to or by contrast with an apparently agreed upon formal sector, writers have discovered it outside the Third World. Similar sorts of con☐fusions and disagreements abound, and authors select terms to make differentiations. Simon and Witt's (1982) underground eco☐nomy is characterized elsewhere as a second economy, irregular economy, subterranean economy, black economy, characterized by clandestine employment, and equated with informal by Min☐gione (1985) and others. Some characterize it by referring to unde☐clared income activities plus crime (De Grazia 1984), or a com☐bination of hidden, criminal and household activity, unmeasured, untaxed, and unregulated (Mattera 1985). Once such economies receive study they are found to constitute an enormous propor☐tion of GDP (see Das 1986: 88 *et seq)* In socialist societies, some of the criteria remain the same, but others are blurred. Mattera (1985) typically identifies private enterprise as the characterizing factor, but clearly there must be a distinction between that activity which is truly underground on the one hand and that which is state encouraged; and between the legal and the illegal.

I can see that most anthropologists, confronted with such identifications, would say that apples and oranges are being com☐pared. Although household activity in industrialized societies may have some points of similarity nonpeasant traditional socie☐ty, if and when exchange is wahr,e6k organized crime and the parallel internal dollar economy of Poland seem very different from informal urban sectors in Africa, Latin America, or Asia. On the other hand garage sales and second hand markets in France or Canada may have marked similarities with peasant markets which seem opposed to commercial firms in the Third World. At this stage I suggest we suspend our immediate impulse to criticism, and pursue the matter further.

Nevertheless, let us note that not a single one of the sets of criteria referred to above, except perhaps rural/urban, refers at all clearly to one major style of exchange which anthropologists study, which is at least equally worthy of being called informal (though in fact, like any style of economy, embodying rules which can be formalized). I refer of course to that nexus of behaviour which emerges from considerations of reciprocity and which can be described as a social exchange system, without intervention of money.

What the anthropologists do with the same kind of issue? How do they handle the conceptual debates of their colleagues from other disciplines? Do we get closer through anthropology to an appropriate and existing classification system?

To partially answer these questions I consulted more or less at random a number of anthropological urban studies (Ansari & Nas 1982; Basham 1978; Cornelius & Trueblood 1974; Eames & Goode 1977; Geertz 1963; Gilbert 1982; Gmelch & Zenner 1980; Khuri 1975; Lewis 1959, 1966; Parkin 1975; Perlman 1976; Red□field 1930; Redfield & Singer 1954;

Rew 1974; Spoehr 1963). Only one author in the sample (Cohen 1974) refers to the range of concepts associated with and including "the informal", although Perlman (1976) gives a thorough history of related concepts. In short, anthropologists have not, as a whole, entered into the de☐bate and have developed their own terms, yet another set of con☐cepts. This is despite the common evolutionary origin from Boeke and Furnivall, and the entry of anthropologists such as Geertz, Peattie and Perlman, into Das, the planner's, cognizance.

Two conceptual problems seem to dominate anthropologists' search for accuracy. The first is to carry forward the argument about the definition of "urban". In one sense the argument is in☐dependent of the sets of issues we have been examining, and has its own complexity. Also, just as formal/informal has to deal with a variety of ethnographic realities, so too does urban/nonurban: cities themselves have to be subclassified for they do not mirror each other in internal structure, in social objectives, in external relations, and in styles of life. Nevertheless, the urban/nonurban or urban/rural dichotomy is germane and sometimes fundamental to the equivalent of the formal/informal debate.

Anthropologists tend to take their first cue from the urbanist Louis Wirth (1938), who identifies two orders of criteria for the urban. Out of data referring to numbers of people, density of settlement, and degree of heterogeneity, towns will have a charac☐teristic physical structure, and defined systems of social organisa□tion, and a set of attitudes which lead to characteristic collective behaviour and social control. Since Wirth does not clearly estab□lish how a generalized urban physical structure, social organisa□tion and collective behaviour specifically differ from the rural, he cannot be said to define the urban. All he does is hint at the dimensions that are relevant, leaving the field open to later wri□ters.

In the process of elaboration and reexamination, anthropo□logists time and again refer to situations in which what they dis□cover to be nonurban, or rural, in fact enters the physical and population entity that defines the city (cf. Ablon 1971, Abu□ Lughod 1961, Levine & Levine 1979, Zenner 1980). Furthermore, movements across the boundary can occur in either direction. Thus the search for a designator is one thing when the referent is the physical city and another when the referent is a style of be□haviour. It is not a paradox that, ethnographically and theoretical□ly, rural life styles may be found in a city which is physically opposed to the countryside.

The second conceptual theme is that of marginality, a theme which may or may not link with that of the definition of poverty, and which tends to replace, in anthropology, the concept of infor□mal, although it is by no means identical Perlman (1976) gives an excellent account of the evolution of the concept, not only in anthropology (there is, of course, a great deal in sociology and in political science, as well as psychology). She also links it to a pre□cise elaboration of the history of the rural/urban dichotomy itself. In addition, she is particularly concerned by the entry of the term into the political and bureaucratic life of Latin America, where it takes on a derogatory and social class connotation, sometimes going so far as to deny the possibility of social integration.

Once again, the criteria of marginality are numerous and in☐consistent Perlman points out that marginals may be defined as poor, as jobless, as immigrants, as different subcultures, as ethnic minorities, as illegal squatters, as any deviants, as not participating in the elite culture, as being below the standard class scale. While some of these criteria are part of what she calls the "myth of mar☐ginality", others can clearly be used as differing criteria for the objective determination of a style of life or a class of people.

Yet the selection of a criterion does not end the matter. Typical of the debates have been those centred upon modifying two classical approaches, the Redfield folkurban continuum (Redfield 1930) and the Lewis culture of poverty (Lewis 1959, 1966).

Out of my sample I found the following points emerging. In almost all instances, the modifications come from the identifica☐tion of places or times at which the Redfield or Lewis models do not seem appropriate. Thus AbuLughod (1961) argues convincingly that rural immigrants to Cairo are more urbanized accord☐ing to the Redfield criteria that longerterm residents of at least one of the eight census tracts of the city. In common with many other observers of international migration, Ablon (1971) shows that the participatory success of Western Samoans in Los Angeles relates directly to their use of modes of social networking they brought with them from Samoa, the opposite of the impersonality that both Wirth and Redfield posit as a characteristic of urban life.

As far as poverty is concerned, Lewis responded to initial criticism by creating a further classificatory distinction (Lewis 1966). He distanced himself from the idea that the occurrence of poverty necessarily implies a culture of poverty. Thus for any so cial group one can ask: Is there poverty? and: Is there a culture of poverty? as two separate questions. The distinction is typical of the method of correction of ethnographically inaccurate classifica tions; i.e. one adds another criterion which suggests a classifica tory distinction. The method gives a hint towards the possible solution to the classificational dilemma. Apart from such consid erations, much of the criticism surrounds the conception that there can be conservative values, and hence persistence deriving from the separated condition of poverty.

Yet when the identifier of the group under consideration is not "poverty" but some physical attribute which superficially seems to be linked with poverty, contemporary trends seem to be in a somewhat similar vein. Such an identifier would be residence in a shanty town, which to most observers implies both marginal ity and poverty, and many other criteria such as immigration. Observations indicate that not all shanty towns are composed of marginal people, not all residents are poor, and there may be both upward and downward mobility. The *favela, barrio,* or *bidonville* can be itself heterogeneous (Eames & Goode 1977) and may have a markedly coherent social organization (Peattie 1974, Perlman 1976).

Running through all the distinctions, and inherent in the con cept of classification, is the idea that there is a boundary between those being grouped together and all others. This was highly evi dent in the writing of Boeke, whose work on Indonesia, extrapo lated to cover "tropical economies", posited a dualism between the traditional and capitalist that was rigid and parallel, with almost no attention paid to crossboundary phenomena. The rigid dualism was not fundamentally necessary to most of Boeke's argument and became a target of later critics, perhaps diverting attention away from more subtle appraisals. Louis Wirth (cf. in Gmelch & Zenner 1980:11), the ancestor of urban studies, parti cularly in anthropology, specifically denied the rigidity of the boundary. As I have already noted, he himself, in his classical paper, did not arrive at clear cut characteristics, leaving it to his descendants to search for them. Wirth provided a check list, as it were, as to what to look for, without predetermining the answers. But when the descendants "discovered" the nature of the charac teristics, and specified them as indicated above, they inevitably created classifications, which implied boundaries.

Anthropological classifications, however, are always subject to the confrontation with the ethnographic real. In this field, where boundaries emerge or are implied, scholars working on single ethnographies can, in the rural setting, abstract out the cross boundary events, or, as do economists with their models, regard them as exogenous. But the isolation of the single culture is be coming less and less acceptable, so that slowly it is being seen more and more as a figment of analysis, of the scholar's need to simplify. Nowhere is this more inescapable than in urban anthro pology.

The urban ethnographic real is almost always, to coin a heavy phrase, multisubcultural or even multicultural. This can express itself in class and educational differentiation, in lifestyle orienta☐tions symbolized by the physical manifestations of sections of the city, in ethnicity, in distinguishable migratory groups, and in numerous other features. Each of the classificatory exercises men☐tioned above, whether anthropological or not, can be closely correlated with such features, and others can be drawn peripheral☐ly into discussion.

It is thus not surprising that recent anthropological literature severely undermines the notion that somehow boundaries are rigid. Such criticism can take several forms. Peil (1981), for exam☐ple (as do many writers with a sociological bent), goes almost to the fullest extreme. While writing of cities and suburbs in West African urban areas, on a comparative basis, almost all her discus☐sion simply ignores the distinction, and her tables of characteris☐tics are based on continuums, without boundary divisions. This result derives from her sociological method and the nature of the quantifications to her hand, and is followed by many writers who depend on statistical aggregates. It is some distance from a study based on ethnographic observation.

Where ethnographic observation stresses culture, values, behaviour drawn "from the ground up", rather than deduced from more macro aggregates, differentiation is plainly there and must be accounted for. But to go from there to rigid boundary is an *a priori* step. Numerous nonanthropologists have shown that under some circumstances the question of being in the

formal or the informal sector (to use the writers'
terms) is not necessarily a matter of destitution
or inevitability but is a matter of choice (Sabot
1979, Sinclair 1978), that persons caught up in
one sector may move in either direction (King
1975 for Kenya, Mazumdar 1981 for Malaysia).
Thus there is what I have called elsewhere
personnel transfer (Belshaw 1969). When such
transfers occur, at least one writer (Rew 1974)
has shown that alterations in norms and values
take place, even suggesting that a single
individual may move during his or her daily
activity from one sector to another, easily
adapting behaviour accordingly. Indeed, this
must be the case, particularly if we include in
our ethnographic sampling bri□colage within a
Western economy. It is also highly consistent
with those studies of religious adaptation which
suggest that syncret□ism is not the only
response to pressures to change, but that
indi□viduals may move without stress between
two religious systems operating in parallel.

Anthropologists also stress such matters as
continuing rural linkages through traditional
networks, and (e.g. Rhoades 1980) the
importance for the total system of return
migration, which can be not only of persons in
the urban informal sector, marginals, and the
like, but of persons who have been deeply
involved in the highest ranks of the elite (the
South Pacific is replete with exam□ples).

For Marxist scholars the informal, the
marginal, the poor, cannot exist in historical or
social isolation. Just as Third World countries
cannot be understood, according to such authors,
out□side of a dependency relationship with
metropolitan power, so class differentiated cities
must manifest a symbiotic relationship between
the classes, or if you like the sectors.
NonMarxists make the same point Perlman
(1976), for example, makes it quite clear that
the diversity of *favela* society involves major
interactions with elite society, interactions which
serve the total system, which help to characterize
the total system, and that are handled with
snobbish resentment by the elite who, however,
cannot do with□out them. Such mutual
dependencies are totally at variance with the
separate dualism of Boeke, but do not derive
from ethnog□raphic differences between Latin
America and Indonesia. Boeke could be
rewritten in precisely the same terms, since it
would not be difficult to demonstrate the same
kinds of dependencies be□tween the traditional
Asian economy and the Western economy, once
the latter had penetrated. i

The study of boundaries in these and other
ways is of fun□damental importance to
classificatory exercises, yet the number of studies
based on classification which selfconsciously

examine boundary interactions is minimal. The mind set which opts for classification is more concerned, it appears, with identifying at least two differentiable groups, and defining them so that they must be separable in research operations. The boundary must be minimized in importance since it is posited to be there as part of the act of classification, and to modify its sharpness reduces the clarity of the classification. While classifications are clearly depen dent on some empirical observation, the characteristics inferred from the observation may be selected almost arbitrarily, depend ing on the scholarly pursuit of the observer. Thus the differences and disagreements rife in the literature are less a matter of objec tive disagreement than the choice of differing objectives of re search among the authors. There can p fact be as many differing concepts within this small field as there are researchers, provided the researchers are aiming at differing kinds of explanations as, indeed, most of them are. If this is so, quarrels about the validity or otherwise of an act of classification, based on the premise that what is to be classified consists of identical phenomena, are doomed, wasteful of scholarly effort, and misguided. This becom es even more valid when we realize that very few ethnographic realities are identical, taking into account the specifics of the char acteristics that are being stressed.

Thus my answer to my first question must be that the method of applying standard classification di the set of problems involved is inaccurate, leads to confusion, is significantly mislead ing. This is not arrogantly to proclaim that it has been unproduc tive. Without such attempts we would not know that, and furth ermore the arguments have served to show that there are condi tions and forces at work which the earliest writers were unable to identify.

What then can we do? Is there an alternative method, and might it be more helpful? Southall (1975) gives us a hint of what to me seems a most profitable direction. He is looking at the kinds of cities in Africa and inescapably notes their enormous diversity, particularly if we include some of the very large population centres which have existed for centuries, without "benefit" of modern commerce or industrialisation. Seeking a method which will serve to explain the differences, particularly with regard to relations with the "country" (i.e. countryside), he writes:

>the apparent diversity ... can be shown to vary according to quite intelligible, orderly and consistent principles if the relevant variables are carefully sorted out, thus demonstrat ing that apparently unlike situations arise mainly from the same sets of factors combined and operating at different strengths >, (Southall 1975).

If such an approach were practicable, it would avoid the ne☐cessity for the kind of classification we have been dealing with, except as a matter of ready reference, without scientific potency. If we applied the above method to all phenomena which one way or another go under the rough name "town" or "city", we could even apply the same variables to units of population which were not ascribed in the same way, were in fact rural. It might be that some of the variables showed up as zero; this then would indicate a substantial difference, by comparison with other units being compared. Exactly what we want. Yet not dependent upon argu☐able classification.

This does not predict that all problems are over. Not at all. Issues will be debated around the selection, strength, measure☐ment, and so forth, of variables. The identification of variables is itself arguable classification, albeit of a different kind. The selec☐tion of variables, also, will differ according to differing objectives, especially in identifying what the research problem is. But it is my belief that the method is inherently clearer methodologically, and is more directly related to acts of explanation which should seek to correlate and account for linkages in the movements of vari☐ables.

At this point I shall take up the issue of boundaries again to illustrate my meaning, though not to assert that this is the only way of proceeding.

In anthropology the discussion of boundaries as natural phe☐nomena or artefacts of the scholar has received relatively little theoretical attention. The existence of a boundary is usually assumed to follow empirically from the identification of a named group, or from the allocation of a name to a group. Thus "doc☐tors", "the peasants of Ecuador", "the Fulani", or in this context "city dwellers", "marginals", "the urban poor", *"barrio* dwellers", by classifying if for no other reason, imply a boundary of some kind. Yet paradoxically, although questions about interactions or the lack of them across the boundaries are of crucial importance for systemic assessment, more frequently than not identification of interactions is based upon general thoughts rather than upon the detailed analysis of boundaries as being at the heart of the matter.

There is, however, on approach in anthropology that has be☐come a *locus classicus*, with good reason. Barth's wellknown essay on the boundaries of ethnic groups (1969) essentially attacks the problem of boundary maintenance as a selfconscious sociopolitical process, a problem which had of course long been post☐ulated as being at the heart of ethnicity. For in the theory of ethnicity lies the proposition that an ethnic group identifies itself by opposition to all others in such a way that its maintenance requires social and cultural instruments for the maintenance of the boundary between "we" and "they". This is true, even though in some instances the boundaries may be fuzzy or open to change. Barth (1969: 15) writes:

«The critical focus of investigation from this point of view becomes the ethnic boundary that defines the group, not the cultural stuff that it encloses.

But alas this is exactly what he unfortunately does not do. He, his colleagues who contribute to his symposium, and the many writers who have taken his position as an excellent summing up of the state of the art, but who wish to add amending perspec tives, concentrate instead on an important but alternative ques tion: how do ethnic groups so identified maintain the boundary (allowing for adaptation over time)? This is not the same question, and it is approached with in fact very little attention, if any, to the mechanisms at the boundary itself.

It is clear that this approach will not help in the present exer cise, except peripherally. If we posit the existence of a boundary, we should surely give it our full attention, as the centre of study, not as an assumed condition. Obviously, significant studies of activities across boundaries are commonplace in the discipline, going back all the way to diffusionism, and covering such topics as migration, intermarriage, trade, political domination and many other themes. What has not happened, however, has been a sys□tematic linkage of boundary issues to issues in the theory of classi□fication, with a bearing upon the way we conceive of systems and systemic relations, and ultimately the way we compare social groups.

One approach I have advocated (Belshaw 1969, Ch. VII) is to start from the assumption that all social groups, whether defined arbitrarily or according to some empirical criterion, have bound□aries physically defined by the observer, which may or may not coincide with a "natural" boundary as experienced and/or defined by members of the group in question. An absolute boundary, in sociocultural terms, would be one with no movement whatsoever across it; only completely isolated populations would meet this condition. In all other situations there is some crossboundary activity, some set of observable transactions. In fact, boundaries consist of sets of variable movements, that is movements which are variable for the same group over time, and variable as between groups which are being compared. It follows that it would be legitimate and profitable to do what Southall suggested above, that is to *see* groups, not as ones falling into classificatory boxes, but as units characterized by the strength accorded to each of a number of boundary variables, i.e. a boundary profile. In such an approach, there is no longer need to argue whether a particular group falls into classificatory box A or B. Each group remains its individual and unique self.

Yet this does not abjure comparison; indeed it assists through the comparison of methodically appraised variables. As Southall suggests, this is in turn an essential step in creating explanations, presumably through the logically supported correlations or lack of them in the movement of the variables. In my tentative approach mentioned above, I suggested that the following vari☐ables would be relevant: the degree to which social roles were completely or incompletely acted out within the boundary; the degree of corporate solidarity addressed to boundary maintenance (Barth's problem); the social direction expressed by the boundary (e.g. parallel or hierarchical segmentation of the society); parity or nonparity in power relationships manifested by boundary in☐teraction; the intensity and frequency of communication across boundaries; the scale and rate of value transfers; the scale and rate of personnel transfer (including such considerations as temporary versus permanent, intermarriage, occupation); activity transfer; transfers of resource control. Such a list was *a priori,* not informed by any specific research goal, and not clear in terms of operational definitions and clarity. That, in my view, is not a fundamental longterm objection to the method, but merely a weakness in my own presentation which was exploratory rather than definitive (as indeed, is the present essay).

Thus, there is an alternative to the kind of classificatory approach to the issues of pluralism and comparison of rela☐tionships between sectors of urban (and other) populations. How might it be pursued further to test its efficacy? There are two steps to the answer. The first is to determine whether the concepts being debated in the conceptual literature, such as the material cited in this paper, can be transformed into statements of variation instead of classification, and what the implications of such a trans☐formation might be. The second is to determine whether the re☐arranged ideas can be linked, say, to propositions about develop☐ment which would suggest the possibility of operational research. In some instances it will be convenient to consider the two steps together.

For example, as I have indicated, running through the litera☐ture is the issue, are urban sectors, however defined, separate or interacting As the discussion on Latin American squatter settle☐ments indicates, the answers given by different authors are di☐ametrically opposed, especially when some authors are guided by political motives. And the answers tend to place the phenomena in one classification or the other. The method of comparative varia☐tion at least avoids this trap. The boundaries between defined sec☐tors may be examined according to the variables I have mentioned two paragraphs above, with a standardized indicator of scale. Obviously, there will need to be thought and ingenuity in arriving at such scales, some of which will be ordinal, a task which lies beyond the scope of this paper. The creation of such scales will enable comparisons to be made, possibly from already existing studies, in terms of the interactions between numerous *barrios, favellas, bidonvilles,* shantytowns, "rural elements" in Asian cities, suburbs, slums, welltodo ethnic enclaves, informal sec☐tors, and any other units on the one hand, and the rest of the urban society on the other. It really does not matter, from the point of view of this application, how the sectors are identified; comparisons can still be made. Some interactions will be low with respect to some variables and high with respect to others. Each set of phenomena being examined will have its own characteristics, laying a foundation for the question why?

I have emphasized the question of boundary for several reasons, one of the most important of which is the underlying belief that the scale and nature of interactions across boundaries will be fundamental to development propositions, if by develop☐ment we mean an increase in institutional complexity. It can also be fundamental for other questions based on other criteria of de☐velopment, such as increase in income *per capita,* growth in pro☐ductivity, increase in the scale of trade and exchanges, and so forth. Once the criteria have been selected for practical or theore☐tical reasons, those criteria of outcome can be matched with pat☐terns of variables on a comparative (historical and geographical) basis.

But clearly boundary is not the only issue of importance, since most of the studies cited above have given only cursory attention to it. The internal operation of sectors, again however identified, can be treated in a similar way, and made subject to comparison. This means the transformation of the criteria of clas☐sification into criteria for the selection of variables, usually merely a matter of the phrasing of the words. Thus, when Emerji (1974) contrasts structured with unstructured sectors, one needs to establish the ideas behind structure and nonstructure, and to con☐ceptualize them from nonexistent or very small to very large and significant. Franklin's (1965) distinction between peasants using a total family labour supply and a sector in which persons use labour outside the family, always leads to such arguments as, «If a nonrelative drops in to undertake labour on a reciprocal basis, which box does the system fit?.. The problem is avoided and the variables clarified if there is a scale which could summarize con tinuously the following kinds of conditions (and others): labour literally confined to the household; labour confined to the house hold and other lineal relatives; labour confined to all named rela tives (a larger pool); labour selected from relatives and persons accorded fictive status as relatives; labour using nonrelatives but limited to those with formalized partnership status; labour includ ing the former but also including very occasional wage work out side the kinship and partnership system; labour entirely depen dent on workers offering themselves for wages. As another exam ple marginality can be broken into sets of variables, such as com parative income, weight accorded to identified values (ideal or ac tiongoverning), degree of political participation, degree of nonmonetary exchange, scale of monetary exchange, rate of capital investment in housing, *ad infinitum*. Marginality in itself then be comes perhaps unimportant as a classificatory concept. Instead, the "sectors" which are labelled marginal or nonmarginal or in determinate can be examined and compared through the use of the variables. Nevertheless, the initial act of classification served the purpose of bringing into the discussion the enumeration of factors in numerous empirical instances, out of which the identification of possibly significant variables emerges.

This is no place to list the whole range of propositions in the study of development. An example must suffice. But before exem☐plifying, one must record that the very concept of development has itself become a classificatory tool with all the ambiguities, in☐consistencies and confusions that seem almost inevitably to arise after twenty or thirty years of debate. Put simply, it means diffe☐rent things to different people. Once again the scientific instru☐ment has been blunted, and needs reshaping in terms of variables, this time variables of output or result. Thus we can talk of such matters as the rate of increase in the complexity of institutional arrangements; the rate of growth in GNP *per capita;* the rate of increase in the articulation of institutions — these as outcomes of sets of variables, some of which have to do with the observation that boundaries exist within cities.

To conclude, I pose as an example an arbitrarily chosen set of questions which the study of comparative variation might help to answer. If a high degree of cultural difference is maintained with relatively frequent communication of ideas and techniques across the boundaries, will the city exhibit a high rate of innovation? If there is a high rate of population recruitment (natural increase, immigration, boundary transfer) in a sector, what factors affect the rate of un or underemployment (not necessarily in market terms)? Does the size of the pool of un or underemployed affect the rate of formation of new enterprises or the rate of expansion of quantities of production in some or all interacting sectors? Does the answer to the last question vary according to the volume of production?

Although existing field studies in anthropology have not nor☐mally been designed to contribute to the comparative examination of the kinds of variables we are now imagining, it is my belief that they do in fact contain a great deal of appropriate data, enough at least to warrant experiments in designing scales and indicators. It is of course essential not only that the scales and indicators are appropriate to the theoretical requirements of the research ques☐tions, but that they are based on ethnographic reality. As anthro☐pologists we would not wish to be trapped like our economist colleagues into according priority to variables simply because me☐asures exist a priori or are technically comfortable. Nor should we shy away from developing scales of qualitative phenomena on the grounds that such scales are apparently less than precise. Precision and refined measurement can be chimerically misleading.

Foundations of Applied Anthropology A Reassessment

First published in Seth, P.K. and S. Seth, *New Perspectives in Anthropology,* New Delhi, M.D. Publications, 1993.

Ever since social and cultural anthropology began to give advice about activities in the real world, there has been controversy over the place of such advice and the accompanying analysis. Is it truly anthropology? Is it inferior in its intellectual pretensions? Sometimes "applied anthropology" has seemed little more than common sense, without reference, for example, to any central body of anthropological literature.

The dilemma is global, and was well put to me some years ago by a Soviet colleague now living in the United States. As we walked to a meeting in Leningrad, he said "What is there in anthropology to be applied? It is hard to see anything." His puzzle can be echoed in a different form by innumerable graduate students in North America who may see effective applications carried out by others but who have difficulty relating their own thesis topic to anything even remotely practical.

It is not my purpose to review the history of the debate. which would take a volume. I am rather presenting a logical exercise in which I select certain assumptions about the nature of sociocultural anthropology and, proceeding from that base, try to answer the questions implied by the Soviet colleague. How can a subdiscipline of applied anthropology ideally function as an extension of its anthropological foun☐dations? I make no systematic attempt in this space to proceed from there to offer a critique of contemporary practice, although I will not be able to resist some remarks, and much can be inferred.

The term "Applied Anthropology" is itself a misnomer which reveals something of the confusion. I take the wo "Anthropology" to refer to a systematic body of knowledge a theoretical

order. While ethnography constitutes a lar part
of its data base, ethnography itself is not
anthropology Out of ethnography come
generalizations about relationships in a social
and cultural order (including change perhaps
limited to the time and place of the culture in
question, perhaps embracing other times, places
and cultures. Such generalizations constitute
anthropological knowledge, often more interesting
when combined together in broader systems of
explanation, including those of other social and
biological sciences.

The validity of such generalizations is tested in
various ways, but it is generally agreed that if it can
be shown that ethnographic data drawn from a
variety of substantive fields (perhaps involving
several cultures, several times, or differ ing
institutional settings) support given
generalizations, then those generalizations will be
thought to be more reli able. In other words, once
a generalization has been formu lated as the result
of a given ethnography, we can test it by applying it
in relevant ways to different phenomena. In other
words, applying generalizations, that is,
anthropological knowledge, to ethnography or
any other body of suitable data is a prime tool for
the testing of validity. It is as well the only tool we

have for interpreting the significance of, and processes embodied in, data.

In short, and to put it bluntly, there is a sense in which every anthropologist of any claim to professional compe tence is continuously in his or her daytoday work under taking applied anthropology, simply by using preformu lated generalizations to understand or interpret ethnogra phy. This is done without any implication of practical results. The analogy is with applied economics: simply the application of abstract theory to the interpretation of the real world, *not* the use of economics for the evolution of welfare problems, a different exercise.

All very well, you may counter, but this is *not* what "Applied Anthropology" connotes in professional activity. What indeed does the phrase connote? It is not particularly easy to find a definition. After browsing through several textbooks and manuals, some infuriatingly without subject indexes, I came across only two serious attempts.'

Of these two, one (Eddy and Partridge, 1978:5) is not rigorous. The authors distinguish between "abstract" and "applied" anthropology on three grounds. The first is that "applied anthropologists study living cultures and contem□porary people". Are not the Jivaro living people, were not the Trobrianders of Malinowski's time, the Tikopia of Firth, or the East Londoners of Young and Willmott?

The second is that "applied anthropologists seek applica□tions of their findings, data and analyses beyond anthro□pology". This is true also of a great deal of "abstract" anthropology since, as I have shown elsewhere (1988), anthropology is fundamentally a discipline that draws from others, contributes to them, and is inextricably interlinked with a wider scholarly world.

Finally, "applied anthropologists conduct research ori□ented toward the problems of those they study". But the authors also say "the problems posed for scientific investi□gation in abstract anthropology may or may not bear any relationships to the needs of living people". The point is that the language of the statement indicates that abstract, or theoretical anthropologists may so contribute. Indeed if there were no such possibilities, applied anthropology would have no link with the main discipline. Since such a contri□bution is possible in abstract anthropology, it fails as a definitional distinction. There are *problems,* practical and theoretical, inherent in organizing ceremonial or curing by traditional means.

The other attempt I found was more direct and simpler. Louise Robbins (Angrosino, 1976, p.18) states that "For most sociocultural anthropologists applied anthropology focuses on the solution of practical problems in the contem porary world usually involving some measure of cultural change." One can pick at the formulation, since what is or what is not a "practical problem" is a matter of Valuation about which there may be differences of opinion between observers and participants. Nevertheless, it is a straight forward and reasonable approach. "Abstract" or "theoretical" anthropologists applying theory to the interpretation of data are not usually concerned, in that capacity, with the resolu tion of practical problems in this sense.

Following from Robbins a little further, I would add that applied anthropology deals with choices about future con duct, forecasting that given activity will result in given objectives, and making suggestions (sometimes recommen dations, see later) that in the light of the participants' preferences certain courses be followed rather than others.

Does this cut applied anthropology off from the rest of anthropology? It should not. I have argued elsewhere (1959. 1988) that the testing of anthropological hypotheses has to be carried out by comparison, either between cultures or, more relevant here, with respect to change over time. An applied anthropologist would be, if the world were a little simpler, in an ideal position to be the grand tester of hypotheses. In principle, his interpretation of sociocultural forces leading to his interpretation of relevant sociocultural dynamics and change is based on hypotheses drawn from the abstract theoretical literature. If he can take into account the relevant variables sufficiently well, his recom☐mendations will in fact constitute a test for the hypothesis if the recommendations are put into practice and when the outcome is known. Since the applied anthropologist is dealing with change, he can observe results even if the participants decide to do something else, thus calling up the possibility of commenting on the validity ofyet other hypoth☐eses which may be more relevant to the new situation.

The kind of operation I have mentioned is rarely accom☐plished. 1 believe that this is because the natural "mindset" of scholars engaged in helping to solve "practical problems" is on the immediacy of the issues and the patronimposed deadlines. It is not inherent in any intellectual division between fundamental or theoretical on the one hand and applied on the other. It is the kind of attitude and perspective that might well be altered through the example of graduate seminars drawing out the theoretical implications of applied work, although this is extremely rare. On the other hand, applied anthropologists do from time to time stand back 'from the immediate issues to reflect on the theoretical implications. One small example would be my own reflec□tions on the factors which result in technical assistance case may be, reflections which resulted from a practicallyoriented survey of technical assistance projects in Thailand (1966). Symptomatically, such papers are seldom written for or published in mainstream anthropological journals, save very occasionally in *Human Organization.*

Many disciplines circumscribe their fields of practical application by reference to constraints of subject matter or theoretical perspective. This would be true of economics and much of psychology. A demanding challenge of applied anthropology is that it is not circumscribed in the same way, because anthropology itself is not thus bounded. True. applied anthropologists frequently limit themselves as spe□cialists in a given set of cultures or draw from bodies of theoretical literature they know best. But they are not disturbed or surprised to find colleagues working in totally different environments and addressing utterly foreign ques tions, a range of possibilities that can be quite confusing to patrons, or to other scholars who demand "what is anthro pology?" or "why should an anthropologist be on the inter disciplinary team rather than a sociologist or psychologist?"

I recently participated in a meeting dealing with the interdisciplinary implications of aspects of economic theory. We decided to pursue the matter further by deliber ately stimulating crossdisciplinary work on topics of signifi cance for economists to challenge noneconomists to pro duce results that forced changes in economic thinking. One such project that I have seen in the followup correspon dence deals with choices in health delivery services in Britain. Incredibly, despite what I thought was a meeting of minds, the economists in charge have not chosen to put their ideas to the test of anthropology, in what is now an intensely multicultural society. That anthropology deals as much with "complex" societies (I do not like the word but have no other) as with shifting cultivators, nomads, or peasants, was treated in discussion as a highly novel piece of information, which clearly did not penetrate. The idea that anthropolo□gists could have something to say about the values and cultural context of health delivery among the English in multicultural Britain, let alone India or Canada, was totally alien to the planners of the study. (My experience is that with some notable exceptions, economists have to them□selves discover the generalizations of other disciplines before they can accept them. Otherwise they consider such generalizations to be irrelevant exotica.)

An economist dealing with practical issues in industri□alized society knows, perhaps falsely, where he is. His language of analysis is tight and restricted, he deals with choice and measurable entities, and he is practised at leaving untidy things out of the analysis. Although his certainty about his tools of trade is being challenged from within and without, more and more, by comparison with an anthropologist, he is identifiable, predictable, and techni□cally secure to a high degree.

We as anthropologists must look elsewhere for our identities and for our reinforcements. Everything we have we share with other disciplines. But we are anthropologists because

there are strong differences in emphasis,
differ ences which must be consciously examined
for us to be sure that it is anthropology, and not
some watered down econom ics or psychiatry,
that we are applying.

The first difference of emphasis is that we study
peoples, both in the singular and in the plural,
and we do so very consciously. This emphasis we
share to some extent with human geography. For
us the study of peoples involves, among many
other things, the delineation of the social
system, a preoccupation of all the social
sciences from varying perspectives, and the deep
examination of cultures, values and symbols. An
applied anthropology that does not deliberately link
the practical issue, whatever it may be, to such a
body of knowledge, that is, to social organization,
culture, values and symbols, is not applied
anthropology. It is something else.

The concern with peoples is of a special
order that results from a methodology to which I
shall refer later. It is intimate and, whatever the
technical apparatus involved, humanis tic. This
is both a positive challenge and a danger. It
involves the possibility of strong identification
with the people in question, of emotional and
political identification which can so easily blind

objectivity and be an Achilles' heel when the anatomy of our work is examined by opponents of it. It can lead to blind possessiveness. Yet it is precious, since the objective parts of our work start with the intimate dramas of human life. When we use statistics and macrodata as anthropologists we interpret their validity and significance in the light of individual human experience, which we, above all, can document. No other discipline has this strength to this degree.

Clearly, all disciplines contain within themselves differ□ing, incompatible theoretical variations. But when we talk of a lack of theoretical cohesiveness in anthropology we mean something rather different. Mostly, in other disciplines, the differing theories can be applied to similar questions and arise from differences in the methodology and logic with which the questions are answered. There is plenty of that in anthropology also: it is part of productive debate. But what we also have is an enormously broad set of quite different questions asked and answered by differing groups of col□leagues who yet, on the whole, manage to talk to one another. The models of conventional economic anthropology and those of puristic structuralism, those of material culture related to museology and those of psychiatric anthropology, are very different. They are parallel rather than competing paradigms. While these too exist in other disciplines, the range seems very much greater in anthropology. Some colleagues deplore the multitude. But it is also stimulating since there are those who can move from one paradigm to another and make links between them. It is the interpenetra tion and mutual stimulation of the paradigms that pushes anthropology ahead.

The relevance of this for the roots of applied anthropology is simply that it would be false and difficult to assert that applied anthropology derives from a consistent set of theo retical foundations, in the sense in which the claim can be made for psychology or economics. Again, what to others seems a puzzle and a weakness should be asserted as a strength to us. The true but awkward position that an anthropologist can be found to handle some aspect of almost every single practical issue makes critics think we are dliletantes and is not the basis for an assertion of strength. It is rather that the insights which come from the internal dialogues and divisions within anthropology represent a much closer mirror of the real and human world than is the case with the perhaps sharper focus of other disciplines. It is a challenge for applied anthropologists to remember and capitalize on the point.

While I believe the above to be true, it is not the end of the matter. There is in fact a theoretical perspective which characterizes good sociocultural anthropology and its ap□plied derivatives. Part of the perspective is *shared* with other social sciences, namely that analysis seeks to establish linkages and interrelationships between elements in socio□cultural systems. In practical terms, we do not study the techniques of agriculture in isolation, but attempt to find linkages with other possible domains, such as religious belief or family organization. Other disciplines are inclined to restrict the scope of such linkages much more tightly and to ignore those which anthropology has learnt to be poten□tially fundamental.

The perspective goes further. Anthropologists tend to posit an ideal theoretical possibility, namely that *alt possible linkages* are revealed and considered together in a single total system, an ideal which we misname "holism". ("Totalism", though ugly, would be more accurate since holism should mean that the totality is necessarily different from the sum of the parts, a proposition implicit in some anthropological theories, e.g. those of Kroeber or Clyde Kluckhohn, but in modern work usually eschewed.) As part of the holistic exercise,

141

anthropologists pay special atten☐tion to the nature and force of culture, with special emphasis on values and symbolism. We do not take this domain for granted, as do economists. And anthropology is the only social science that gives this dimension such primacy. Materialists must confront this element in theory and real☐ity, which is why Marxist anthropologists have to be neo☐Marxist to carry conviction.

If we consider social science and humanistic disciplines to be built around emphases on orientations of study —political science dealing with power, sociology with social relations, geography with space, economics with choice, and so on — it can readily be seen that no problem of significance to humans can be the domain of any single discipline. Human problems involve all social science approaches si☐multaneously. The issue translates into the work of the anthropologist. Intent on studying matters totally, he or she must draw relevant perspectives from as many of the rel☐evant disciplines as practicable, internalizing them into a inherent in such an ambitious synthesis, which no anthro☐pologist can overcome, and in practical terms the issue is often resolved by attempting to use collegial specialists in interdisciplinary teams. The precise emphases that the anthropologist commands clearly vary with training and temperament: there is no preordained solution. But the attempt, derived from the nature of anthropology itself, is creative and unique to the discipline, leading to new insights which do in fact justify the term "holism" if applied to theoretical synthesis between disciplines.

Applied anthropology, then, must reflect to the degree that it is practicable to the total system of interrelationships surrounding a given problem in the context of culture, values and symbolic systems, with a mode of thought that attempts to synthesize strains of theory derived from the broad spectrum of human, social, arid biological sciences.

The sheer impossibility of such a task should, but often does not, induce a suitable modesty of claim. Since each scientist approaching a task must select a number from the infinite range of possible linkages, he or she must leave many out of consideration, either deliberately and consciously, or inadvertently. The omissions are not predetermined, as when economists use the "other things being equal" tech□nique (a technique our theorists might try to learn to use on occasion), but specific to the task and to the investigator. The sensitive investigator will be aware of this, and will never claim 100 per cent accuracy in forecasts or advice. The applied anthropologist who fails to make this clear has to be suspect, even if the disclaimers lead more arrogant and dogmatic colleagues from other disciplines to draw the false conclusion that by this very fact anthropology is less accu☐rate than they are. In human issues, certainty is a false claim. One of the great potential contributions of anthropology is to make more precise the limits of certainty, to show that it can never be achieved, and to assist authorities, scholars and peoples to understand those limits and to carry out their tasks with confidence nevertheless.

Obviously, any problem which attracts the work of an applied anthropologist is rooted in time and place. It is culturally, environmentally, and ethnographically specific. Many patrons, and anthropologists themselves, seem to believe that such a situation gives a certain primacy to anthropological knowledge. Anthropologists, so the argu☐ment would run, can draw upon an existing body of ethno☐graphic knowledge about it relevant facts which can be incor☐porated into diagnosis. If by some chance there is no written ethnography, they can carry one out (if time permits) or draw upon knowledge of analogous systems. For this reason, anthropologists are often relegated to the role of fact finder, and some are prepared to accept the point.

At one level, there is some truth to this, although ultimately it would deny the validity of what I have written above. Nevertheless, a major contribution of anthropology is the act of interpretation from one culture to another. Anthro□pology might be characterized as the science of the interpre□tation of cultures, though as a definition this is overlimiting. If a scholar analyses his own culture without such crosscultural interpretation, he is being sociological rather than anthropological.

The point is not as limiting as it may sound. An Ibo scholar interpreting Ibo institutions may be regarded as belonging to a culture which, by reason of advanced educa□tion and similar influences, is no longer Ibo in the sense in which rural Ibo would conceive of the term; furthermore in his professional writing he is interpreting not to the Ibo themselves (though this is not ruled out), but to the national or international culture of anthropology, more broadly of social and hui nan science. Applied anthropologists are interpreting to a variety of audiences, including authorities, other professionals, the national citizenry of a multicultural state. It is essential that applied anthropologists interpret their analyses with the specific culture of their intended audience specifically taken into account.

All this having been said, the assumption of accurate predetermined ethnographic knowledge is one which can be extremely dangerous. It simply cannot be taken for granted. An applied anthropologist working among Sikhs or Northern Italians in Canada, or for that matter among Anglo Canadians, cannot simply assume that ethnographic mate□rial about Sikh culture, or Northern Italian monographs, or sociological statements about AngloCanadians, will be ethnographically relevant. By the very fact of living in Canada, such peoples have changed in potentially signifi□cant ways, yet have brought with them undetermined con□tinuities. As an essential part of the task, an anthropologist must determine the degree to which this point is applicable.

In the case of sociological materials, the techniques used are quite likely to present information in an ethnographically distorted way, particularly if rooted in questionnaires. In addition, there will be significant ethnographic differences between different parts of Canada, or even sections of communities with differing class and educational back ground. Both time and geography, to say nothing of the complexities of cultural and other influences, will cause variable adaptations in Sikh and Northern Italian communi ties, and differentiations within them. The first task of an applied anthropologist is to know what he is dealing with. and that cannot be determined without some form of fresh ethnographic enquiry — whether it be light and quick if differences are known not to be great, or extended and deep if there are large unknowns. Yet, for practical reasons, the applied anthropologist has to develop techniques which enable this to be done expeditiously, without losing sensitiv ity. I shall refer more substantially to technique in the following paragraph.

The resolution of the difficulty is helped through the re affirmation of a principle that we often take for granted, sometimes then allowing it to be forgotten. Ethnographic data, and many of the interpretations of its significance, come from the people themselves, supplemented by direct observation. To put it bluntly, good anthropologists do not impose systems on an unsuspecting culture. They derive systems from cultural materials. In other words, anthropolo□gists, in every piece of empirical enquiry, must themselves learn, and it is the people who teach them. The principle is embedded in everything we do in the field (modified as we shall see). Applied anthropologists have to understand this and to use it consciously and conscientiously. We are pupils being taught. These are not "our" people whom we patronize. We are "their" anthropologists.

The implications of the last three paragraphs are pro□found, and quite different for anthropology titan for any other discipline. Every piece of applied anthropology has to be based on ethnography, definition of problems, insights, elicited from the people said to be under study, who are not being studied in the normal sense of the word, but who are teaching us. They do so because they cannot be taken for granted as stereotypes derived from previous studies. Every situation, in anthropology, must be treated as novel until it can be shown to be otherwise.

Would it then be sufficient for an anthropologist, or a journalist for that matter, simply to sit down with a few people and to write a book or report based on what they said without any prompting? Clearly, no. At the most elementary level, such a work would not be understood, would be misinterpreted, by any, audience which did not share the culture. At the very minimum, a translation of language is required. But more than that, questions of power aside, if this is all that ig involved, then there would be no need for anthropologists, economists, or anyone else. Yet something like it is often assumed by nonanthropologists (even by some anthropologists turned administrators). "We don't need anthropologists or sociologists in this organisation because all the officials come from the culture concerned, and therefore know it inside out — they don't need any interpretations."

We know the answer, even if we do not always succeed in making it clear to administrators. The significance of social forms and cultural expressions is more frequently than not lost upon the participants, unless they have a body of scholars to draw it out. In industrialized countries we know this well, though even here it can be disputed by authorities who are insecure when their own ethnosociol ogy is called in question.

The task of the applied anthropologist is, if you like, to ask informed questions, and to put those questions in forms which permit of disciplined answers. The questions should come from theoretical insights, from comparative knowledge about how institutions work, how they tend to be interre□lated, how change takes place, what factors tend to be relevant. The questions lead to answers provided by the participants, supplemented by observation confirmed and debated in discussion.

The ability to raise the right questions is the anthropologist's major contribution, not the presumed knowl□edge of ethnographic fact. The creation of the anthropologi□cal analysis is thus an intimate partnership. At the same time it carries immense dangers.

The dangers are inherent in any investigative process, whether it be in journalism, natural science, police work, or anthropology. Since our skills are in the formulation of questions to ask, we can misconstruct the questions to bias the answers. Anthropologists should be trained to avoid the danger, but the issue appears rarely in graduate work, and tends to be dealt with intuitively in field experience. In opinion polls, police detection, television journalism, the problem is endemic, rarely avoided, and often deliberately used to achieve a desired result (how often have you seen television journalists forcing respondents to answer ques□tions which lead to automatic responses, especially in contexts of personal or political crisis?) Anthropologists are not pure in this matter, though are usually successful in avoiding the more extreme forms.

But our ability to ask the "right" questions depends on our previous theoretical and comparative knowledge. Hy□potheses are derived from this. There is a natural and human tendency to raise the questions in the expectation that the answers will be as predicted. We see this in extreme forms in police work and in journalism, but it is also endemic in anthropology, however much we assert that theories "emerge from the data". Just ponder for a moment how many different theoretical interpretations there are of very similar Melanesian societies.

The warning is a caution, a call for alertness. It does not in itself alter the fundamental point that applied anthropol□ogy consists of raising relevant questions in forms that can be answered by the people involved who provide data and discussion.

It might also be argued that applied anthropology is anthropology because enquiries make use of techniques of investigation specific to the discipline. In this discussion, I will ignore those techniques which are common to other disciplines, and handle only those I feel are specific to anthropology.

Essential to the anthropological enterprise is the construction of abstract or large scale paradigms from the minutiae of daytoday evidence drawn from the uninter□rupted life of ordinary people. While social surveys may or may not be used, and while some anthropologists have taken the trouble to devise and use laboratorystyle controlled experiments, in both instances the influence of intimate individual observation and conversation is apparent. Thus, questions in surveys will be strongly influenced by a knowl□edge of the complexities of daily living, and will not be thought of as reliable evidence without confirmation from other behavioural sources. And laboratory experiments are influenced strongly by endeavours to replicate elements in ethnographically described circumstances (McFeat, 1974).

A pertinent illustration may be drawn from the use of social exchange theory, though the relevance of the perspec□tive is by no means limited to this. In social exchange theory, the primary source of data is information about interactions between individuals, involving a mix of material, symbolic, even emotive characteristics in transactions. As the net of transactions widens, so too does the conceptualization of regularities which come to be seen as social structure and social organization, and indeed of operating culture.

If an anthropologist is to enter the domain of interna□tional monetary transactions or hospital organization or communication in the workplace, his study will not rely on paper reports, statistics of money movements, even ques□tionnaires. To be anthropological, it will see the players first of all as individuals and endeavour to trace their actions, values, communications not only with others in the same institutional setting, but also in the wider contexts of family, friendship, values, play, culture, language, meaning. In this way, individual behaviour becomes enmeshed in a socio□cultural nexus to which no other discipline gives the same priority. To do otherwise is to lose the strength and unique□ness of anthropology, and to move toward the banal and commonsensical.

Admittedly, to make the connection between conclu□sions derived from a base in personal cultures to, for example, regional, national or international generalizations is fraught with difficulty and danger. To create methodolo□gies which minimize such problems is one of the major challenges to anthropology's future, to which the applied anthropologist can no doubt make major contributions.

It is obvious that this perspective, even bias, of anthro□pology is a consequence of the primacy of participant obser□vation in modern fieldwork. Without entering the estab□lished literature on participant observation, I should per□haps note some cautions. I have observed, for example, that scholars in other fields, and some of our own graduate students wrestling with intractable field problems, some□times use the phrase loosely, indicating a situation in which the investigator is simply in individual contact with sources of information. Admittedly, participant observation is never full participation and full observation, since there are always limitations of one kind or another in the investigator's role. But to use the term when there is no participation, and sometimes even no observation (only talk), is to destroy the special characteristics of the idea.

Participant observation is not always possible and some□times is inadvisable, yet it remains one of the strongest elements of anthropological investigation which sets us apart from most other investigators. Where it is not possible, the absence does not destroy enquiry: considerable progress may be made in building on the knowledge of individuals in culture without it. But where that is the case, it should he recognized that the enquiry has limitations other than those of participant observation, and the term should be avoided. Participant observation itself imposes serious limits on the scope of enquiry of the individual investigator — limitations of time, contact, and ability to observe beyond that which immediately confronts the eyes, and so on. But it is possible to extend enquiry far beyond these limitations, combining sharp indepth focus with wide angle lenses. I have described some of the issues elsewhere (1980).

In this context, it is perhaps useful to concentrate on one underused possibility. The use of field assistants is now commonplace. But if we put together the concept of participant observation with the idea that anthropologists are in the business of learning from the people, then I would suggest that one kind of field assistant stands out as more important and more creative. This person I would call a "paraanthropologist", a person who is essentially an investigator in his own right, though under the direction of a fully trained anthropologist. A paraanthropologist would have training in the kinds of work that are useful to his role, either directly from the anthropologist in the field or, perhaps, in collegiate classrooms or schoolrooms where they could be developed.

Basic to the concept is the point that a paraanthropolo gist is not at work full time in the investigation. Indeed, a key to the concept is that he is, quite apart from the investigation, living a full life in, or connected with, the community. We all know of important "informants" who have worked with anthropologists over many years and decades, inevitably absorbing points of view from their association with enquiry, and learning, sometimes to the detriment of objec tivity, from the investigator. They could be sometimes re garded as paraanthropologists, but what I have in mind is more farreaching.

The most obvious kind of person I am thinking of is a member of the community who works in a defined role —medical dispenser, teacher, priest, nurse, veterinary officer. Obviously, since some form of authority is embedded in such roles, and since the persons concerned have their own ambitions and perspectives amenable to manipulation through knowledge, selection and training with an eye to objectivity are crucial. Since that can never be 100 per cent, there is also an enormous responsibility for the principal investigator to take precautions to delimit the investigative role of a paraanthropologist to prevent or minimize possible abuses. Remember, however, that not "even" the anthro☐pologist is pure in this regard.

I am convinced that a corpus of paraanthropologists would provide over the long term a significant asset to applied anthropologists, and perhaps even more to their more theoretically minded colleagues. I am also convinced that doctoral candidates need training in the use of such helpers, and that fieldwork funding should make possible their employment so that up and coming anthropologists would be trained to supervise teams including such personnel.

In one important sense, applied anthropology adds an additional dimension to anthropology itself. It subtle blend of information transfer and persuasion (in the erstwhile Soviet Union, applied anthropology and sociology were sometimes defined as "propaganda"!). Applied anthro☐pology, in other words, has an essential element of education embodied in it. A report, however coldly written, is not intended to gather dust, though it often does. It is intended to be read, used, and hopefully agreed with. Two aspects are of interest.

The first is, whose ideas are being communicated? I have said that the anthropologist is himself learning from the people. He or she introduces questions. Above all, I would add, the anthropologist is in no position to impose his or her analysis on the actions of either people or patron (if patron is different from people). There are moral and ethical limita□tions, especially when we know that *no* analysis will be a perfect descriptor or Predictor, and that *no* analysis written by an outsider will be 100 per cent accurate as an interpre□tation of the values, will, and conditions of the people whose fate is at issue. The implication is clear.

The conclusions which an anthropologist presents are anthropological only in so far as they have been arrived at by the very people with whom he is working and represent their analysis, arrived at with the anthropologist's help. This conclusion, it seems to me, is valid no matter who is paying for the enquiry. I have to admit that this is an ideal statement, and that very frequently it is not possible for the people concerned to verify, for example, an anthropologist's report, even with the best will in the world. In other words, anthro□pologists are sometimes forced to present less than anthro□pology.

The second aspect is just as fundamental. Be^ause anthropologists work with people, learn from people, and endeavour to translate from one cultureto another, their results are available for educational communication to the public, whatever that public may be. By the terms of the work, it may sometimes be legitimately reserved to the patron. More often, this is not legitimate. The work is then open to communication to a very wide range of possible auditors. sion, in anthropology itself, then the communication takes on special characteristics. This is something I myself have learned through experiences related to the XIIth Interna☐tional Congress of Anthropological and Ethnological Sci☐ences in 1983.

Prior to the Congress, which had the theme "Anthropol☐ogy and the Public" a group of interested people, a mix of anthropologists and nonanthropologists, worked to draft ideas about conveying anthropology to the public of British Columbia. In a way, this was a kind of academic extension service. Anthropology conveyed in that way is of course educational, but the context, which must reach out to the interests of clients is in fact a branch of applied anthropol☐ogy. The manner in which the projects emerged made it even m o r e s o .

The Action Anthropology of Sol Tax's Fox Project and its successors was part of the stimulation, but those who participated started afresh. They made few assumptions about what anthropology could or could not do to meet public interest, and did not assume that the public would necessarily be disadvantaged in terms of the total society, that anthropology necessarily knew answers a priori, or that clients would be represented through an organization.

The most important principles that the anthropologists involved had to come to grips with were those of client participation and learning from clients. Interestingly enough, although I have argued that the principles are embedded in the very nature of anthropology, the academics, very few of whom had experience of applied anthropology beforehand, found these to be the most difficult to conceptualize, at least at the outset. This can be illustrated by analysing the steps undertaken to design projects (for reasons of financing, manpower demands, and Congress complexities, none of the projects moved beyond the design stage, and financing was not available to design most of the innumerable ideas which emerged.)

Working teams approached interest groups consisting of organizations or individuals, usually with an anthropolo gist, an adult educator, and a member of the interest group. The initial approach was along the lines, what are your concerns, as interests or problems? It avoided the approach, anthropology knows about this or that, why don't you use it? The approach derived from first, the notion that a successful programme should speak to interest and need as defined by clients, common enough in applied anthropology; and sec ondly the realistic assumption that the clients' stereotypes of anthropology were far removed from reality, so that the initial use of the word would conjure up mistaken notions. (Despite the passage of thousands of students through university and college anthropology courses, time and again information about the scope of anthropology was received with surprise and even incredulity in professional as well as lay circles.) The interest groups were selected because there seemed probabilities of interest and/or because there were anthropologists in the community with applicable interests.

At this point an anthropologist and a member of the interest group. with an adult educator or similar person acting as intermediary, interpreter, and catalyst, would share ideas and work up project designs. The intent was that if the project designs were of interest to the client, funding would be obtained under client control and responsibility; otherwise it might be assumed that the level of interest was low. However, as I have said, in most instances preliminary funding was needed to get the project to this stage, arid that funding was lacking.

Nevertheless, the various design beginnings revealed a number of relevant points. First, since most anthropologists were academics with little or no experience of applied anthropology, they had great difficulty in working from the fundamental principles to viable projects. The expression of the difficulty took many forms. One was that the initial format of an idea coming from anthropology would normally be extremely conservative — the academic anthropologist conceived of activities such as lectures, slide shows, video□tapes, all part of his or her familiar world.

It took adult educators to shake us out of this rut, using their own principles, which were entirely consistent with the anthropological fundamentals we have been addressing. In the first place they stressed varieties of communication, and their variable relevance. As is now commonplace in many parts of the Third World, they suggested using theatre, University of British Columbia Museum of Anthropology despite accusations that this was "not a Museum role".) We quickly discovered that the artistic community was ripe for involvement, and saw this as an outlet for their own inter□ests, furthering their own creativity, and providing, in the long run, potential new sources of interest and income. A high proportion of innovative ideas came from this group,

Secondly, both graduate students and faculty often had difficulty relating what they regarded as abstruse anthropo□logical interests to the practical concerns and interests of the neighbouring world, which also they tended to see as rela□tively banal and uninteresting. This to me was an enlighten□ing hangover from the days in which anthropology appeared to be the study and translation of the esoteric. We had to take such colleagues step by step with the process of returning them to the comparative fundamentals of the discipline. It is not possible here to give systematic illustrations of the problem, although to write journalistically about the rel☐evance of such materials is a task I would like to set myself for some time in the future. A fictional example must suffice.

Imagine a doctoral thesis dealing with the structural symbolism of death ceremony and ritual in a Burundi culture. It appears personally difficult for the writer of the work to carry out the *intellectual* task of moving his or her mode of analysis out of the ethnographic context to that, for example, of ethnicity in a modern industrialized city such as Vancouver. Yet by use of the far away example, it turns out that inhabitants of that city can be fascinated by applying the same sort of analysis to themselves or to their neighbours, to learn about the handling of grief, to become sensitized to cultural differences within their own society, to add to counselling knowledge. The use of participatory investiga☐tion relieves the anthropologist of having to *know* the ethnography relevant to the application. He or she *must,* however, develop a flexibility in dealing with new materials, and an inventive exploratory approach to thinking about subject matter. He is drawn into discussion, talk, empathy within the context of the Vancouver culture, even though his speciality is Burundi. Usually this turns out to be highly stimulating. In addition, the public interest turns out to be not merely enlightened curiosity, but once the discussion is opened up it includes a concern for practical matters such as psychological counselling, interfaith communication and collaboration, architecture, law.

The third point that adult educators stressed, which anthropologists should have known a priori, was that the clients do not constitute the uniform population tacitly assumed by most lectureslide show presentations, or extension courses which emerge from the educational establishment or brief television courses. Themes such as alternative approaches to therapy, experiences in the human life cycle, the sociocultural format of immigration, strategies of individuals faced with unemployment — and any others you might think of in broad anthropological terms have differing implications for differing groups of potential clients. An approach which lumps them together misses the point of relevance. Thus, the format emerged in which slide or video show would be divided into segments, some segments of universalistic comparative questionraising intent, some zeroing in on closely identified target groups — nurses, educators, general citizenry, lawyers, political movers, youth, the elderly, and so on. For any given client group, the segments would be combined to suit its special requirements.

The fourth observation consisted in the bias and limita tion embodied in such terms as "client", "target group" and so forth. It is very difficult to avoid the notion that anthropol ogy in this context is selfserving — indeed there is an inevitable element of this, since a long run result of such projects would be to raise consciousness of the anthropo logical contribution, ultimately providing new opportunities for employment. But, if overstressed, selfinterest can lead to heavy persuasion that client groups ought to participate or they will lose out, resulting in topdown design and reluctant participation which is uncommitted and ultimately selfdefeating. The terms underplay the important principle of learning from the people, so that the better term is "partici pants". The lecture and passive slide show format works against this principle.

Hence great pains were taken, once the issue became clear, to induce in every project mechanism to ensure participation and creativity as it were from the "audience" side. This is similar to the activity of the field applied anthropologist in seeking discussions, information, and as psychological counselling, interfaith communication and collaboration, architecture, law.

The third point that adult educators stressed, which anthropologists should have known a priori, was that the clients do not constitute the uniform population tacitly assumed by most lectureslide show presentations, or extension courses which emerge from the educational establishment or brief television courses. Themes such as alternative approaches to therapy, experiences in the human life cycle, the sociocultural format of immigration, strategies of individuals faced with unemployment — and any others you might think of in broad anthropological terms have differing implications for differing groups of potential clients. An approach which lumps them together misses the point of relevance. Thus, the format emerged in which slide or video show would be divided into segments, some segments of universalistic comparative questionraising intent, some zeroing in on closely identified target groups — nurses, educators, general citizenry, lawyers, political movers, youth, the elderly, and so on. For any given client group, the segments would be combined to suit its special requirements.

The fourth observation consisted in the bias and limita☐tion embodied in such terms as "client", "target group" and so forth. It is very difficult to avoid the notion that anthropol☐ogy in this context is selfserving — indeed there is an inevitable element of this, since a long run result of such projects would be to raise consciousness of the anthropo☐logical contribution, ultimately providing new opportunities for employment. But, if overstressed, selfinterest can lead to heavy persuasion that client groups ought to participate or they will lose out, resulting in topdown design and reluctant participation which is uncommitted and ultimately selfdefeating. The terms underplay the important principle of learning from the people, so that the better term is "partici☐pants". The lecture and passive slide show format works against this principle. Hence great pains were taken, once the issue became clear, to induce in every project mechanism to ensure participation and creativity as it were from the "audience" side. This is similar to the activity

of the field applied anthropologist in seeking
discussions, information, and After having
conjured up principles and questions, videos
and slide shows would elicit information and
analysis out of the participant group experience.
(Had this been carried through, it would have
resulted in an enormously increased body of
anthropological information and perspectives
of equal interest to the "fundamental"
anthropologist as to the "applied"). Plays, musical
events, and the like would contain elements of
participatory involvement and subsequent
dis□cussion to draw out implications, often
comparatively.

Finally, this implies that the anthropological
contribu□tors to the process have, if you like, an
intellectual role, drawing attention to relevancies that
might otherwise be missed, opening up underlying
questions, injecting com□parative information.

Very frequently applied anthropology takes place in
an institutional environment which appears on the
surface to be entirely different from the participatory
and voluntary activity to which I have been referring.
The applied anthro□pologist is a consultant or an
employee, in both cases owing a primary duty to the
source of professional income. Never□theless, I think it
important to stress that, if the work is truly

anthropological, the differences are tactical rather than matters of principle, and a significant part of the anthropologist's role is to assert and achieve the primacy of the principles. The task is to establish participation in the applied research endeavour in a manner that adds an interactive dimension outside the preestablished hierarchi□cal rules, yet without threatening them unless changes in hierarchical structure turn out to be part of the solution. Clearly, we are asking for unusual diplomatic skills, sensi□tivities to differences in cultural norms, an ability to secure participation at different levels of interest, even at times an ability to ensure discussion between parties with very differ□ent ideas of authority and social objective. Indeed, quite frequently we hear it said that the major contribution of anthropology has been the capacity of the person concerned to act as a catalyst, to bring people together who consider themselves to be competitors, or who have avoided knowing one another.

Therein also lies a danger. ,The worldwide community development movement at one time adopted a similar stance, becoming in many of its manifestations only concerned with intermediation, a kind of community therapy group, eschew□ing any pretence to substantive competence. It would be a tragedy if applied anthropology followed the same route. Its practitioners must retain their competence through special□ized comparative knowledge and knowledge of the principles of social and cultural organization and processes which give rise to the questions introduced in participatory discussion. In this they cannot be mindless neutrals.

Inevitably, anthropologists will be dealing with widely differing interests and interest groups in the process. From time to time one gets the impression that only one set of interest groups is significant, namely those who are at the receiving end of authority, if you like, the people rather than the bureaucracy or the professionals. To the extent that this is true it can be a grave and selfdefeating error. Few anthropologists are likely to have the political power or influence to change a political or bureaucratic system, at least in the sense of altering time established hierarchies, save in unusual revolutionary contexts. Their influence modifies and does not restructure. Indeed quite radical solutions are usually not the kinds of solutions that emerge from participation, though in some contexts they may be.

When this is the reality, anthropologists need to talk on equal terms to all the relevant groups. Under various codes of ethics, they are supposed to be careful not to reveal information or propagate conclusions which can be seen to be detrimental to the interests of those they study. In participatory applied anthropology, even in fundamental anthropology, such a rule is impossible to observe. If an anthropologist (on the basis of participation) comes to a conclusion that change is in order, the conclusion is almost certain to be detrimental to some group's interest. Since the applied anthropologist adopts a totalistic approach, the group that is adversely affected is part of the arena of study, *ipso facto* must not be adversely affected, which is patently impossible. If, as some colleagues apparently feel, the an swer is *not* to include the adversely affected group in the arena of study, then the anthropologist is being less than totalistic and credibility, even the likelihood of results being successful, is compromised. If the context of problem in volves the bureaucracy, the bureaucracy (even the military) must be studied equally with the people, and the implica tions for selfinterest and change that is detrimental to their perceived power are part of the subject of examination, whether or not it has its detrimental costs. Indeed, no worthwhile project of change will be without costs, detrimental to someone.

The point raises questions of a more technical, perhaps less politicized nature, namely that of the direction and language of communication. Factual and analytic reports are often directed first at the patronal authority, with an availability or a repeat report in alternative language to the participant clients. Most applied anthropologists are famil iar with this process, which is, moreover, partly enjoined upon fundamental anthropologists working in other coun☐tries, by ethical codes or government regulation.

I am, however, prompted to extend the issue as a result of conversations some years ago with Dr. Barbara Lane, who with her husband Dr. Robert Lane has been operating for some years a consultancy dealing with North American Indian Law. The Lanes have a highly effective success rate, which I have not seen described in the professional litera☐ture, in the provision of advice and evidence to legal firms and courts involved in settling disputes with Indian people. Contrary to the experience of some other consultants and expert witnesses in this domain, this does not consist merely of uncovering ethnographic data and presenting the anthro☐pologically sound conclusions from it. It consists rather *of* deliberate acts of cultural translation, carefully thought out and applied. It involves a careful study of the culture of lawyers, laws and courts *in addition to* the Indian culture. The concepts which are present in the ethnographic mate☐rials and in the anthropological analysis are deliberately translated into formats which fit the culture of the legal system in the United States. It is no use, argue the Lanes, leaving it to the courts to make the translation. It is essen☐tially an anthropological exercise returning with great skill to the fundamentals of the discipline as involved with inter☐cultural translation.

In the end, I wish to draw together some of the implica⬜tions I derive for the professional training of anthropology. For reasons I have not fully expressed, I see the future of anthropology as lying as much in its applied professionalism a in the increased sophistication of research and theoretical knowledge. Both go hand in hand. But it is already evident, though not much a matter of public consciousness, that careers in anthropology now stretch well beyond the con⬜fines of the academic tower, and rare indeed is the anthro⬜pologist who will not be challenged to apply knowledge and perspectives to the task of dirtying his or her fingers in the fertile soil of the world of human problems. This, it is not hard to predict, will become more and more the case, and, frighteningly, since anthropology deals with almost every aspect of human living, the range and scale of demand for anthropologists could grow *ad infinitum*. Instead of restrict⬜ing entry into anthropology courses and graduate programmes, we should be opening them to as many as are qualified and who can be handled by teaching faculty — in fact more, as has been demonstrated in several countries, such as Spain.

That having been said, most university departments have not adjusted to the reality that most of their graduates will have careers outside of academies. The structures of undergraduate syllabi need adjustment to provide for a professional stream leading

to the training of paraanthro□pologists. Since
anthropological research is intensely labour intensive, it
would appear that there should be greater
opportunities also for the training of professional
anthro□pologists at the bachelor's and master's levels,
who will, in fact, be qualified to participate in
investigatory teams, though not to lead them. And
doctoral candidates require funding to enable them to
receive training in the creative use of such personnel.
The suggestions imply considerable change in
undergraduate and graduate programmes with more
delib□erate orientation to professional as well as
academic need.

I would hope that courses would be amended to
permit of the deliberate analysis of links between
fundamental arid applied or problemsolving
anthropology, and that in this process scholars would
seek to learn and cooperate with those elements in
adult education who have, knowingly or unknowingly,
borrowed techniques and orientations from the
fundamentals of anthropology which we ourselves tend
to take for granted and then lose sight of. I would trust
that scholars would take steps to create in their own
communi□ties and in those in which they work corps' of
paraanthro□pologists to assist creatively in getting the
job done And in this process, I would insist that
enormous stress be placed on the skills of
communication, at all relevant levels, from addressing

the major international journals to journalism, from analytic report writing, bearing in mind the specifics of the audience to openended interactive tech□niques for involving in a twoway flow the people with whom and for whom one is working.

The time is ripe for applied anthropology to be conscious about what it is already doing and will do more creatively in the future. To coin a phrase, the sobriquet Applied Anthro□pology should move beyond Action Anthropology and its derivatives to become Participatory (or Interactive?) Com□municative Anthropology.

ACKNOWLEDGMENTS

The author wishes to thank the WennerGren Founda□tion for Anthropological Research, Inc., of New York, for financial assistance.

REFERENCES

Angrosino, Michael V. 1976 *Do Applied Anthropologists Apply* Anthropology? Athens, Georgia: University of Geor□gia Press for *Southern Anthropological Society. Proceed□ings* No. 10.

Belshaw, Cyril S. 1959 The identification of values in anthro□pology. Am. *J. Sociology* 64: 555562.

Belshaw, Cyril S. 1980 The data base in economic anthropology. In *Currents in Anthropology: Essays in Honor ofSolTax* (edited by Robert Hinshaw). Berlin: New York: de Gruyter. pp.4264.

Belshaw, Cyril S. 1988 Challenges for the future of social and cultural anthropology. *Int. Soc. J.* 116: 193202.

Belshaw, Cyril S. 1988 *Some Limitations of Classification in Comparative Studies Exemplified by the Analysis of Parallel Economies, with Implications for Development Theory.* L'Uomo. 11 (2): 295318.

Eddy, E. M. and W. L. Partridge 1978 *Applied Anthropology*
in America. New York: Columbia University Press.

McFeat. T. 1974 *SmallGroup Cultures.* Elmsford: Pergamon Press.

The Evaluation of Technical Assistance as a Contribution to Development

First published in the *International Development Review* VIII No 2 June 1966. It was the outcome of the experience as a member of as term created by UN ECOSOC to report on the effects of all technical assistance programmes in Thailand which reported in 1995 and was written when I was a Fellow of the U.N. Research Institute for Social Development in Geneva. Although written from an anthropologist's perspective it uses economics terminology.

THE EVALUATION OF TECHNICAL ASSISTANCE has been of concern to international officials for over fifteen years. During that time there have been some attempts, more or less sporadic, to develop techniques of evaluation, but very few of the attempts have been coordinated with others, and one cannot describe a continuous evolution of thought about the matter. The symposium on techniques of evaluation which took place in 1955 under TAB auspices, summarized in the *International Social Science Bulletin,* might have taken place today. One is struck by the fact that there is in existence no bibliography of evaluation reports, and that most evaluation teams or studies pro☐ceed with little attention to what has happened in the past. Even international and bilateral agencies some☐times lose track of what they have done before. Another impression is that the evaluation efforts of international and bilateral agencies proceed with only slight contact, so that learning and the transfer of experience between them is minimal, and the growth of technique and con☐ceptualization is slow.

This article is not to make up these deficiencies, but to consider a point which has been lost sight of because of the considerable duplications of conceptual effort. The nature of evaluation depends entirely upon the purposes of the evaluation, and so far very few attempts have been systematically concerned with the effects of technical assistance upon the development of a country (a polity, a society, an economy) as a working system. Concern with this overall approach to technical assistance has s been growing in recent years, and is reflected in the debates and resolutions of the Economic and Social Council which have led to the appointment of a number of evaluation missions. Such missions, however, must work out their own technique in the short space of time available to them, and must therefore build very largely t upon the past with the minimum of innovation. This paper grows out of the experience of one such mission and attempts to reflect further upon the possibilities. It is of course a personal paper, with which the other members of the mission, and the United Nations, are not associated.

LIMITATIONS ON PROJECT EVALUATION

Most approaches to technical assistance evaluation are concerned with the question, to what extent did the project achieve its goals in the most efficient manner?

Such a question can often be answered with a great deal of accuracy, which varies according to whether we can assume that the goals are specifically defined, and whether the analyst can obtain sufficient data about results, timing, and the resources used. When the approach is develop techniques of evaluation, but very few of the attempts have been coordinated with others, and one cannot describe a continuous evolution of thought about the matter. The symposium on techniques of evaluation which took place in 1955 under Technical Assistance Bureau auspices, summarized in the *International Social Science Bulletin,* might have taken place today. One is struck by the fact that there is in existence no bibliography of evaluation reports, and that most evaluation teams or studies pro□ceed with little attention to what has happened in the past. Even international and bilateral agencies some□times lose track of what they have done before. Another impression is that the evaluation efforts of international and bilateral agencies proceed with only slight contact, so that learning and the transfer of experience between them is minimal, and the growth of technique and con□ceptualization is slow.

Yet to describe this as an evaluation of the contribution of technical assistance to development would be to give a false emphasis: the operation is simply an extension of research into the techniques and methodology of agricul□tural, health, educational, industrial, or other operations, with special emphasis on problems which are of frequent occurrence in technical assistance.

Even within this conception there is a major limitation to the approach. Frequently the goals of technical assist□ance projects are not specified with a sufficient degree of precision to make such an assessment possible, and the methods used involve skills and intangibles which weaken attempts at quantification. This is occasionally a matter of careless project formulation, but very often it is delib□erate, since the objective is to probe, to test, to explore, to stimulate, and since, if the goal were predefined, it might dictate an apparent solution which would other□wise not be appropriate. This is true of openended scientific exploration, of most institutional change, and of projects which involve the formation of ideas and values.

Linked to this limitation is another, namely that im□portant effects of technical assistance, both positive and negative, are sideeffects. These are not only unforeseen results in closely allied fields (the use of a school text□book offending mores and creating antipathy to the school), but ramifying results over many areas (a road creating a demand for markets, transportation, drainage, organized water supply). To concentrate solely on the specific goal of the project might mean the setting aside of extremely significant conditions.

Another consideration is the analysis of the goal itself. To accept it as given may be to avoid asking the question, was it the most appropriate goal under the circumstances, or would some other uses have been more effective?

And finally sometimes, though not always, the evalua☐tion does not distinguish between the technical assistance component of a project, and the total project itself. Thus, for example, it is fairly easy to state that a tuberculosis eradication campaign was associated with a reduction of disease incidence which in turn was associated with a sharp drop in mortality attributable to tuberculosis. But it is not always so easy to decide how much of this result is attributable to the skill of government action itself, to the W.H.O. key assistance, to the actions of U.S. aid financed teams, or to alterations in the habits of the population in turn linked with improved housing, water coupled with an examination of possible technical alter☐natives, it can lead to an improvement in method, and often increased results with fewer resources. Evaluations of this kind are necessary to improve the technical capacity and economy of the agencies providing assist☐ance.

Yet to describe this as an evaluation of the contribution of technical assistance to development would be to give a false emphasis: the operation is simply an extension of research into the techniques and methodology of agricul tural, health, educational, industrial, or other operations, with special emphasis on problems which are of frequent occurrence in technical assistance.

Another consideration is the analysis of the goal itself. To accept it as given may be to avoid asking the question, was it the most appropriate goal under the circumstances, or would some other uses have been more effective?

And finally sometimes, though not always, the evalua tion does not distinguish between the technical assistance component of a project, and the total project itself. Thus, for example, it is fairly easy to state that a tuberculosis eradication campaign was associated with a reduction of disease incidence which in turn was associated with a sharp drop in mortality attributable to tuberculosis. But it is not always so easy to decide how much of this result is attributable to the skill of government action itself, to the W.H.O. key assistance, to the actions of U.S. aid financed teams, or to alterations in the habits of the population in turn linked with improved housing, water coupled with an examination of possible technical alter natives, it can lead to an improvement in method, and often increased results with fewer resources. Evaluations of this kind are necessary to improve the technical capacity and economy of the agencies providing assist☐ance.

Yet to describe this as an evaluation of the contribution of technical assistance to development would be to give a false emphasis: the operation is simply an extension of research into the techniques and methodology of agricul☐tural, health, educational, industrial, or other operations, with special emphasis on problems which are of frequent occurrence in technical assistance.

Because of factors such as these, some approaches to evaluation are more openended and discursive than the tight technical ones which are superficially precise. Thus Professor Charles Madge, for example, attempted, on behalf of UNESCO, to tap the experience and knowledge t of a limited number of technical assistance experts who had been working in Thailand in fields where the rural human relations component was highly significant in   the work. The experts were asked to keep diaries indicative of their experience, including interaction with counter parts and with village people, to answer questions about their experience and its results, and to add their own analysis of the impact and significance of the project in a freeflowing manner Similarly, Professor Herbert Hyman and his associates at the United Nations Research Institute for Social Development, have made a detailed statistical and analytical study of the views of over four hundred experts in ten countries, again working in areas where rural human relations are of great significance. The most immediate value of such studies is to cast considerable light upon the attitudes of technical assist ance experts who are, of course, key elements in the I chains of interaction which ultimately bring about a technical assistance result. The views of Resident Representatives, as surveyed by the Technical Assistance Board, are of a similar order.

In a limited way the experts are also used to reveal the processes at work during the course of their project, and since they are intelligent commentators and observers they can record many events and interactions which are extremely instructive, and can add an element of depth and humanity to otherwise mechanical studies.

Nevertheless, they cannot do the whole job of analysis. What one observes depends on what questions one is interested in. Field experts are very seldom economists or sociologists, and if they make observations of interest to economists or sociologists, it is quite often because they have absorbed appropriate knowledge as intelligent men and women stimulated by an overseas environment that has intrigued them. In the same way, anthropologists made use of missionaries and other field observers in t the early days of the discipline, and now contact other anthropological colleagues for information o fa comparative kind. But anthropologists interested in generalizations are continuously frustrated because their colleagues have not recorded information which is essential to other new theory, and in many instances were not even aware of its significance when they were in the field. The dimen□sion added by the knowledge of the field experts must eventually be supplemented by more systematic valuefree observation which can go beyond the theories at present currently circulating among the professional fraternity.

OVERALL CONTRIBUTION OF TECHNICAL. AID

These types of investigation are leading into much broader fields than those indicated by the problem as to whether a project is being handled in the most efficient or effective way possible. They are leading in fact to□wards the question, what is the contribution of technical assistance to the overall socioeconomic development of a given country? At first sight, it would seem that this question, being even broader, is less capable of being answered.

To some extent this is true, particularly if one expects quantitative precision in one's answers. It would be feasible to select particular types of technical assistance where relations between inputs and outputs are direct, and measure impact on the economy at least. But most technical assistance, and perhaps the most significant, is not of this order at all. How would one translate the effect of an adviser on national planning in such terms? How would one put together the effects of a fellowship concerned with the administration of social welfare and the advice of an expert who suggested that the time was *not* ripe for a national standards laboratory? To add up, for example, the monetary value (in terms of salary and other costs) of the fellowship and the expert project would not give a comparative indication of significance, and would not take into account the ramifying effects of decisions which flow from the two enterprises.

One is therefore forced back into a process of analysis which endeavours to place the technical assistance project in an organic framework, and which endeavors to ascer☐tain what the implications of the projects are for the economic and social environment in which it is placed. One must analyze what happens, and what the linkages of events might be. This implies the selection of infor☐mation according to judgments about its significance for organic relationships rather than for its significance for quantitative measurement. (The two concepts are not necessarily opposed: it is a question of starting point. One method starts with observations which are measur☐able now, and builds a pattern of significance around them; the other starts with patterns of significance, and ultimately tries to measure what one can within the pattern.)

Thus in the analysis judgment is all important. Judg☐ment in such a field is systematized around propositions, explicit or not, about the crucial operation of significant relationships. There is in fact a theory of the operation the circumstances of the country at the time. There is no doubt that we have here a basic factor in social development.

However, no single criterion is likely to be good enough. One of the difficulties is that an increase in skills is not an independent variable, and that it may be supported or counteracted by other variables, which ought there☐fore to be taken into account. It is not difficult to think of instances in which a dramatic alteration in the avail☐ability of physical resources called forth, to some degree, an increased supply of skills (mining linked with the sup☐ply of engineers, roads with the development of market☐ing skills). On the other hand, examples of the over☐supply of skills are legion, and there are countries where scientists and engineers are available, but are not being used to capacity because of lack of appropriate forms of organization or institutions. A single criterion which hides such factors will reduce the significance of the evaluation as a diagnostic tool.

SOME RECOMMENDED CRITERIA

I wish now to set out a series of propositions and ques☐tions which in my view are closely linked with the devel☐opment process. Since there is no clear agreement among scholars and administrators as to the theory, or the nature, of development, or as to the weight to be attached to such factors as are considered to be significant, it is most unlikely that this series will be generally accepted. Nevertheless, if it has merit as an approximation it will lend support to the idea that evaluation exercises should endeavour to make explicit the development theorems on which they are based, and to relate these to the specific technical assistance programs they are examining. It should be stressed that there is no implication that proj☐ects should, to be effective, contribute in terms of all propositions, or that they are better or more effective if they contribute to the first rather than the second. At this stage, evaluation of the impact of technical assist☐ance upon development is not to be achieved through arithmetical summation but through qualitative analysis.

> (1) A technical assistance project contributes to de☐velopment if the program of which it is a part perma☐nently alters the effective demand schedule, or con☐sumption pattern, of the country in such a way that an increased level of satisfaction is achieved, and the gap between effective demand and the preexisting potential demand is narrowed. This is the most difficult propo☐sition to formulate

succinctly, and also by far the most difficult to assess. Note first, the phrase is "preexisting" potential demand, because it is very often the case that the satisfaction of one series of wants at one level opens up a whole range of other unsatisfied ambitions, or brings them into consciousness in such a way that they can constitute goals for further action (see proposition two). Note secondly no attempt has been made to distinguish between economic, cultural or social wants, or to state which have prepotence or greater importance. The distinction is unsatisfactory analytically, and in any case. Within the context of this propositions, the choice is for the people to make themselves. The difficulty of assessment lies in the identification of the effective demand schedule, and even more in judging potential demand. Work being done at the United Nations Research Institute for Social Development on levels of living may contribute to the solution of the first problem, and the second may be solved approximately or temporarily by the convention that the government's assessment of plans and aspirations is the one to be used.[22]   We

---

[22] It is of course necessary in 2011 to add the qualification that this sentence can only apply to establoished

cannot, however, rest content with the mere acceptance of government priorities, particularly since some governments may be out of touch with the aspirations of its citizens, or may not be able to analyse the implications. It must be admitted that most evaluation teams will of necessity judiciously and somewhat subjectively combine information gleaned from government plans with indications from market behaviour, statements of opinion, sand social and economic analyses.

(2) A technical assistance project contributes to development if the programme of which it is a part increases the satisfaction in such a way that other unsatisfied wants, some of which may be new, alter their position in the potential demand schedule to such an extent that they become goals for further action. In other words an increase in consumption (material or immaterial) spurs people to try to obtain more, constituting a dynamic force for change. This by no means always happens, particularly in marginal communities, but unless it happens, development associated with selfsustained growth will not be present. It must be admitted

---

democracies.

that neither economic theory not empirical analysis has yet given adequate guidelines for the assessment of the multiplying or ramifying effects of particular forms of consumption.. Nevertheless, judgements about this are implicit in the evaluation of the impact of technical assistance.

(3) A project will contribute to development if it assists a programme to increase the range of indigenous resources utilized or increase the range of commodities produced (provided this is justified economically) or to remove bottlenecks in the system of resource exploitation and production, thus liberating further productive forces.

(4) A similar result will occur, other things being equal, when technical assistance contributes to an increased division of labour (sociasl concomitant: increased diversification of social roles), provided that this contributes optimally to production or to the direct satisfaction of wants. It should be stressed here once again the wants will be material, cultural or in the nature of social welfare satisfactions, and that a *priori* judgments of appropriateness or

imbalance should, in this context, be eschewed.

(5) A further proposition linked with (4) is that development reflects innovation, and that the rate of in□novation, other things being equal, is associated with the size of the pool of relevant ideas and information on the one hand, and the ability of the potential innovators to question, observe, generalize and apply knowledge. There□fore one should ask, does the form in which technical assistance is given add to the pool of ideas *permanently* available to the society (the visit of an expert who took his knowledge away with him would not qualify) ? And does it equip personnel, not merely to apply knowledge statically, but to develop it in the circumstances of the country? It should be noted here that innovation is not merely technical in a physical sense, but also implies alterations in modes of organization.

(6) Just as an increase in the velocity of circulation of money may be deemed to increase the quantity of money, so an increase in the velocity of circulation of ideas and information may be deemed to increase the effective size of the pool of ideas. Thus communications are of vital significance in development. But communi□cations have a further effect, namely that of assisting individuals to adapt to one another. They are a vital element in the articulation of a society, a culture, a polity, an

economy. Does technical assistance contribute to in☐creased effectiveness of communications?

Here the evaluation must look for several types of indicators. The use of twoway transmitter/receivers, the improvement of the stock exchange (or its foundation), the state of the commodity market, the use of telephones and the mails, the extension of reliable freight services, the use of computers, may be areas involving technical assistance which have profound social and economic consequences. The problem for assessment may link equally with boundaries in social relations (for all com☐munication flows along lines indicated by social struc☐ture and social organization) or increasing the effective☐ness of symbol systems (the basis of the means of com☐munication), whether these be conventions such as legal contracts, or language elements such as literacy, mathe☐matics, or weight symbols. What does technical assist☐ance do, both directly and indirectly, in these connec☐tions?

In most countries to which technical assistance is given, the spectrum of organized institutions is either not as complete as in developed countries, or does not constitute an articulated whole in such a way that the society operates as a set of interacting organizations.

Technical assistance will make a contribution towards the establishment of a modern articulated society if it meets some of the earlier criteria. But in addition, as an aspect of the division of labour, and as an extension of the fourth proposition, it will make a contribution if it assists in the creation of specific institutions. The func□tional emphasis of these is likely to be the following, although functions need not be limited in this way: (a) the creation of institutions which produce skills and knowledge, (b) the organization of production and serv□ices (including cultural and welfare services), (c) the organization of units of public administration, (d) the organization of institutions to remedy societal ills which are frictional to the operation of the system.

It should be noted that the emphasis is upon the "training of trainers", to use the current jargon, and the creation of institutions. If a technical expert simply produces a new textbook, teaches a number of children, succeeds himself in removing malaria from a village, cures a number of opium addicts, secures the production of x quantity of a raw material, his impact is limited to an effect, probably temporary, on growth rather than on development, unless in addition his action meets the requirements of propositions one and two. Such wants or ills cannot be dealt with permanently unless perma nent institutions are available to assess and act. Tech nical assistance thus tends to be geared to institution building, and rightly so, for this increases the complexity of effective social organization, and the capacity of a society to take its own responsibility for increasing its output, and its performance from the point of view of satisfying wants.

(8) Organizations themselves are small socioeco nomic systems usually capable of improved performance. If the operation of organizations is improved so that their contribution to the overall social system improves, they will be changed and developed and will be part of a development of the social system. Technical assistance is likely to make a contribution in several fields, which would include increasing the efficiency of operation, an improvement in adjustment mechanisms (both internal and as an aspect of adjustment to external conditions and to other institutions), and the creation of an orien tation toward growth and expansion.

(9) Finally (but this is implied throughout) technical assistance will make a greater contribution to develop ment the more it results in the internalization of the above factors, so that they are not dependent on external arti ficial stimulus.

Any technical assistance project can be linked with the above propositions, and analyzed according to which propositions (if any) it fits. Presumably, if it does not fit any of the propositions it does not qualify as technical assistance which contributes towards overall develop□ment. There are indeed technical assistance projects which can be ruled out on these grounds, or on the grounds that their contribution is minimal

But beyond these extreme cases, the propositions as they stand do not in themselves give a clear indication of the relative merits of alternative technical assistance projects or proposals. I do not believe that any firm agreement on the technique for achieving this next step is at this stage probable; indeed, at this stage it may be undesirable, since in the present state of our knowledge a further period of trial and error, of experiment, and of observation, is probably to be preferred over a too hasty commitment to one line of thought.

A STRATEGY OF DEVELOPMENT

Insofar as there are principles to be discerned or worked out, they will probably crystallize around the notion of a strategy of development. This is simply a short way of saying that projects vary according to the weight of their impact. Conceptually, such variation is in the degree to which projects have multiplying or ramifying effects throughout a socioeconomic system, and it may be argued that the greater the multiplying or ramifying effects the more strategic the project. This refers to the objective of the project, and its indirect consequences. In addition, technical assistance may not be concerned with a total project, but only part of it, and here again the possible alternatives may be judged according to the proliferation of their effects.

Unfortunately, this criterion, necessary though it is, is not only a matter of evaluative and analytic judgment, but is also predicated to some extent on the existence of a working socioeconomic system which has a high degree of internal articulation. A project may have highly ramifying effects in one country, because the effects travel, as it were, through the social and com□municative links of the system, and effects take place as various institutions adapt to the new conditions. But in another country the same measures may have little or no effect beyond the immediate implementation of a target, because communication does not exist or because institutions in the linkage of social interaction are miss□ing, or because they are nonadaptive. This suggests that a strategy of development may need to place greater or prior emphasis upon institution building and the communications system in some countries, or for some sectors.

In any event, the contribution of technical assistance to overall development cannot be judged finally without some fairly specific assumptions about the strategy of development in the circumstances of the country.

The Data Base in Economic Anthropology

First published in Hinshaw, Robert, ed., *Currents in Anthropology: Essays in Honor of Sol Tax*, The Hague, Mouton, 1979

My acquaintance with economic anthropology goes back to the 1930's when, as a New Zealand schoolboy, I read Raymond Firth's (1929) *Primitive Economics of the New Zealand Maori*. The success of that work was dependent upon the author's skill in assembling, recognizable as anthropology. Only rarely have they been equaled since, and not once have they been surpassed[23].

Meanwhile, on the other side of the Atlantic. and at approximately the same time, a few American anthropologists aimed at similar results. Allowing for differences in society and field conditions, Sol Tax's work in Guatemala, begun in the mid'30's. showed the same pioneering ingenuity in obtaining figures and using them to discover relationships and back up propositions. While some of the Tax Guatemalan material was ready and appeared much

---

[23] Also, through my economist father, I learned something first hand of the contemporary life of the Maori, as mentioned in *Remuera: Memories of a New Zealand Boy between he Wars*

earlier, the primary economic study. *Penny Capitalism: A Guatemalan Indian Economy,* was not published until 1953. (The delay in publication could be attributed to the intervention of World War II.) Still, enough was known of the Firth and Tax achievements to prompt debate in the graduate seminars of the late'40's and '50's which were influ□encing the focus and methodology of oncoming younger anthropologists.

That debate was not by any means always favorable to the trend which Tax and Firth, with others, were pioneering. I well recall a not unusual remark: "Who are economic anthropologists? They are people who count the number of coconuts on coconut trees. There's nothing in it." The implication was clear: counting was dull and intellectually derisive. It resulted in delayed publication because of all those tables which had to be wrestled with, and, in field conditions, it was nearly always impossible to do (despite the Tax/Firth demonstration to the contrary). A few of the mature figures, for example, Audrey Richards and George Foster, took no notice of these objections and in their own contemporaneous work provided materials which, again, from this point of view, could be taken as models. Some of the fresh generation also were sufficiently deaf to persist in an attempt at quantification.

In the subsequent years, the relevance of quantification and formalized methods of analysis has expanded, particularly in anthropological linguistics, kinship analysis, and archaeology. In economic anthropology, however, the advances beyond the techniques of *Penny Capitalism* have been episodic. Apart from the appearance of the essays in *The Craft of Social Anthropology* (Epstein 1967), which is in part a handbook of quantitative field method, there has been little replication of techniques shown to be workable. Even courses in economic anthropology pay little attention to this aspect of the subject. and in a distressing number of studies the most elementary data omissions are shrugged off. In common with much of anthropology, economic anthropology has addressed itself far too little to the problem of cumulation in knowledge, and the approach of many of its practitioners has been to dabble in datagathering techniques with little attempt to build upon or learn from past successes and failures.

What was done in *Penny Capitalism?*

In the first place, it should be mentioned that Tax initially suffered from the common North American condition of spending short rather than long periods in the field. This will not do in economic anthropology, because of the absolute necessity of correcting quantities for seasonal adjustments. Further, Tax did not have the benefit of a tradition of earlier studies which would have given him guidance. Thus a considerable part of his first field experience can be regarded as exploration. During sub□sequent visits of longer duration, spread over many years, the questions that he saw he had to answer became sharpened and organized, and what was originally a disadvantage became an advantage. He was able to obtain additional data and amend his technique over time. Further, and this is most important, he obtained the cooperation of a school□teacher, Juan Rosales. who later became an anthropologist in his own right. This extended the fieldwork team to two, permitted data gathering between Tax's visits, and made possible more or less continued inter□action with the field.

There are two prime obstacles to obtaining quantitative data by field methods. The first is manpower. One person can only do so much, no matter how much time he spends. To take the observations or ask the systematic questions which are necessary is extremely timeconsuming One must always be taking the measure of opportunity costs and deciding when more value will be obtained by inquiries aimed in other directions. The critics are right to this extent; a field study limited entirely to systematic figures would be very dull reading, unless it were handled with considerable theoretical ingenuity. The second obstacle is the boredom and irritation which can be engendered by the routine questioning, the continual repetition of observation, and the persistence which must characterize the gathering of significant material. We have here the socialscience equivalent of the tediously repeated experiments of the natural sciences, which turn to gold only when large numbers are ac☐cumulated or when controlled action leads to an unexpected observation. In our case, however, we are not dealing with inanimate matter, and the irritation and boredom can come to be shared by our informants. At that point, the information gathering becomes not merely a normal cost of fieldwork, but a hazard, interfering with the supply and validity of the information. The anthropologist must stop this line of inquiry, or take measures to avoid or minimize the problem.

The pioneering studies did not address these questions directly, but they nevertheless were successful in dealing with them. Both the Firth and Tax studies assembled data from two fieldworkers. Both made use of official statistics as background material. Both seized the opportunity when it occurred to make regular quantitative observations. Thus Firth made an incredibly onerous daily sixmonth record of the catch of 20 liftnets on a halfmile length of beach, sampled rice production on 222 contiguous plots, made a census of 331 households, and recorded the budgets often households for periods of from one to five months. Tax was able to check the acreage devoted to specified crops on the first day of each of twelve months for a total of 1,638 acres. He assembled a complete survey of land ownership, withsummary wealth data for 132 families, and a more detailed study of ten households chosen to represent economic differences. Marketing data included the observation of produce carried to market by vendors at stated hours during each day of eight separated weeks. He obtained a detailed, ex post facto, annual budget for four families, linked in his calculations to the detailed checking of the actual consumption of six families for a sevenday period.

The material gathered by these processes was still insufficient in itself; huge gaps in data of significance to the general analysis emerged. These had to be filled by calculation or estimation. Clearly, such deductions are reliable only to the extent that the initial samples are adequate and the logic of calculation is suitable. Firth makes the point that the mere counting of the physical catch landed on the beach was insufficiently reliable, since sometimes the boats transferred the catch to other carriers or agents at sea; the direct observation had to be supplemented by pointed questions. If such problems have been controlled, however, it is, for example, possible and legitimate to calculate fishing income from one's knowledge of quantities landed and transported to market, cor rected by a factor to allow for nonsale, domestic consumption, nonmarket exchange, and spoilage (each based upon some observational data). These quantities can then be multiplied by a market price figure, which in turn is based upon detailed observation, questioning, and the analysis of the nature of market pricing and variation. While this is com☐plicated, each observational step may be more practical, reliable, and acceptable than the direct questioning of fishermen as to their cash income. Furthermore, such a procedure has a chance of revealing the processes which lie behind the results.

Tax leaned on calculations of this sort very heavily in *Penny Capitalism;* indeed, looking back on that study I feel that one of its most significant contributions was the demonstration of the possibilities of ingenuity in calculation. While most of the data assembled are based upon inference and calculation rather than direct observation, and while occasionally Tax is not always explicit about the calculation method, I doubt that there are more than three or four studies in the literature which approximate the richness of his final data. In general, he achieves this result by using normal anthropological inquiry and observation to obtain as precise a description as possible of relevant roles and categories of action. In addition, he is systematic and thorough in his coverage of the range of relevant behavior. Thus, for example, he works through every conceivable occupational role in the community and builds a careful analysis of the conditions of that role and the requirements which affect such matters as the distribution of time. He uses the information obtained to calculate the distribution of work, to examine age and sex differences, and to arrive at a macro account of labor distribution for the community as a whole.

The method of indirect calculation is exemplified by his account of the way in which he built up a table summarizing time devoted to marketing. The table, he says (p. 132), comes from two surveys, with different Indians, and several years apart, plus the innumerable observations of years. The Indians talk about markets, and prices, more than anything else, and merchandising activities are well known. However. the primary data are not all as detailed as table 49 would indicate. Questioning was done in terms of households and general custom. For example. an informant's statement that a certain "whole family" went regularly to Sololã. was true even though part of the family went one week and part another. Thus while it is true that 102 men, 112 women, and 60 children regularly went to Sololã, the number that went on any one Thursday or Friday is a question. Without a count of Indians on the road for a sample period of time, or some other spot check, the figures in the column "Times per year" are based partly on general observations such as that the 82 households regularly patronizing the Sololá market are regularly represented there 50 times annually (some occasionally going twice weekly), but that the total days are reduced because inclement weather, sickness, and fiesta days keep all of the families away some days. and in cases of compound families, all of the members do not usually go to the market at once. . . . The figures for "Hours each time," based on reliable statements and observation, are highly accurate. The totals calculated for "regular" visits are probably accurate to within 10 percent. Those for "irregular" visits on the contrary could be off as much as 30 or 40 percent.

 A detailed account of the manner in which consumption data were arrived at (p. 164) has very similar implications: meticulous observation and calculation constrained by the physical limitations of observation, the combination of various sources of data to provide a chain in the link of calculation and to reinforce conclusions, and the indication that such calculations contain the potentiality of error. The frankness about margins of error is not usual in other fields of anthropology. Perhaps this is the reason that subsequent searches for more accurate methods have not been particularly sustained or enterprising.

Although Firth added a short methodological postscript to his work, neither the Firths nor Tax presented their studies as consciously arrivedat advances in technique. Nor have many later writers. One is tempted to say that this is partly because later writers, with very few exceptions, did not advance the techniques; indeed, a high proportion of subsequent work fails to reach the same standards. This in turn is perhaps because the significance of an adequate methodological base, although it should be obvious, has not been made the subject of sufficient discussion (with the exception of accounts in Epstein [1967]) or a criterion for grant support.

Yet at the same time the range of theoretical questions which could be addressed has expanded considerably since the Tax and Firth studies. The advent of the computer means that a vast quantity of data can be handled; there is no danger now of gathering too much, as long as it can be of significance. We can use simulation techniques and give meaning to "pieces" of data, even if we lack the whole picture, enabling us to work with the principle that scientific advance consists in replacing one ap□proximation with another that is somewhat less approximate. Further□more, the chances are that students and the present generation of research workers are much more knowledgeable about calculation techniques and statistics than Tax, Firth, or the students they dealt with in the late '40's and early '50's. This is not the place to attempt a full statement of the new theoretical issues, but a few can be mentioned which have a sharp implica□tion for data gathering.

One of these has been the focus of interest on

choice and decision making, for which intensive and detailed information of limited kinds about a few individuals can be theoretically revealing, as can linear programming and laboratory experiment (cf. Davenport 1960, Prattis 1973, McFeat 1974). Perhaps the most satisfactory linkage between data and analysis has been in market studies, for example, the work of Davis (1973) and Beals (1975). Here the best practitioners either take the greatest pains to ensure that the data samples are representative or frankly use qualitative judgment in the standard anthropological way. Unfortunately, the best studies are supplemented by other work which falls into most of the methodological traps without recognition that they are there (see, for example, essays in the collection edited by Brookfield [1969]).

One field in which there has been some cumulative advance has been the examination of presentation and exchange that have a nonmarket base (though often linking with market forces). This advance has proceeded slowly, however, usually through comparative analysis of existing field materials. The number of persons who have made new contributions through using new techniques is small (Schneider [1970], Salisbury [1962], and Cancian [1965, 1972] are among the exceptions). The insights gained are of course important when the work is well done. They are also, however, a little dangerous, particularly since they establish a model for graduate students, who may feel they must use their field opportunity to establish yet another ethnography which will meet the standards if some little original guess or new philosophical twist can be incorporated. One of the results is a tiresome series of studies of, for example, Melanesia or New Guinea, or Latin American peasant com munities, which tell us nothing that was not fully known by the mid'50's.

At the same time, very few are addressing themselves to the important issues: What are the exchange *networks?* How can decisions within them be interpreted? What are the communication flows? Where are the power and influence links? It is now agreed that such questions can no longer be raised adequately by internal village studies and that some sense of sociogeographic perspective is mandatory. This fact alone places a tremendous burden upon the investigator. It also seems to be agreed, though often by lip service rather than by practice, that dynamic rather than static models provide the best perspective and that they must incorporate external as well as internal influences. History (with ethno□history) is still the dominant source of information here, and much can be achieved creatively (Salisbury's [1969] *Vunamami* and Burridge's [1960] *Mambu* should be required reading). The timescale involved, however, is often too long to provide the dynamic models which can be of utility in interpreting the here and now and the microsocial. At the same time, the link between the microsocial and the macrosocial demands that at least the models we already have be filled out by data.

These are but a few of the issues, and I have not attempted to deal with the extension of anthropological analysis into such uncharted territories as the interpretation of contemporary corporate behavior or inter□national politicoeconomic transactions and organization (cf. Belshaw 1975) or the analysis of socioeconomic achievement (cf. Belshaw 1970). It is true that there seems to be a gap between grand theoretical demands, issues of public policy, and the minutiae of field investigation. Yet our discussion of such matters will continue to be speculative to the extent that we do not root the arguments in some samples of empirical inquiry. Let us come back to the minutiae again and see what the problems are.

The basic data problem throughout anthropology is to obtain samples which have some analytic meaning. On the whole, most anthropology records a range of uniquely observed events which are then analyzed in terms of a discovered logic in their relationships. The representative nature of the events is inferred or assumed, and the problem of sampling is seldom addressed consciously. The single statement of a myth is an event; it occurred, it is recorded, it is therefore a datum to be analyzed. A single wedding ceremony is observed in all its complexity. Since the population studied is that of a small village, the investigator counts himself fortunate in having been there at the time, and although it is physically impossible for him personally to follow the whole event, he can combine observation and information to reconstruct a description. Perhaps he is lucky enough to note several births, and of course he can find aggregative data for more static or frequently occurring material, such as that involved in kin relations or a household census.

For matters of production, consumption. and exchange. to say the least, more formal approaches to sampling are essential. For somewhat different reasons, the same is true for ceremony, which is, after all, a special form of exchange. The problem also bedevils other areas of anthropology, particularly those concerned with the regularities and variations of social relations. Obviously, one event in these fields cannot strictly be taken as representative of a general condition, either for the individual or, still less, for any group. What we generally do is to obtain a great deal of surrounding information, for example, idealized accounts, or the observation of subsidiary events, or partial observations of greater numbers. If the detailed observation is consistent with the surrounding information, we are tempted to consider the detail to have some sort of representative or typological value. Furthermore, it can be used to illustrate the operation of processes, for example. of exchange and decision, as individuals make their choices when confronted by particular concrete circumstances. Such analysis, if properly carried out, can be of great merit and constitutes one of the strengths of anthropological inquiry, but it is also a source of vulnerability. Critics can question whether our individual, our event, even our village, is representative, and we have little by way of persuasive answer except our own faith. Furthermore, even under the best of circumstances, evidence of single events is weak when our interest is in dynamics rather than statics. I am confident that this is the reason for the traditional static bias of much of anthropology, which, in turn, has limited the growth of formal theory, since the propositions of formal theory can only be tested adequately in a context of dynamics.

Yet, at the opposite extreme, the collection of vast amounts of quantitative material through statistically valid sampling can only be achieved for limited kinds of information under special field cir□cumstances. Statistical validity is a goal which must be in the mind of every anthropologist, but his skill in the field will be demonstrated as he uses ingenuity to increase reliability when he is denied full statistical validity. I assume that, except for limited special fields, the anthropologist must rest content with smaller than desirable samples, and yet he will not be content with episodic isolated instances. The real problems. for which anthropology has bit by bit worked out a few answers, lie in this intermediary area. I will now set forth what I think we have learned.

Observation, limited to one observer, often is unable to encompass the complexity of the interactions which together constitute one institutional event. Ceremonial (particularly of marriage, death, and the more complex religious occurrences) provides an appropriate illustration. In my own work in Fiji (Belshaw [1964]) I found it fairly straightforward to obtain general accounts of the institutionalized steps involved in these matters and to use them to organize information with respect to particular ceremonies. My task was also simplified to some extent by the broad geographical coverage of the study, since I had earlier determined that it was unrealistic for my purposes to confine observations to one village, or even to one structurally united group of villages. As a result, I knew about a sizable number of appropriate events, whereas from a single village base I would only have been drawn into one or two, except insofar as the villagers themselves were caught up in "external" activity.

Even had I been able to be present for all ceremonies in all villages, I would have lacked an adequate sample for statistical validation. The basic constraint was that as a single fieldworker I simply could not gather the quantitative data for all the numerous institutionalized exchanges linked to any of the major ceremonial events. Therefore, why should I bother about quantification? Why not rest on the laurels of qualitative and ethnographic description? The reason was that for Fijian society, as for so many others, there existed an ethnosocialscience myth, which permeated all levels of government and public opinion, to the effect that "ceremony" involved "wasteful" and disruptive expenditures inconsistent with economic growth and development. It was of fundamental importance to test the validity of this myth. A qualitative ethnographic interpretation could have been misleading, and it would not have carried conviction if it asserted principles contrary to the prevailing theory. Hard data were necessary to provide me with my own basis for interpretation and evaluation, to give a clear indication of the flow of goods and services, and to provide material for discussion and argument. How could they be obtained?

In the outcome, I was aided to a great extent by the custom of Fijians nowadays to keep records of who gives what. Where such records existed, they could be used. In many instances, however, they were imperfect or needed a great deal of interpretation through inquiry after the event, and even these accounts had to be doublechecked. The end result was that my account of ceremony consisted deliberately of combining elements, closely observed, from a series of *different* events, to build, as it were, a composite picture. This method did at least enable me to assess the flow of goods and services and to challenge with hard data the prevailing view. (1 did not succeed in destroying the prevailing view, which has abysmal results for policy, but at least I have the satisfaction of knowing that, up to now, my opponents have not been able to put together equivalent information.)

This method did not, however, achieve another possible objective. Too often we are presented with accounts of ceremonial which indicate that this or that must be done if traditional culture is to be observed. What we do not often obtain is an account of variation, not merely over time but in a given period, as individuals manipulate custom for specific purposes, or as differences in power, social position, income, scheduling, occupation, residence, and similar factors bear upon decisions. These issues I could only deal with by inference, with some quantitative backup drawn from a totally different source — a housetohouse census which included questions about ceremonial involvement. (The study which has attempted to grapple with this problem most successfully, though not with all the factors mentioned, is Cancian's [1965] *Economics and Prestige in a Maya Community.)* Nevertheless, because I was drawn into or observed what seemed to be an infinite number of *yaqona* drinking ceremonies, I do have in my notes, waiting for analysis, material which ought to provide a base for the analysis of variation and manipulation for that ceremonial institution. It can be done.

The census and the questionnaire are of course instruments of ever increasing importance in anthropology. Unless deliberate steps are taken, however, they tend to be static instruments, and it is most important, wherever possible, to check the results over time. For example, in 1950 I spent very short periods in some selected communities in southeastern New Guinea. As part of this expedition I spent two months on the island of Ware, not nearly long enough to provide the intuitive and qualitative judgments which would alert me to the falsity of initial impressions. Naturally, I administered a household census, which told me among other things who was living in which houses. By a stroke of good fortune I administered a shorter version six weeks later; it told me that, out of a total population of 233, 35 of the children and the unmarried had changed their residences in that short period. While I might have been aware of one or two movements, I would certainly not have seen the phenomenon in that light (Belshaw 1955). How often, one wonders, do such matters go unobserved?

The census and the questionnaire do have severe limitations. Anthropologists are correct to treat them with great suspicion. In our kind of work. they should never be used in isolation; indeed. it is possible that our vision of our own society is becoming seriously distorted by the tendency to use questionnaires without correcting factors derived from more qualitative sources. They are particularly open to challenge when they attempt to elicit opinions rather than a statement of events or a description of things; when they pose hypothetical questions; or when they place a considerable burden on memory. Many anthropologists, including myself, have incorporated questions such as "How many weddings did you attend this year?" "What did you provide for those weddings?" "What income did you receive during the year from garden activity?" The accuracy of responses to such questions is open to very serious challenge. Nevertheless, aggregated data of this kind can *sometimes* be useful, to compare, for example. the situation of coastal and inland communities, or one occupation against another.

Such questioning has the advantage that you can reach a fairly large sample, even if you are the only fieldworker, by devoting considerable time to the questioning. Its defects, however, are such that it is always desirable to supplement the broad questionnaire with smallsample intensive inquiry over short periods. Such investigation is usually applied to areas of concern such as income and expenditure accounting, domestic consumption, exchange relations, and the like. In this manner an impression of quantities can be built, often taking into account time changes, adjustments in response to pressure, and comparison between social categories. In theory the method should provide almost infinite data, but the practical constraints dictate otherwise.

Ideally, for the households or individuals involved, the data should be obtained for every day for the whole year. if they are to be used to detect and interpret variation. The most important reason for this, and the inescapable one, is seasonal variation, however small, and attending rhythms in the work pattern. In addition, one must be able to allow for the impact of ceremonial involvement.

It is simply not practical, however, for a fieldworker to impose his presence day after day on the same households or individuals. He will soon be shown the door, confronted by bored respondents, fed misleading answers, or told to mind his own business. Further, the only time available for such questioning is, almost by definition, time during which the respondents are not engaged in other activities. Such times often are the same for all respondents (i.e., very short periods of the day or evening, perhaps at mealtime), so that even in the most favorable circumstances the lone fieldworker can perhaps cover only five to eight households in a day. One response to this situation, distressingly frequent, is to produce tables on the above matters which, typically, read "Real and Cash Income for Five Household Heads Obtained over Three Weeks." Such a table, despite the labor that went into it, is hardly worth publishing. One must do better than that.

A possibility is to visit the households or individuals, not daily, but periodically. This has the merit of extending the time coverage, but it must be balanced against loss of accuracy. In some communities it is quite feasible, and may even be helped along by persuading cooperative householders to keep notes. Similar principles apply to market situations, in which it is necessary to collect information from individual vendors, stallholders, or established buyers. Where there is a great deal of mobility in the market, it may be desirable to concentrate on a single corner of it, even though the personnel who move through that corner change each market day. The control points become fairly obvious when one is in the field, but their use is not always practicable. I was fortunate in Ware Island because all external trade had to be seaborne, and the movement of vessels had to take place from the village beach. At Wagawaga on the mainland, such certainty of observation was impossible because the coastline was longer, and the numerous trails in and out of the extended village provided several channels of movement. In some inland Fijian villages a single horse trail gives the route of trade, and toward the coast I was able to obtain information about the market produce of a dozen villages because they all had to converge their activities onto a single road and then move their produce by bus or lorry in one direction.

All the above situations require conscious decisions about the structure of the sampling, which cannot be taken adequately until some broad outline of the socioeconomic situation is available. Census taking, with the conversations and observations that accompany it, and language acquisition provide the initial opportunity to gain appropriate insights. As a result, the first one or two months in the field are too early to start to apply systematic sampled inquiry, unless one is prepared to jettison or amend the sample. Clearly. one must endeavor to draw into the sample individuals who seem to be representative of socioeconomic variation:

Lineage differences, since these may imply differences in landholding and in the size and importance of kinship connections; occupational interest; capital and prestige; sex and age; family or household size.

If there is only one fieldworker, the result of all this activity may well be only one example of each category. To aggregate such data to provide a total for the community is clearly dangerous and potentially misleading. To put the categories into one table labeled "Data from Six Households" is also at least indeterminate. It is probably rather better to keep the information separated and to use it as indicative, not necessarily representative, of the conditions which apply within the specific categories. This comes close to using the information as part of individual case histories, which, if properly analyzed, can be most useful and revealing of conditions and processes.

It is not necessary, however, to remain limited to this level. Provided one does not claim statistical reliability, but is merely endeavoring to search for further information and to provide some rough basis for comparison, then it is worthwhile to go further. One technique I devised in Hanuabada (Belshaw 1952, 1957), for example, where I was aiming at covering the lineages in inquiries devoted to such matters as household transactions and consumption, was as follows:

I selected three lineages with six or eight households in each and administered a daily inquiry for one week in Lineage A, another week in Lineage B, and a third week in Lineage C, with a break from the inquiry in the fourth week. I repeated this sequence for two to three months, then abandoned the process for one or two months, then started again.

Such a recipe reduces the chances of irritation among household members, since they are only being visited for a week at a time. It extends the sample in two directions — temporally, to cover such variations as seasons, and socially, across lineages. By keeping the records identifiable, one can aggregate them in ways which will emphasize comparison across lineages or through time. Further, it is not difficult to extend the sample in other ways. In the conditions of communities such as Hanuabada it is possible to capture memory reasonably accurately over two days. Thus it would have been possible to use eightday units instead of oneweek units, and cover twice as many households by calling on them on alternate days only.

Most of the above remarks are predicated on a single fieldworker, but Tax and the Firths achieved what they did in part because they were not alone. In my opinion, current standards, and the need to break through to new levels of data gathering, require even more than this. In Hanuabada in the early '50's I was most fortunate in obtaining the goodwill of government departments; three of them each made available to me a member of their staff for onthejob training (Belshaw 1951). Not only did they work regularly and hard to extend my sample, but they perused such anthropology texts as I had in the field with me. (Moral: anthropologists should consider taking relevant books into the field; they can be eagerly consulted.) In Fiji the climate had already changed. The bureaucracy could not see its way to helping out. But after all, the records that are necessary do not require a high standard of literacy or even a sophisticated education. It is obviously better to seek helpers who can have a career or professional interest in what they are doing, for the work contributes, if only modestly, to the extension of their awareness and their skills. In Fiji I could not do this. Nevertheless, by squeezing a little money from my funding (at the expense of my family), I could provide a reward for a number of assistants who proved adept at census taking, checking market movements, and the like. The process of increasing the team's manpower has perhaps gone farthest in the case of Cancian's work (1965, 1972); he, like other American anthropologists working in Middle America, acknowledges assistance from a number of students and local people. Similarly, Beals's latest marketing study (1975) acknowledges help from a very large team including American students and educated local residents.

There is no doubt in my mind that serious work in economic anthro☐pology, if it is to produce quantitative material for the new demands, must be based upon teamwork, and that the team composition will vary according to the general field situation and that of the country where the work is taking place. Yet, at the same time, numerous cautions must be entered. I do not believe that the Middle American solution is the ultimate, or even that in the conditions of those countries and of the modern world it is ultimately wise. If economic anthropology is to be pursued by scholars who are not a part of the academic structure of the country where the research is taking place, they are by and large confronted with one of two situations. Either there is an academic establishment with personnel resources in place, or else the academic establishment is absent or overloaded. In the first instance, it now seems obvious that the extension of the team must be designed in partnership with national academic personnel, and not used as a training ground for the foreign student. This is difficult to achieve, because many national funding agencies have not yet accustomed themselves to providing the money for students or personnel who are not nationals of the funding country. I for one am now making it a practice to point this out to funding agencies and to recommend refusal of grants which are built on the premise that the faculty member takes a team of eager students with him, rather than exploring cooperative links with the country of his research.

By the same token, students who are applying for support for thesis research frequently do not apply for the necessary funds to enable them to hire junior students of the country where they will be working as research assistants, or to pay local people to keep records for them. I do not know of anyone, for example. who has yet succeeded in establishing a network of "observation posts" in New Guinea villages held together through prestatory exchange, or in tracing the exchange movements between the highlands and the coast, although there have been innumerable studies, particularly theses, which touch upon such topics. In many instances, the funding agencies, while perhaps sympathetic to the idea of paying "informants" (in my opinion a barbarous practice in all but a few special circumstances), do not recognize the need in their rules. The paradoxical result is that we often allow graduate students to go to the field unaware of the demands upon their technique, and where they are aware of these we cannot provide them with the necessary funding. The result is that students must learn anew in the field, almost as if no one had learned it before, that datagathering assistance will be virtually mandatory. Unless they are very fortunate or ingenious, they cannot put into practice the true basis of their craft until they can apply for funds as faculty members.

No wonder that economic anthropology, despite its manpower needs, is grossly understaffed.

There is yet another phenomenon which I feel requires more funda mental explanation, and which perhaps it is particularly appropriate to raise in the context of a *Festschrift* for Sol Tax in view of his continuing and deep concern for matters international. The craft of economic

223

anthro⬜pology, as traditionally defined, is even more highly concentrated in a few countries than is the remainder of anthropology. The United States, France, Britain, and Canada are the main sources of studies in which extensive quantified data are available. The Netherlands, India, and Latin America are making analytic contributions to economic anthro⬜pology, often in the latter case under the rubric of the analysis of peasant society. In Africa and Asia, most anthropologists seem to prefer to tackle other questions. Yet surely, eventually, it is from outside Europe and North America that the new insights, carefully founded in controlled data, will emerge.

Standards for a data base in economic anthropology were created by Sol Tax and the Firths and reinforced by their colleagues in the 'SO's. Since that time there have been not more than a dozen studies which, by the exercise of ingenuity and the extension of manpower, have *added* to the repertoire of techniques, and only somewhat more which have been roughly equivalent to *Penny Capitalism* in their data base. The great majority of studies have not come up to these requirements. This is patchy cumulation at best, and we owe it to Tax and Firth, who were the pioneers, to see to it that future work builds on their foundation. Is the younger generation heeding? Or is it being forced to learn from scratch all over again because those of us who teach the subject have not adequately drawn attention to the issues?

REFERENCES CITED

BEAL5, RALPH L. 1975. *The peasant marketing system of Oaxaca, Mexico.*Berkeley: University of California Press.

BEL5HAw, CYRIL *S.* 1951. Using Papuans in social survey work. *South Pacific* 5. 1952. Port Moresby canoe traders. *Oceania* 23.

1955. *In search of wealth.* American Anthropological Association Memoir
   80

1957. *The great village.* London: Routledge and Kegan Paul.

1964. *Under the lvi tree.* Berkeley: University of California Press.

1970. *The conditions of social performance.* London: Routledge.

1975. *The Sorcerer's Apprentice.* Elmsford: Pergamon.
BROOKFIELD, HAROLD C. Editor. 1969. *Pacific marketplaces.* Canberra:
   Australian National University Press.
BURRIDGE, KENELM 0. L. 1960. *Mambu.* London: Methuen.
CANCIAN, FRANK. 1965. *Economics and prestige in a Maya community.* Stanforth Stanford University Press.

1972. *Change and uncertainty in a peasant economy.*
   Stanford: Stanford University Press.

DAvENPORT, WILLIAM H. 1960. *Jamaican fishing: A gametheory analysis.* New Haven: Yale University Press.
DAVIS, WILLIAM G. 1973. *Social relations in a Philippine market.* Berkeley:
   University of California Press.
EPsTEIN, ARNOLD L. Editor. 1967. *The craft of social anthropology.* London:
   Tavistock.
FIRTH, RAYMOND. 1929. *Primitive economics of the New Zealand Maori.* New York: Dutton.

1966. *Malay fishermen: Their peasant economy.*
   London: Routledge.
FIRTH, ROSEMARY. 1943. *Housekeeping among Malay peasants.* (Monographs in Social Anthropology 7.)

London: Lund, Humphries.

McFEAT, TOM. 1974. *Small group cultures.* New York: Pergamon.

PRATrIS, J. I. 1973. Strategising man. *Man,* n.s., 8(1):46—58.

SALISBURY, RICHARD F. 1962. *From stone to steel.* Melbourne: Cambridge University Press.

1969. *Vunamami.* Berkeley: University of California Press.

SCHNEIDER, HAROLD K. 1970. *The Wahi Wanyaturu.* Chicago: Aldine.

TAX, SoL. 1953. *Penny capital1L~m: A Guatemalan Indian economy.* Smithsonian Institution, Institute of Social Anthropology, publ. 16.

The Bedrock of Innovation.

This article is reprinted with minor amendments from my book *Fixing the World: An Anthropologist Considers our Future* which set out a *holistic* view of the nature of global society and institutions. The theory is based on passages in *The Conditions of Social Performance*.

There are some general principles which underlie my optimism and belief that a practical utopian world is achievable. is possible by the end of the twentyfirst century. These are the principles which govern and account for innovation and change. The recognition of them demonstrates that Utopia has moved from science fiction and fairy tales to potentiality.

First a couple of definitions or we will be misunderstood. *Everyone* invents, throughout their whole lives. Invention is simply to do something not done before – washing the dishes in a different way, disposing of garbage using procedures not done before. We *invent* for ourselves all the time. No culture is immune.

Often we teach our family to follow suit. This is the beginning of much *innovation* as the new methods are taken up by others. There are thus differing strengths with which innovation percolates from the individual inventor through institutions, enterprises and eventually perhaps global culture.

How does societal change occur? As a boy with left wing ideals my critics often said to me "But human nature will never change". Biologically there are limits. But in fact, culturally, there are none, with one exception. This is that where we go is dependent on where we are and have been. We must build the future on our past history and our present situation. In the past, that has put serious limits on our imagination of where we *can* go. But today so many options are open to us that such a limit is now of minimal importance.

If we wish to play our part, as individuals, in the movement of society we may preach to influence others (as perhaps I am doing) or, to the extent that it is in our ability, to *live* our beliefs. Not many of us can be political leaders of countries, let alone of world "government". But in family, business, or creative life we can do so insofar as the world around us permits. As more and more are doing, we can, if it suits our temperaments, exercise influence in associations and in whatever political process is open to us. We can become activists for pushing toward the achievement of the world we want. As I shall show we can do much of this simply by adapting our own individual, even family, behaviour.

Since, by definition, we are working toward change (or such behavioural change would not be an issue) it is not going to be easy. It is hard to think of changes in ourselves managing the control of depression, working fewer hours, dealing with conflict that will not be noticed by others, thus giving rise to comments and judgement. We put ourselves on the line, we are stating who we are, exposing our identities.

Those who run the gauntlet of possible criticism, however, can be comforted by the phenomenon that *any* action or belief, at least in industrialised society, will be criticised by some, open to the charge that it is mistaken, immoral or evil. (The obverse is not true: murder, child abuse, rape, are not likely to be approved by anyone, though killing is often condoned, ethnocide is often advocated, and some may excuse sexual assault.) A good football player, idolised by crowds, is condemned as a macho bonehead by others. Mother Theresa has her critics, as did Albert Schweitzer. A computer whiz or brilliant mathematician is scorned for being outside the real world. Giving to charity is blessed to some and tabbed as posturing by others. Discipline a child in the family circle, and neighbours will comment when does it become abuse? A manager who promotes an able woman attracts gossip and jealousy. How many are they who have been hurt and disappointed when they find that their wellmeaning, generous, or innocent actions have attracted derision, hostility or suspicion?

In many small societies in which I have worked, success is both highly sought after and dangerous. A successful person is one of power, manipulating the ties of kin, friends, or compadres to create obligations. The reciprocal bonds of indebtedness ensure that the successful person is one who is owed much by others, ensuring that he gets material, moral or political support when he needs it. It is his generosity that makes this possible, for to give creates an obligation. But too much success attracts competition, envy, hostility, so that it must continually be managed sensitively. The successful person must speak in the idiom of family, tribe, community, ancestors, not of himself alone. If generosity falters, then it can be seen to be blatant, selfserving, and selfish. Dislike of aspects of behaviour failure to perform a ritual properly, slighting a relative, the failure of a crop leads to resentment that masks envy. Of a sudden, success is dangerous. There is illness or a string of bad luck attributed to sorcery or the success of competitors. The mana, the power, is gone. The high are toppled.

Complex societies have not evolved very far from reciprocal dependencies and the levelling influence of envy. We sometimes mistakenly think this to be so because of the ideology of individualism, and the perception that "simpler" societies were somehow noncompetitive because they had ideologies of kinship, family, clan, tribe. We must address this issue, the way in which *ideologies mask the empirical realities*, the way in which they can disguise the realities of the system they represent. Until I raise that question more systematically later it must be reserved as part of the background to some of my arguments, held as a continuous modifier to interpretations.

Anthropologists do not have much difficulty in demonstrating this. The public pretends reciprocity is not there. Yet ceremonial events birthdays, weddings, Christmas tie in dramatically with each other. The intensity, or lack of it, in personal and family relations, by which is meant personal interactions, create networks of giving that are dynamic, and in which what happened before influences what happens now. That the giving is generous does not remove the fact that it recognises past obligations, and creates new moral ones too. And the proportion of consumer spending that can be attributed to ceremony and friendship is enormous.

The impersonal market system of commerce and industry is not impersonal. Yes, contracts may be up for bidding. Yes, they are usually awarded on price and quality. The strict rules that apply to governmental contracts demonstrate, by the very "need" for them that something other than "objectivity" is significant. Of course it is. Reliability, the return of a favour, security based on personal knowledge, are of key significance. Entrepreneurs want to *know* their clients and suppliers, both to favour them and to exploit their weaknesses. Why else should there be business clubs, entertainment accounts, golf, exchange of gits, horse racing, networking…….. and corruption?

I see pros and cons as I make judgements about such features. As a "scientist" my orientation is to understand without judging, to try to elucidate *how* it is that societies and cultures work the way they do, *how* did present conditions arise, *what* makes phenomena functional or dysfunctional within the system that is presented to me. By attempting to understand what goes on in one society and culture I may be able to arrive at principles or intuitions which can be applied to the interpretation of others. Some principles may be extended to apply to numerous, even all, "societies", that is to global society.

Indeed it has happened already. The study of the classical prestatory (giftobligation) societies North West Coast Indians engaged in potlatch, Trobriand Islanders, then many others throughout the world enabled anthropologists to hypothesise, in fact predict, the occurrence of such dynamics in as yet undescribed cultures, and, as mentioned above, in a reinterpretation of what goes on in the "individualistic" West. Clearly, because so many things are otherwise different, prestatory dynamics will not, empirically, be identical or even similar in different contexts. But they will be there, in some form or another, in all "societies", because giving (not only in material forms, but in emotions and communication) and receiving, and the psychological demands and moralities of the exchanges, are the essential bricks out of which the regularities of social organisation and of social predictability are built. One of the most noticeable applications of this theory is in the observation of negotiations between nation states on trade or military policies.

Let us continue, bearing in mind that we are leading up to thoughts about the nature of innovation, for we have determined that the necessity for change is pretty well axiomatic, and change rests upon just that. Innovation in the context of reciprocity..

The dynamics of prestation suggest that individuals pursue their goals through the creation of networks of social exchange with others. In some societies the networks may be hierarchical or kinoriented. In the industrialised world the networks are far more open, although hierarchy and kinship are still very much there.

It seems difficult for many, including some of those in the intellectual community, to apply the concept of social exchange that underlies prestation. Most economists, with the exception of those who follow Gary Becker, have escaped from their ancestors into narrower concepts of exchange, confined to goods and (commercialised) services, or to market, that is monetised, transactions. Even many of my fellow anthropologists still speak of "the economy" or "the economic" as being related to material things, relegating services such as the provision of ritual to some other domain. The concept can be not only confining, but mistaken and ethnocentric and undermines our holistic principles.

It is mistaken, from the point of view of the subject matter of this argument, because such separations are artificial rather than real, because the material and the nonmaterial are inextricably blended together by webs of value and meaning, and because ideas, values, concepts, emotions, spiritual thoughts, philanthropy, the search for power, are all there, in competition, both as instruments for a satisfying life (resources) and as competing goals for our actions – and hence for where we want the globe to go.

It is ethnocentric, for the ideas of money and the market are used to separate "market economies" from the rest, a separation that denies continuities between the two categories, postulates the near impossibility of the one evolving naturally into the other, and obscures analytical similarities. I have argued elsewhere that "money" is a matter of degree, not of kind[24]. It is not coinage and bank balances, but the *degree* to which whatever it is (materially) serves such functions as medium of exchange, store of value, and so on, in which other elements such as liquidity and confidence are embedded. There is nothing new in this; indeed it is

---

[24] See my *Traditional Exchange and Modern Markets*, Englewood Cliffs, PrenticeHall,, 1965

oldfashioned. It is mistakenly ignored especially when we talk of nonindustrialised economic systems.

So, as it were, we must turn things on their head. In the context of innovation, we talk of *exchange* not market, and we recognise that the things that are exchanged are not simply commercialised goods and services but all those other things that link one person to another, the immaterial, the intangibles, power and love, altruism as a goal, those other things that are never "equal".

Almost by definition, human beings cannot be totally in isolation from one another. Some groups such as some monasteries can separate themselves more or less, and some individuals may opt to be hermits. These are decisions which result from previous histories of social interaction. Furthermore, in this day and age, supplies are almost always, if minimally, required from elsewhere. A completely localised and bounded exchange system is impossible to sustain. Those who advocate reducing consumption, especially of foods, to those produced within a hundred mile radius are advocating a social and psychological consumer impossibility (which also falls foul of one of the most significant precepts of economic knowledge: that development is based on "taking in each other's washing" or, in anthropological terms, some form o reciprocity).

The desire of individuals to link with groups is among their decisionmaking goals, and as such will be a subject of later discussion. Here it is sufficient to note the tension between the individual and the group, whether that group be a family, an association, a church, an ethnos or whatever. At one end of the spectrum, the group in question may succeed in subduing the individual and creating authoritarian conformity.[25] (Even here individuals are not carbon copies of each other, so that some degree of tension is present.) At the other end the individual attempts to reject a group, to find his own path, to seek isolation, to be a total rebel or to find another association.

For by far the majority of persons on this earth, linkage with one or more groups is an essential element in the construction of personal identity. We cannot live alone; the choice of whom we associate with, in varying contexts, is part of our selfexpression. This is true of even abstract communication, such as my writing this book.

At present it is almost an accepted truism in therapeutic ideology that it is not an appropriate goal for an individual to be so surrounded by inescapable group influences that he or she has lost his or her identity. Such individuals must seek their identities from a renewed consciousness of what lies within especially if pressuring group has been a dominating family. Early family influences, once regarded as almost the inescapable creators of the persona, are now seen as the enemy, to be rejected in order to find one's self. The specifics of such an argument are for later chapters. Here, let us simply note that this is an example of the tension to which I refer. Moreover, the individual is in fact often replacing one group with another the family (which he or she has probably already lost) with the cultural group constituted by therapists and their clients and likeminded others.

Tensions taken to this degree can be horrendously destructive. But some degree of tension is the source of creativity and hence innovation, since tension implies that there is a problem to solve. Awareness of a problem, its solution, is part of the process of innovation, of change. An alertness comes with reasonable tension, an alertness in which the mind identifies ranges of problems.

Problem solving, that is creativity, however modest, can draw its ideas from within the identified group, for this is where the idioms of communication will be fairly clear. In such groups there are shared languages. Mostly, a modicum of security is needed for the innovator to take the risky step of not only thinking, but of doing, something new. That security comes from group membership. And the innovation comes from mixing the ideas that lie within the group in new ways, and is extended when ideas enter the group from the neighbouring cultures. We can see the tensions, opportunities and restrictions at work very clearly in immigrant groups not only now, but over the centuries. Overseas Chinese constitute the most wellknown and marked example, reinforced by immense international networks of friends and persons who can be called kin. But almost every migration has had its stimulating effects Huguenots, the nineteenth century movement of Swiss, English, Scots, and German; Lebanese, Punjabi, Ismaili, the list goes on.

Of course, the group can be selflimiting and inwardturning. If it is not open to outside influences, absorbing and using them, the capacity to innovate will be limited to the mix of ideas already present, and that limitation will be reinforced if there is an isolationist ideology. This is particularly true of some religious groups, who place an emphasis on their uniqueness, and the superiority of their ideology and ethics. The current phenomenon of extreme Christianity and Islam is an example.

Another significant aspect of group identification is the use of innovation to reinforce that very identity. We must be careful not to confuse innovation with only socalled "utilitarian" considerations. Spectacular ceremonies and extravagant festivals are the most cogent examples of other kinds of pervasive innovation. Note the widespread extensions of carnival and similar group festivities since World War II, especially as communities have more wealth to spend on them.

In a world where so much of our living is related to the anonymity of functionaries, where we interact with people of whom we know very little, when we must make meanings for ourselves as tiny particles in an infinite universe of others, where we are lumped together as being of a certain age, or sex, or tax bracket, we must, the therapists tell us, know ourselves. What better way than to see ourselves not as part of the whole world, but as a member of an association, an individual who can make a creative contribution in a cultural group when "out there" we pass almost unnoticed?

When western developers first pondered the potential of Third World communities to "grow", they almost unanimously decried the existence of "wasteful" ceremonial. It took time before they could understand the anthropological truism that such ceremonial was often a way of redistributing wealth and sociopolitical power; that it created dynamics of social exchange without which the economic system would be dead; that it embodied positive goals, part of the economists' "competing ends" to which "scarce resources" would be allocated.

Surprise, surprise. As income increased, so did the amount of resources devoted to ceremonial even to the extent of reinventing activities that had been apparently gone, as with the famous medieval football game of Florence, proscribed under Mussolini.

And most such activities are still further segmented. In Florence and Siena the activities are organised over months in parishes of the city, to which loyalties are addressed. In Rio and Basle the competing carnival enterprises are handled by long term associations. Throughout the world there are events of a similar kind, let alone weddings, funerals, and Christmas giving. Embedded in them are values of power, fame, pride in the group, selfidentity (look at me, I belong here), companionship and often spectacular innovation. Are the competitions of sports, both professional and amateur, not similar for athletes, "owners", coaches, advertisers, and the home fans?

But wait. Competition is dangerous. Associations have their own charters, their own rules, the procedures that set themselves apart from others. Like professions, which are restrictive by definition, they set boundaries to acceptable activities. An innovator may get away with enormous power; or by contrast the very fact of being too ambitious may lead to him being dragged down by envious rivals. To be successful, he must work within cultural rules and norms. Go too far beyond them and the power slips away. Nowhere is this more clear than in Industrialised political parties both internally, and externally as the electorate expresses envy at perks and the symbols of power, and stretches out claws to tear down the "improperly" powerful. It is everywhere.

An innovator, then, must often express a different kind of personality from his fellows to give expression to his ideas. He must often break with his group; his creativity is perhaps first expressed by doing just that. He may even be expelled or excluded by suspicion as to his motives, his intellectual nature, even his strange powers. He may find that the group with which he is associating simply does not have the imagination, the resources, the drive, or the interest, to support him when he needs it.

His risk taking assumes a new dimension. It is not only the risk of failure in the eyes of those who have trusted him, but the risk of selffailure. It is not only the risk of bankruptcy or that his ideas are not functional or ahead of their time, that they won't work, that others won't recognise them. His own self is on the line. Can he fight through the reverses and disappointments? Can he find the niche in society that will allow his talents to flourish?

So many innovators discover themselves to be different, must live with those differences, become outcasts at least for the moment. In this age when we study almost everything, writers have drawn attention to two kinds of individuals who, except for a few perceptive observers, are somewhat like this. One set consists of those many differing individuals who have brain damage or sensory handicaps. The fact that "normally" equipped people have difficulty communicating

sensitively with them hides their interior lives from all but the closest companionobservers. Those who do communicate find enormous resources of intellectual activity, artistic sensitivity, and creativity that comes from the narrower but more intense focus of their perceptions, which, when expressed, may be highly compulsive, yet innovative and valuable when made known to the rest of society. Autism is the major example of this and may have been present in, for example, some of the great philosophers and mathematicians.

And there are the "eccentrics", people who in effect say to the world "I'm me. I shall concentrate on behaving the way I like. If you wish to learn to live with my foibles, good. If not, I'm sorry, but I laugh." Britain was once renowned as a country that valued its eccentrics, turned them into the subject of warm satire and playful cartoons. Britain defended their right to be eccentric to the hilt. The most recent small example I ran into was at a pedestrian crosswalk in London. A tweedy gentleman with a cane stepped forth. The oncoming car kept moving at the crosswalk. The gentleman stepped into its path, waved his cane angrily, went to the driver's window and gave him a dressing down.

Take that little incident for a moment. Trivial? Not at all. To an observer like myself it was a warmingly welcome incident, with which I identified, but perceived as unusual, hence eccentric, probably part of a personality that would express many other similar actions. In some parts of the world, doing that would have been a high risk matter. Here, in this part of London, it seemed to carry little risk, denoting the thought that such behaviour was still tolerated. But it carried another thought, namely that if there were a growing number of incidents of that kind, if it were on the rise, so to speak, then drivers would begin to realise that infractions of this kind, the inherent threat of danger within them, was no longer a matter to be taken for granted. In other words, the eccentric act of one individual at one time, if repeated and taken up by others, could become the norm. Is this why, now, I do whatever I can to make my anger known to drivers of rowdy motorcycles, unsuppressed car mufflers, and heavy metal emerging from 4 x 4s.

Individual actions *are* significant. It is through them that norms become established.

"Eureka" he shouts in the bath tub, "I have it!" The dramatic flash of insight that in a moment changes the world..... Coming from nowhere, into a brilliant mind.

Not so fast. There are many components to innovation. An innovation is, by definition, a new cultural artefact. Innovations flower in a thousand ways. But they all have one characteristic.

They make use of *already* known cultural components. The components must be *recognised* by the innovator, they must have meaning for him.

Even in dreams, in the wildest imagination, the elements that combine to make the fantasy are each, if taken apart one by one, already known. The angels do not send down a flash of lightning with the message here is something, dear innovator, for you to use, something that is beyond the comprehension of your culture. Even if that were so, the innovator could not be expected to understand its significance unless he were mentally ready, unless the novelty were composed of elements he recognised, unless he had some understanding of how it fitted into already established life or thought. An innovation may be revolutionary, may have uncomprehended consequences, but in itself it combines in a new way characteristics that are already there. The novelty may come from accidental observation, the insight of a dream awakening, but the components of what is observed must have meaning; or it may come from painfully elaborated abstract logic.

Whoever first used fire to cook something, maybe meat, already knew that fire burned, already knew that meat was good to eat. Perhaps he dropped the meat in, but his senses were ready for the result.

Obversely, it is no use preaching the value of platinum to a culture which does not yet recognise the uses of the substance, directly or in trade. And the outcome of mathematical logic depends on the elaboration and manipulation of concepts that have already been developed, doing so in new combinations, creating more substantial or simpler concepts. Each concept, once established, adds to what is there, expands it, and becomes a stepping stone for the next stride.

That axiom is at the root of what follows.

For it follows that if you have very few components in your culture the likelihood of recombination will be slim, the changes slow. But if you have limitless components, then the possibility of recombination is also limitless, and the pace of innovation is fast.

It used to be argued that "traditional" societies were "innately" conservative, lacking an "achievement orientation". Not so. In the first place, *all* societies value achievement where they differ is in the objectives of achievement. It may be good hunting, producing children, warfare, riches, spiritual attainment, leisure, or of course in combination. It is true also that some societies, or social groups, value the security of stability or unchanging continuity; but so strong is the appeal of innovation that they can only do so by attempting to place strict boundaries around themselves, trying to prevent the enlargement of their cultures. And there, of course, in this modern world at least, they fail, with the result of change, of schism, or of loss of population.

In a previous work I wrote, confusingly, of an "orientation" toward innovation. It is probable that it would be more useful to place innovation within the list of culturally valued goals as a variable. This is most easily illustrated with art. In some cultures new pieces of work are valued for their continuity with past forms; in others they are valued for their "originality", their change from the past. Such goals have to be balanced with, and to compete with, other goals perhaps some aesthetic principle to become effective. The explosion of the art of the Northwest Coast Canadian Indians would provide a beautiful case study – incorporating new materials and presentations on a basis of new arrangements of old continuing symbols.

Certainly, *individuals* differ the one from the other in their ability to create the recombinations, to innovate, that is they differ in their creativity. In the simplest of societies there are those who think, who tell stories imaginatively, who philosophise, who tinker, who adventure, who explore, and thus stand out as different.

As I have pointed out earlier a new idea or artefact is not in itself an innovation. It must somehow spread beyond the individual's own world, be communicated to others, and embraced into the cultural world of others. If it stays privately with the individual, it is lost to culture. It is the individual's private toy.

The individuals to whom a new idea or artefact is presented judge it from the point of view of their own thoughts, interests and goals. That is, does it somehow fit into their conceptual framework? A proposal that is "ahead of its time" may simply not fit well; it must wait until the rest of culture has changed to make the fit more apt, more useful, more acceptable.

The impact does not have to be acceptable to everyone. On the contrary, its value may be in stimulating further debate, further change. The point is that it has entered the pool of ideas, become part of the capital stock of culture, available for yet further recombination, known to other minds.

There must be hundreds if not thousands of material inventions which are in themselves inherently sound, but which have not been recognized, or have been rejected because their creation does not fit into the mind set of those to whom it may be targeted. One current example is that of the Skegway. This is a battery operated device which moves the human body making use of the body's own inherent attributes of balance and adjustment which come into play when we walk. Its foundation is a platform on two specially tired wheels which the user's body manipulates by linking the body to the device through a rigid handle. It replaces the single occupancy car, is environmentally safe and energy efficient and, with adaptations, can be used all terrain. The inventor could not get financiers, policy makers, and certainly not vehicle manufacturers to take up its production and distribution. Despite this, through his own efforts, the device has been successfully demonstrated in many contexts, is now in manufacture, and is being adopted in numerous industrial contexts (such as the Vancouver International Airport) to move people around expeditiously. For that use it was ready. But it has had some but limited use by private individuals, many of whom were not ready for it, or were facing bureaucratic obstacles.

In other words it is more likely that not that initial inventions will meet naysayers who have vested interests in reducing competition, or who, unlike the inventor, are still thinking blindly within a dark box.

If this is true of material inventions, how much more true it can be of nonmaterial and policy innovations. Don't rock the boat, there are too many risks and uncertainties, are common objections to the most innocent of proposals, let alone those which have world changing attributes. Indeed, innovative ideas in this book are bound to attract opposition as a matter of blind principle as well as a matter of genuine thinking. It will be a task of what follows to show that such objections are open to challenge and that they can have consequences which are often dire as well as obstructive. Nevertheless it behoves the innovator to consider the sociocultural context in which heshe is working, and to bring the ideas and proposals into touch with those elements of culture and knowledge which are already in place to be tapped and recognised.

To sum up so far, the rate of innovation in a culture is a function of the size of the cultural stock, that is the pool of ideas, knowledge and material resources, interpreted widely, plus another factor I will introduce shortly..

Material resources are included for two reasons. The obvious one is that material resources provide some of the raw materials for innovators to play with, to help them communicate their ideas, and to put them into effect.

For this to happen the resource must be recognised in some form. When a resource crosses from one culture to another, it is frequently the case that its meaning, and therefore its function, will also change. Guitars will be used for different purposes in Nova Scotia and Pernambuco the outflows in music and in the social context are not identical. The aluminium and wires of an abandoned aircraft in Kenya will not go to a recycling depot, but will be turned into articles of bodily adornment. To sell the benefits of oil production to a culture that does not know the concept "oil" as it applies to underground liquids and industrial use or consumption requires conversation and persuasion to introduce the relevant notions, that is to add to the stock of cultural capital.

In other words the material is never just the material. It does not consist of objects isolated from cultural linkages. Whether it be coins or a chair or women's adornments, or a rock by the side of a road, or a road itself, it is irrelevant except insofar as it has meaning, can be interpreted, and unless it communicates that meaning, which may have utilitarian, aesthetic, personal, or even spiritual overtones. It is with the manipulation of such meanings that material innovation takes place. Hence, from an innovative point of view, the elements of the material that are significant are those that are immaterial. Remove the legs of a table and replace them with rollers; change the shape of the table; replace the wood with glass; etch the glass; place flowers on it; put a Japanese screen behind it; place food on it; put your feet on it; all these changes take place through the use of concepts. Put the table in a Melanesian thatch hut and it may be out of place, not wanted unless another idea comes into play, that of prestige, oneupping the neighbours. The material consists of concepts, then, and those concepts are available to the innovator in the same way as are the ideas translated into a book or a painting.

I have already pointed out that the size of the cultural stock affects the chances of innovation taking place, that is the quantity of innovation which results. Let us do a bit of innovation ourselves along the lines of the principles I have been enunciating. From economics we know the concept that the size of the money supply consists of the quantity of money modified by its *velocity of circulation*. It seems sensible to borrow the concept here.

For surely if two men sit side by side, each with differing ideas, but don't talk to each other, i.e. with a velocity of circulation of ideas of zero, the size of the sum of ideas of each of them will be minimal if not zero. Minimal rather than zero because mew thought combinations may be occurring in their brains.. Zero velocity, minimal innovation. Even if one of the men has enough ideas in his head to think up something new, he is not communicating by talk, hence minimising the potential innovatory impact.

Once they start talking, the chances increase. Expand the conversation to others, they increase further. Circulation is happening within the pool of ideas. And so it goes on. It is no accident that the exponential innovation growth of the twentieth century was founded on profound changes in communication. And it is no accident, either, that mediaeval scholars, often quite isolated in their own communities, placed enormous emphasis on travel to scholarly centres to expand the limits of their communication. Was not the need for communication, for disputation, for the interacting of minds, in times when travel was inefficient, a most powerful impetus for the founding of universities? And did not a lingua franca, Latin, contribute to that possibility?

So, the rate of innovation is a result of the size of the pool of ideas modified by the velocity of communication.

In later argument I will be writing of cultures as imagined entities, that is as being in some sense bounded, a concept that raises many issues. For the moment, however, let us assume that this is so, despite what I have written about the global culture being the only "natural" one.

In this model we can conceive of culture as something like a liquid containing millions of moving cells not people, but ideas, concepts, values, moving through talk, gestures, facial expressions and embodied in recognised institutions and items of manmade material culture. To conduct empirical research on culture, in connection, say, with my theses, it would be ideal to be able to quantify the number of those cells. To do that one would have to break down everything ideas, elements of material items into both their smallest parts that can conceptually stand alone and into those combinations (a table, a table leg, a table top, a mathematical equation, each of the concepts which make up that equation) which also have meaning. An enormous and literally impractical task.

Failing that, and failing the ability to conduct hypothesis testing on the basic of such a necessity, a major conclusion stands out nevertheless, which will have an impact on later chapters. We have come across one of many limitations to the certainty of knowledge. Our knowledge about the kinds of matters we are discussing cannot be perfect. It can be indicative, approximate, subjective. As individuals facing the future we must reconcile ourselves to ***the certainty of imperfect knowledge***.

To return, however, to the concept. If a cultural boundary is tight, with no movement over it (almost an impossibility as is the economist's "perfect competition") the number of cultural cells contained within the boundary is finite at any given time. But there are more of some than of others. There may be ten mathematicians and a hundred boat builders and five thousand lovers. The number of cells related to these conceptual domains will be affected by the complexity of the thoughts in each domain (let us say 1,000 cells mathematics, 500 boat building, and 50,000 lovemaking not very realistic, but illustrative), by the number of individuals sharing those thoughts, and by the velocity of circulation, that is communication.

To draw up an account of what is going on, one would in fact be drawing up an inventory of the cultural stock, and analysing modes, patterns and intensities of communication (which would have to allow for the possibility that the receiver did not absorb the communication in precisely the way it was sent that is, filtered it). This inventory I call a *profile of culture*.

Profiles of culture do, approximately, exist. They are called thick ethnographies. Most of them, for the nonspecialist, are terribly dull to read, because they describe in minute detail elements of the daily life of a people, as completely as possible, preferably based on participant observation, a technique in which the observer merges as closely as he can within the daily life, using the language as the medium of talk. They are indeed inventorylike, and they make interpretations and generalisations based upon the way in which elements in the inventories relate to each other, that is, communicate.

Because such profiles describe the here and now of the observation, they are also the *only* data that approximate what the economist calls effective demand, that is what people actually do with their resources at any given time, whether that be of a material or nonmaterial nature. In practice, economists deal with only little bits of effective demand, treating some of the most important wants (or goals in life) as outside their models, or as "other things being equal". Not many of them read ethnographies, even of modern communities.

In fact the ethnographies also fall far short of the objective. The writers do not have, at least in these decades, the scientific objectives that would be implied in the questions of this Chapter. Paradoxically, once upon a time the objectives would not have seemed so strange, for anthropologists in the early part of the 20th century were obsessed by what they called "cultural traits" that correspond very roughly to the cells, and they were guided in doing so by a search for the influence of cultural traits upon each other within and across cultural boundaries. Many of them did so out of sociological context, that is without observing meanings working *in practice*, and with inadequate attention to context.

Studies of profiles of culture are also hampered by manpower, its training and its distribution. Doctoral candidates are seldom given the finances to employ research assistants to gather data in ways that permit quantification. Their theoretical orientation suggests, anyway, that this is less worthwhile than the creation of a range of studies, each focusing on a theoretical problem which does not require such minute quantification. In most cases, discussion is by way of *example*, minutely dissected. If there were enough of these examples, the data would be there, but there cannot be through these methods.

I myself, in looking at the interlinkages between ceremonies in parts of Fiji, in which scores of individuals were involved, with the massive exchange of goods, and large feasting, and me working alone, could not cover all the significant detail of any one marriage, for example. I had to attend several, and combine the observations. And then do the same with funerals and other events for they were all interlinked. But I did not count the *number* of such ceremonies in the observation period. It could have been done, quite simply. But other things.....the number of first fruits ceremonies performed? I would have had to redirect my four Fijian parttime assistants, who were very busy doing household budgets and tracking cargoes on the trucks going to market......

We can improve, if the questions are deemed important enough. We are not likely to improve enough to give certainty, even in the quantification mad 21st century. I have argued before, and state again, that in the absence of appropriate techniques we can never truly know the operable values in a culture or predict its movement. We can only approximate.

I think the questions *are* important, because I believe there are significant generalisations about the way in which innovation translates into societal change, which are capable of being investigated more closely. (I first expressed the ideas in the late 'forties as a result of thinking about agriculture in the Solomon Islands, and tinkered with them from time to time later. No one has told me I'm wrong, nor yet debated them.)

Begin with the notion that the profile of culture is not a random hodge podge of cells accidentally linked to each other. The cells are linked by communication, which is the electricity that attracts or repels them, and by the power of thought that binds those that are attracted into conceptual nuclei. Add to this the notion that societal change takes place not when a single nucleus is altered, but only when it spreads within the system to some degree. The system is just that, a system, its parts influencing each other.

A changed nucleus can bring about ramifying consequences. For example, the introduction of reading skills can bring about a demand for reading materials, newspapers, books, libraries; can lead to changes in other ideas as a result of the fusing of concepts contained in the written word with ideas already in place, and so on and on. It can also have multiplying effects, that is for more reading instruction given to other persons, children or adult. However, such effects may be no more than potentials, if the means of satisfying them are not there, or are too onerous to be used. When I was in the Solomon Islands in the 'forties the ramifying effects were primarily limited to religious literature and the writing of letters which sometimes had almost mystical connotations of power, for there was almost no other reading material. (Paperbacks from the U.S. forces were snapped up, and a typewritten "newspaper" I created engendered a flow of story and article contributions which totally surprised me.) But after the war the resource base changed, and the potential demand was translated into a vigorous and effective search for high school and university learning.

To disentangle a viable *potential* profile of culture, in precise terms, is almost impossible, but in approximate terms it must be attempted. If asked, individuals will certainly express their hopes, fears, goals, values. But when it comes to the point, when actually confronted with the possibility of achievement, many of the thoughts fall by the wayside. The precise costs, the alternatives that have to be downplayed or given up, the price in terms of time, emotion, or material things, turn out to have a reality that differs from the fantasy. Such conundrums are the bane of social workers, community developers, political activists, reformers of all kinds. Many of the suggestions that come later in this book will be wrecked, at least in the short term, on this sharp rock. If this were not so, we might already have reached Utopia.....

There are conceptual ways of getting around this problem. The economists' notion of *elasticity* of demand, adequately rearranged for sociological purposes, provides a framework. It would postulate that the true measure of valuation of a thing or an activity consists in the degree to which individuals are willing to suffer costs to get more of it, or to pay increased costs (including the psychological and emotional ones) to hold on to it. The empirical test of values through elasticity runs up against the problem of differing kinds of costs, of measurement of changes, and of the fact that it is *ex post facto*, which limits the power of predictability. Nevertheless, more serious attention to the concept could result in approximate advances in what we know, and some data observed from segments of the population might provide bases for predicting what could happen in others.

Certainly, if we wish to know more about future innovation, attention to the concept is essential. At the very least, it indicates that assertions about the future, and about what is *likely* in fact to happen, whether by politicians, by pundits or by preachers, must be taken with mountains of salt. *The harsh truth is that they do not know what the consequences of their actions will be, and nor do I.*

We must live with approximation. We cannot stand back from the world or fail to act because our informed guesses about the future are just that. Further, the limitations of predictability increase the desirability of normative analysis. We *can* articulate where we *think* we want to go. We *can* change our minds if we find the costs too high, or the satisfactions of achieving the goal are less than we had anticipated. We can and do live with uncertainty, and that does not and should not prevent us from doing things that we imagine, anticipate, will bring about a better world. Dealing with uncertainty is an adventure, an emotional challenge, a value in itself. Uncertainty is no excuse for sitting on one's butt.

We all learn to live with our inconsistencies. We handle them, tell ourselves they don't matter, or we follow one idea at one time and another at the next. There may be objective inconsistencies that observers could agree are manifest in our expressions or behaviour. We can ignore them, and are usually unaware of them.

Sometimes, though, they become uncomfortable, to the point of interfering with our actions, rising to obsessive dominance in our thoughts, and arguments with our fellows. The inconsistencies demand resolution. We seek to amend our thoughts and our world until our internal peace is reconstituted; we are in equilibrium again. *Incompatibilities* are once again reduced to compatibility, by some adjustment in the cultural nuclei. This is a constructive path to societal change, one that, ideally, we would all like to follow, since it posits an outcome, a psychological resolution. Peace and wellbeing return. There is a sense of having achieved something. There are some of us who innovate in this way continuously, thriving on the succession of problems, resolution, problem, resolution and sometimes other related rewards, such as the respect and prestige it can bring. (Don't forget the costs: failure, envy.)

Here we are on the very edge of *dysfunction.* There is no law that states that a cultural system has to be perfectly adjusted. If it were, there would be no demand for change whatsoever. Functional (and its offshoot structural) anthropology reacted to the popular conception that many cultural traits were irrational, strange, inexplicable, savage. It was and is a major tool of understanding to actively seek the explanations, the rationalities that underlay the apparently irrational, the common sense of what was being done in the light of the total context, the damage that systems would suffer if one such significant trait were to be destroyed by outside thoughtlessness. The sources of change to functional or structurally sound systems did not come from stresses within. They came from without, and caused pain and problemsolving as the outside influences ramified through the culture, creating inconsistencies and incompatibilities that cried to be resolved.

In the modern world, there is still much to be said for the humanistic values of such an approach. But it needs to be amended. As analysts were quick to show, what came from outside did not descend on an inert body waiting for injections of new nuclei. The body of culture had its own immune systems, and chose from the invading viruses those they could handle and those they rejected. (Not literally: individuals did not have the power to resist biological viruses.....) Of course, power played a part, the power of the outsider to use force and blandishments; and the power the insider sought to gain by adopting new strengths. And while this was happening, the functional systems had their own problems to handle, and were involved in the ongoing adaptations of their cultures. Invading ideas had to fit the dynamic, force the dynamic into another path, or be adapted to fit the dynamic.

When competitive nuclei refuse to accommodate in such ways, when individuals hold to them as precious, as so highly valued that they will pay high costs to keep them, and the accommodations can be resolved only by a clash, often of titans, sometimes of dwarfs, we are led straight into *dysfunction*. In individuals it manifests itself in depression, alienation and the like, which, if treated, can return to the functionality of solutions. But as a manifestation of a cultural system, or two in a clash, we have measures of adjustment which aim at control, an inability to compromise, and often force in one form or another. Divorce, violence, antisocial behaviour, war, totalitarianism, racism, family violence, the attempt by groups to *impose* their will on others, the list goes on.

The processes I have mentioned in this summary form all imply that one can abstract a culture, talk about it as an entity, and think of it as being composed of a multitude of interacting parts, which not merely gear together in some mechanical way, but rather influence and change each other. The conceived culture is *articulated* insofar as rules can be discovered which guide the effects of nuclei upon each other. One such theme is that the powers of nuclei to adapt and to change others are based on their psychological component, manifested most significantly in perceptions. It is the *perception* of compatibility or incompatibility that counts, not some outside idea of functionality. Wouldbe reformers must constantly be reminded of this. An idea is much more likely to move into the system, or through it, if the persons involved *perceive that it fits*, and, based on that perception, judge that it will be good for them. Good for them usually means that it brings a benefit to their thought or behaviour that is worth the costs and sacrifice involved.

Here we are close to the endsmeans relationship that is essential to the thinking of economists and some other social scientists. I adhere to the use of this relationship in the form I understood it to mean among the *pioneer* economists. That is, what is an end and what a means is not an objective external definition, but depends upon the personal evaluations and concepts of the actor. Influenced by their need to measure and to manipulate quantities, economists have largely dropped this notion, and they themselves attempt to define what is a means and what an end, what is productive capital and what is a consumption good.

There are signs of trends back to what I regard as basics. This is coming about because economists have been forced to become interested in factors of production and social objectives that link with finance but have nonmaterial components health, social policy, education to take the most obvious. Once seen as social objectives and thus calculated as "ends", they are now recognised to have effects on "production", must be picked apart as "factors of production" *as well as* ends in themselves.

The circumstance that education has both characteristics, that is as a valuable end in itself, and as a means to greater productivity, should give us pause for thought. It impinges on arguments in various sections of these essays. But more profoundly, it raises the hypothesis that ***all*** *behaviour and objects contain **mixtures** of means and ends.*

A grand cathedral is a means to spirituality, but it is also a direct provider of awe and aesthetic satisfaction in itself. Tourists are shown Gaudi's buildings in Barcelona, not because they are functional but because they challenge the eye. A craftsman carves or builds a boat to make money for his family; but the activities are chosen because he loves them, he is prepared even to take a loss or a pittance of profit because he values the work in itself.

Once again, reform has often stalled because the element of satisfaction in something the reformers define as having only pain can so easily be overlooked, or put down to "innate conservatism". Why should shifting cultivators give up their forest digging sticks for "more effective" spades and shovels, and their clearings for fields, when they *like* the way their bodies move in traditional agriculture, enjoy the leaves around them, are happy with the schedules of work and rest in their present system? There can be good reasons, but reformers need to be absolutely sure that the benefits they dream up are real ones, do not have hidden unexpressed costs, and above all fit well into the perceptions of the cultivators about what they want from the world.

If there is confusion about ends and means, there is equivalent confusion about the material and nonmaterial. The distinction seems so straightforward: the material is something I can touch. If I can't touch it, it is nonmaterial..

Material objects are, though, a collection of symbols put together in material form. In that, they are at one with nonmaterial symbols like language and thought. They are in fact composed of thoughts, of the recognition of meanings. Buildings are libraries of concepts, so are coal mines, so are piles of grain waiting to be shipped, so is a pavement. Without their embodied concepts they are meaningless, they do not exist, they rot away.

And the meanings and concepts are subject to change according to the same rules we have been discussing. All the things we think about them, all the recognitions, ambiguities and puzzles, are nuclei in the profiles of culture. At one time a building is ripe for demolition; at another a historical treasure. At one time it is a school, another a warehouse. Coal is something dirty for domestic fires; or an alternative source of energy. The mine is dangerous and dirty, or a work place with perhaps high wages, or a source of tourist dollars, or something to be closed down. The pavement is hard on the feet and needs replacing, it is the route to the nearest good restaurant, it is composed of ugly stones, it is the embodiment of the history of the feet which have passed over it. The house on the corner is environmentally destructive, to some its staircase is beautiful and functional, to others it is something to be taken away to an antique market, what happened to the trees?, it accommodates too many people, it interferes with my view, I don't like the idea it is a halfway house.....

Once my father and I had to invent a new word for a building, where my grandfather preached. It was built as an ordinary house, to which someone had added a belfry. We couldn't decide whether it was a "chouse" or a "hurch". (His innovation was for the family only)

Is it not a common complaint about certain "functional" buildings that we don't know from the outside whether they are supermarkets, schools, hospitals, or prisons?

Material innovation and cultural innovation are one and the same. Cultural and social changes arise from the dynamics contained in the profiles of culture. The move to, or from, Utopia, is a cultural event. Within that context, politics and economics are not even subdivisions. They do not exist except as part of the changing cultural whole.

You may of course be wondering why I have used the word "innovation" instead of "creation" or "creativity".. One reason is pragmatic. The word "innovation" focuses on a process which results in something new. Much of creation does too. But in my view quite significant creation does not. A woodworker may turn out chair after chair of quite skilled handcraft. His original concept may have been innovative, but thereafter it is repetitive. Yet he is a creator of good things.

The other reason is that much confusion surrounds the analysis of creation, so that there is good reason to break away from it. One of the most recent compilations of perspectives and analysis, with the words :Theory and practice" in the title is almost encyclopaedic in its range of examples[26]. It even suggests that the religious stories of "Creation" are part of the subject, not because they are creative fables, but because the subject they deal with is one form of creation – that is not due to human hand. This is going to far, but the author correctly notices that the approaches of creative individuals differ widely according to subject matter – in literature, music, engineering, for example. Then the matter is left up in the air – there are many creativities and no overarching theory[27] A set of propositions which accounts for the process? Considering innovation in all domains of human endeavour enables us to approach understanding in a theoretical way. And having undertaken such an approach, we can use it to inform ourselves or our own innovative behaviour, and that of the institutions of which we are a part.

---

[26] Pope, Rob. *Creativity – Theory, History, Practice.* Abingdon, Routledge, 2005. The book contains an extensive bibliography.
[27] There is one attempt, quoted from Henry Petrovski, *Invention by Design* on page 267 with hints towards a generalisation.

There is also a psychology of innovation. Studies of innovative individuals ha ve revealed that for the greatest of them psychological props help. My favourite example is that of writers or composers who must settle to their work at a particular time of day, must have their pen or keyboard just so, with a cup of favourite coffee of just the right blend and strength, and the page open at the end of an unfinished sentence which gets them back in the mental swing. If any of these items is missing, it takes time to get settled. Thinkers are noted for their walks in the words. A sculptor or a painter must have the work space arranged (however chaotic it may seem to an outsider) to hiser satisfaction, and maybe spend some moments reflecting on how his creation meets his ambitions in the new morning. And should we speak of chefs with their *batterie de cuisine*. So it goes on. .Each one of us can find ways to refine our innovative actions and thoughts.

An understanding of and an application of a theory of innovation gives us the opportunity to be more effective in changing our world towards that of a magnificent place to live in the 21st century.

Reformed Education is Imperative

This chapter may be regarded as the cornerstone of my holistic view of global society as set out in *Fixing the World.* An earlier draft was part of the text which was awarded the 12005 World Utopian Championship.

Education is the foundation of reforms in every sphere. The reorganisation of the approach to engendering maturity in youths is interwoven with the concerns of every other chapter in this book. We must try to tackle it alongside all other reforms, which will be weak without it. It will minimally take a generation to experience maximum results in other spheres. So we had better get on with it.

You think this is not necessary? Examine the state of education in the most advanced countries and you will find it necessary to think again,
This is where we begin.

Take a moment to examine critically the ways in which official policies relate to the maturation of youth, primarily through the educational system, primarily but not only in richer countries. More and more frequently schools are being confronted by manifestations of societal ills – violence, depression et al. This is not new. But they have not been equipped to remedy the problems they face, and there are bureaucratic and communication difficulties bringing other community resources to bear on the issues.

Once we identify the tasks and challenges necessary to optimize the ways in which youths mature into responsible citizens, we may then design appropriate institutions to do the job. That design will be a major goal to achieve well prior to 2100 – in my view it should be achievable fifty years before that indeed very soon in much of the world. Special adjustments will be required to modify the institutions and ensure that they are effective in the poorer countries. In all instances the interaction of these ideas with indigenous values and systems will need careful culturespecific appraisal.

I start with suicide in its several forms.

In many parts of the industrial world, high school age youths are committing suicide in increasing numbers. As their age group rises as a cohort in the demographic scale, so the general figures of attempted suicide rise. In other words, the tendency toward suicide carries on into higher age groups.

Recently I do not know for how long the elderly had the highest suicide rates in such countries. Now the rates among the youth cohorts match those for the elderly. Unless there are fundamental transformations, the changing attitudes towards euthanasia coupled with the entry of present youth cohorts into the ranks of the elderly could produce a suicide explosion in forty years[28], if not before, that could shake the capabilities of society to respond.

I accept and advocate the right of the elderly to take their own lives, though I would prefer it to be in the context of psychological peace rather than ageinduced depression. I do not accept it as a necessity in other age groups, for which the future is still an open possibility. That would not be my idea of the toward which we strive.

In Japan and other countries suicides take place as the young take their lives for fear of failing examinations or similar tests. Family and peer pressure play a role: so do induced or real feelings of selfworthlessness in a demanding society.

A further form of suicide is ideological. This is particularly the case in Arab society, where young, welleducated people, notably including women, undertake acts of terrorism in which their own deaths are virtually certain – acts of martyrdom.

Close to suicide, perhaps virtually the same, are thousands of young boys and girls who are recruited into guerrilla and sometimes national armies, indoctrinated with the fever of killing, and

---

[28] Despite sentences of this kind it is not my intention to imply certainty about future trends.

thrust into the front lines where they are most in danger. It is well documented that many, indeed the majority, have been kidnapped to serve as cannon fodder.[29] They are often in hysterical or druginduced excitement, at the dangerous age of susceptibility. They take risks, voluntarily or under pressure, in which the likelihood of death or lifelong injury, before or after episodes of looting and socially destructive seemingly inhuman acts, is high. They are removed from the world of normal society, pariahs to civilisation.

And then there are those whose alienation is not that of the body, but of the mind and its spirit. These include the habitual criminals, so often and so long behind bars that they are seriously unable to function outside of prison, and who, when freed, commit acts so that they can return. They do not kill their bodies, but their way of life has become virtually suicidal – often, at a young age, because of experiences "inside" prison, that breeding ground of antisocial behaviour.

The correction of the tendency among those who have already moved beyond school and university can only be modified by a changes throughout culture, especially in the institutions which are held to be responsible for social control including police and prisons an issue that is fundamental to our goals, as we shall see in Chapter V.

However, the first step in tackling the issue *throughout all age groups* lies with education.

Suicide is part of the nexus of concerns that include violence, bullying and harassment in schools, truancy, youth prostitution, youth homelessness, the recourse of youth to violence and gangs on the streets, abuse in the family, and drugs. These are not just urban problems. Until the idealisation of rural life in the second half of the last century, it was well known that sexual abuse, family instability, incest, and violence were typical phenomena of **rural** living. They are more dramatic, more concentrated, less hidden, more newsworthy, and more frequently observed because the populations are higher, in cities. Although this is so, it is doubtful whether the statistical incidence is higher than in earlier centuries, and it is certain that there have been periods in modern history, for example the nineteenth century, when the situation was much worse.

That is, though, beside the point. It doesn't matter what the trends are, except insofar as wrong publicity overcreates immoderate anxieties and backlashes. What *is* to the point is that there should be zero tolerance of any of these phenomena in a civilised society. I am not referring to the superficial remedies of authoritarian crackdown. I mean getting to the remedial basics.

The basics consist in the *positive* upbringing of youth, presently a joint responsibility of family, schools, youth organisations, religions and the State.

The family is having great difficulty. It has *always* had great difficulty, among rich *and* poor. Let us be freed from "traditional family values" which have done such a horrible job, and been the cover up for abuse. That does not mean throwing everything out. It means rethinking responsibilities and dynamics.

Guilt. Anxiety. Hopelessness. From time to time these strike at all parents who take their responsibilities seriously. What, oh what, am I doing wrong?

What parents tend to do is to bring forward the learning that they acquired in their family of origin, and as they acquired a philosophy of parenting in their twenties and thirties. Parents themselves survived troubled times, in the late 'sixties and 'seventies battling authority with the assertion of permissiveness. When adults become responsible for loved children themselves, the two themes fight for dominance and balance. Parents blame themselves for not getting the balance right, for not foreseeing.

They cannot get the balance right by themselves. Nobody knows what that balance is, for any individual child. The outside influences are so powerful. Parents must count themselves fortunate and extraordinarily sensitive if their offspring make the transition to adulthood reasonably well as most but not all do. Quite frequently, the path is first one of natural rebellion which can take extremely dangerous turns beside the abyss of drugs and alienation. Quite frequently, parents find that the children, now "friendren", have survived, matured, found new solid roads.

This is not to argue that, if parents do not *know* they should not try. Of course they will. Their efforts, whether misguided or highly sensitive, *will* have an effect, a positive one, when guided by love and support, come what may. It is almost the only principle that counts for sure. Parents, after all, are not the only variables.

There is the child itself. Life never will be a cakewalk. Despite the incidence of trouble, by far the majority of children become reliable adults. Even when they have inner pains, they function well, even creatively.

And they live in a challenging environment in which they are led by a myriad of influences toward a myriad of choices.

In what follows I am somewhat neglecting the influence of religion. This is a pity, but I can't do everything at this moment. Despite refusing the concept of a God or gods in human form, I am not one of those who believes that religion, or at least the search for spirituality, is insignificant. On the contrary, the search for spirituality, within or without the churches, is a major preoccupation, a resource, an intellectual and emotional drive, that has a major part to play in the lives of an increasing number of men and women, even traditionally dominating in some cultures. On the other hand, the influence of formal religion and the spiritual beliefs of parents on children is a part of family life, determined by parents. Further, the range and variety of belief and of the types of searching are now so great as to defy summary. For the growing young, seeking their own paths as they enter the enquiring teens, the range and variety are part of the almost infinity of choice with which they are confronted. It is that infinity of choice which evokes creativity, thoughtfulness, anxiety and despair, an infinity that continues well beyond school into adulthood. As each decade passes, the conscious part of that infinity expands, life juxtaposing simplicity and resounding chaos, in which the ears as well as our other senses defend themselves against both aggression and sensuality, often not being able to distinguish this from that.

The school is the place in which family influence confronts the perspectives of other families through the filter of other children's presence. It is the place where the influences of the media, of adult role models, of professional teachers, the contributions of churches and voluntary youth organisations, and the policies of the State, come together, working out their pressures and contradictions in the minds and behaviour of children.

It is inevitable that education should thus be the focus of power rivalry, conflict and cooperation, demands and compromise. Ideally, the State should be in a position to take a detached view, to consider the meaning, objectives, philosophies and methods of education. This is not the case. The State is governed by men and women whose basic philosophies are *a priori*, joined with those of political allies in a mostly confrontational competition with oppositions. The State is strongly advised by bureaucracies who control data and implementation, who are a force for conservative continuity which fortunately somewhat counterbalances the potential swings of elected political opinion. Theocratic States are additionally dominated by clerics and religious authorities. Powers are variously filtered through intermediary bodies down to the school, or in some instances tightly controlled by the central government or a recognized religious hierarchy. Powers relate to the official objectives and philosophy of education (sometimes ideology), the curriculum, and budgetary influences on school practice.

Teachers, like any other professional corpus, have the responsibility for the direct contact with their clientpupils, and to a lesser extent with the semiclientparents. It is this responsibility, together with their common experience of professional training, that binds them together, and constitutes the reality of their power base. Furthermore, the most significant reality in the exercise of educational policy is what teachers do with it. A fiat from above is useless if it does not fit well with the perceptions that the teachers themselves have of their realities, their philosophy, their responsibilities, and, increasingly, their material conditions. Even unintentionally teachers internalise their beliefs and practices in ways that are difficult to change, and of course sometimes they don't want to change, because what they do is a sacred pursuit.

It might be said that the way to change teaching is to change teacher training. Indeed, without this, change would be even more difficult. But if serious changes are to be contemplated and I have not yet made my case for them we must recognise that young newly trained teachers have limited influence and, perhaps, none at all within a religious hierarchy. It is not only that time must pass before they rise in seniority and their proportions increase with the consequence that even newer ideas must enter the system with the young cohorts now the conservatives. It is that they are posted to schools as individuals, surrounded by those whose training belongs to an earlier period. They meet in committees, socialise, discuss issues, are rewarded, with and by those who belong to an earlier generation. Inevitably, most of them will unintentionally modify their positions to conform to those of their peer group. Their impact is reduced. (They could have greater impact if posted en bloc to specific schools, more or less taking them over, at the expense of experience.)[30]

Some of this can be modified by major refresher training. This is not readily achieved by North American style "professional days", or by uncontrolled sabbaticals. It would require periodic freedom from classroom activities for substantial blocks of *required* refresher education.

There are other difficulties in teacher formation. What is to be taught to them? Subject matter? Pedagogical philosophy? The State's requirements? In these matters, wherein lies the "academic freedom" of the teacher? Does the teacher in fact have "academic freedom" that a university professor is supposed to have? I think not. The teacher has a responsibility for the vulnerable children of parents, and is thus morally responsible to those parents, whereas university faculty are supposedly guiding young adults. The teacher interprets responsibility by using skills the best way possible to influence young minds. In my view, those skills have technical components that can be taught, and personal, human components that training can influence but not control. Because of the latter limitation, the effectiveness of the classroom has, ultimately, to depend on the

---

[30] In the late 'forties I had the experience of conducting research amongst units of the British armed forces. The then government was determined to change the culture of the by now professional officer corps. Young officers were indoctrinated with the new ideas, but as they were posted one by one to their regiments or squadrons they rapidly succumbed to the values and culture of the officers' mess.

individual teacher who makes the institutional framework operate through personal qualities which technical skills support but do not suffocate. The freedom of the teacher lies in his or her application of those skills, *not in deciding what the ultimate classroom goals should be*.

Ultimately, then, I argue that innovation in the school system is the same as in any other context. It comes through the interplay of ideas and concepts that can come in all forms, formally and informally, which the individual teacher rejects or accepts. The rate of acceptance will be proportional to the degree to which the concept or practice "fits" the profile of culture of individual teachers, and can be incorporated into that profile.

You will find only a few small countries some Pacific Islands, perhaps where the main corpus of teachers individually share more or less identical cultural profiles. In all others, there is considerable variety. Within that variation, individuals who approximate each other in ideas and point of view may be grouped, more or less categorised. If one wished to do so, one could identify such groups. Educational innovation would have differing impacts on each such group. This is one potential influence towards diversity in the school system. Teachers with differing philosophies and methods can, theoretically, operate schools with differing philosophies and methods.

If there is truth in this, how much more so is it true of the third power group, the parents. Whereas teachers, despite their differences, have some common ground derived from occupational considerations, parents do not. Their variability is much greater, except in rural tribal communities. And in developed and developing countries they increasingly demand more variation in education. States, and teachers, confront increasingly multifaceted parental cultures.

Some argue that the more varied and complex a society, the more important it is to use schooling as a cohesive force. (In some times and places, compulsory army service was justified in this way.) I confess to doubts about this, if the objective is Utopian, for we have seen that diversity adds to the size of the profile of culture, and hence to innovation, and because, as I shall argue in a later context the State is not, fundamentally and as we know it, holy. Yet in the shorter term, this is a practical consideration. Do we want the cohesiveness of the State to be weakened? Let us keep this in mind.

What should be the functional objectives of the school? Do they imply major innovation? In approaching these questions I am not implying that, for any function, the school is the only influence that is relevant or that is needed. The school, however, works with children for long hours, day after day. Its potential influence, through both teaching and the influence of peers, is as great as that of parents and it may be identified as the primary institution which exposes children to nonfamily society in a societally coordinated way[31].

Such influences embody major ethical problems. If State schools were fully effective in carrying out their mandate, they would be imposing a single universal philosophy on children. The authoritarian and centralising dangers are modified by the essential individuality of both teachers and children, the existence of programme choices, and the counterbalancing effects of family and other outside influences. Yet a single, universal, little modified, State system could move in the universalising direction and is contrary to my sense of the ultimate goal of a diverse creative culture[32].

There is also an incipient conflict between the goals of particular schools and the goals of parents, individually or collectively. One of the most dramatic illustrations came from special Indian schools in British Columbia in the nineteenth and early twentieth centuries. A now discontinued type of school, known as "residential

---

[31] Other institutions such as churches, sports associations and so on normally deal with segments of society, whereas schools, one way or another, penetrate all corners.

[32] This is not to say that authoritarian regimes cannot achieve amazing results in limited highly concentrated teaching, usually in technical areas. In Soviet Moscow I was astounded at the ability of a seven year old attending an elite language school to converse easily in English.

schools", deliberately removed young children from their parents and communities (considered to be retrograde influences), transferring them to boarding schools. Later, in more subtle ways, Indian community day schools were sometimes staffed by dedicated, earnest and responsible nonIndian teachers who, as individuals, considered it their duty and mandate to be agents of change. In itself, this indeed might have been a legitimate mandate it would in effect have been impossible for a school to have operated *without* engendering change of some sort. The issue here, though, is that, at least to begin with, many of the teachers did not have the skills or incentives to match their ideas about the goals of change to those of the parents. The child, unintentionally, became the location of a battleground between two sets of adults, overt or unseen. Even teachers in village schools were drawn into such conflicts. In extreme cases the tensions and misplaced mandates brought despair, neurosis in both teacher and pupil, and revolting abuse in the residential schools.

This is an extreme form of a tension which is frequent, teachers considering some parents to be irresponsible, uncaring, harmful to their offspring, ignorant about the educational needs and strengths of their children, causing antisocial behaviour; parents considering teachers to be using wrong methods, presenting irreligious values, encouraging laziness or pushing children too far. The obverse of this is the rote and ideological learning of schools in extreme religious contexts.

To advocate no tension at all would be unrealistic and false. A major part of learning, as I shall reinforce, is to deal with tension and to work out the implications of inconsistency and conflict. It is from such bases that innovation takes place. However, whatever I may suggest by way of resolving issues, I am in no doubt that differences will continue in the ultimate world, and that, in reasonable ways, they should. When I set forth ideas about objectives for ultimate achievement I know I shall be establishing a battleground or, I would rather hope, a platform for debate.

By way of opening the subject, I once had ideas about an ideal base curriculum for a modern world. It was oriented toward mobility and the growth of the individual. The underlying theme was to maximise the child's potential for communication as an adult. Thus the threer's were essential few disagree about that today. To literacy, numeracy and communication skills (including logic and rhetoric) were added those languages which worked as *linguae francae* across major segments of the world English, German and Russian (for much of eastern Europe), Arabic, Spanish, French (for parts of Africa and Asia), written Mandarin, Malay, and Swahili (for East Africa). To this would be added comparative anthropology, world social and political history and geography, medical diagnosis, data searching and processing, and, for real mobility, basic motor mechanics, horse riding, sailing (with navigation) and outdoor skills. Such a curriculum was predicated on one specific goal making it possible for young adults to move through the world anywhere with confidence and to move forward (with specialised advanced education) into their professions anywhere.

While such a model programme may be teasing to some, **all it does** is to demonstrate that current curricula are not writ in stone; that what is taught depends entirely on objectives. The major limitation of the above imagined programme was that the objective was narrow, too much based on instruction and too little on the nature of the child, and not suited to the needs of our ultimate goals. But the limitations of the above extreme case are also present, if to a lesser degree, in *all* curriculum models. The very idea that one curriculum serves the needs of all students in all parts of society is and should be a nonstarter. The major thread running through all good curricula is that they establish standards of rigour, mental discipline, clear thinking, and the processes of continuously acquiring and using knowledge, old and new.

If the above is not currently satisfactory, then what should most, if not all, schools do, in principle? There is a great deal.

Particularly in the second half of the twentieth century and into the twentyfirst, schools have been experimenting with our children, often in the light of general theories which can be misinterpreted when put into practice, theories which, in the nature of things, have not been properly tested in terms of results. What I write now is of the same order. It is opinion, linked to some observation, some experience, and, I hope, some logic. In particular, *it is linked to ideas about what the end results should be*. Recall one of my foundation statements. There is no complete knowledge; anything put into practice will lead to unexpected results. What we do in schools will have profound effects on the future. The cautions of this paragraph will have major implications for the organisation and dynamics of schools.

In 'fifties Canada I saw schools in which uniforms had been abandoned as a matter of theory. Uniforms were felt to be authoritarian, representing an expense for those not so well off. At the same time schools emphasised the skills of social interaction, the ability to get on with one's fellows. The solitary pupil was an anachronism. The children themselves stepped into the gap. Peer pressure dictated clothing, both boys and girls decided that what they wore had to be what youthful fashion dictated. Those who wore different clothing were open to derision. Within the peer dictates, some of the better off were seen to be better off by the expense of the clothes, the cars driven, the hairdos and makeup of the girls. The concern for the visible aspects of group personality seemed to take priority over the content of school work, where conformity emerged naturally.

By the 'nineties more individuality was expressed. But the use of externals and clothing is still an identifier. This time it identifies group *difference* as well as juvenile peerconformity. Gangs have their markers. Certain conformist schools mistakenly attempt to enforce clothing standards which reduce ethnic identification. They are kinds of uniforms without the admission.[33]

The most marked change in school ethos in many industrialised countries since the late 'sixties has been the formal redefinition of the appropriate tension between conformity and individuality, a redefinition which affects major changes in adult perceptions. In one sense, the group is reasserted. Group projects frequently take the place of individual ones. Seating arrangements create eyetoeye contact in the classroom, emphasising interactions, and hence peer control, in place of the more individualistic lines of desks.

On the other hand, the self is reasserted. Therapies dealing with relationships in adult society often emphasise selfawareness, selfknowledge, the discovery of the past and of the child within; and selfassertion. Mishandled, as therapy often is, the "other" becomes secondary. The right kind of concern for the "other" will emerge only after the "self" has been discovered.

---

[33] In a recent visit to New Zealand I was impressed by the groups of high school boys and girls in smart uniforms. They are also common in most of the once colonial world.

So in the school. In both schools and universities, there have been times, teachers, and classes for which selfexpression is valued simply because it is the expression of self, with little or no regard to the quality of the expression. The fact that I thought it is quite sufficient to give me top marks. Indeed, since everyone in the class thought something, let's give them *all* top marks. Such caricatures have been realities.

However, even where such naive extremes have been in place, it is interesting to see both teachers and the public striving to establish something else, "standards". And it is more interesting to see children discovering that there is more to creativity than simple effort; discovering, as they step into the world, that they have been betrayed because they were not prepared for "standards"; that much of peer pressure "out there" is indeed about standards and performance rather than superficialities; and that there is excitement to be obtained from meeting intellectual challenges. The cliché has it: if there are rigorous and demanding standards in sports, why not in thinking?

Both themes need expression, and never will either disappear. To equip children for a world in which there is extensive adult nonwork that I envisage for the better world[34], it is essential that

---

[34] See Chapters X and XI. Our desired world will have less mandatory employment, more nonemployed activity.

they know themselves. It is a fundamental part of creative education that children learn how to explore, out of their own interests. They will not fully discover themselves in high school. Currently, most children do not discover their creative capacities until well into young adulthood. No school can place before a young person the whole total richness of the world and what the human capacity is capable of; no school can provide the total basis for choice[35]. But all schools can aim at encouraging intellectual in which I include artistic and psychological exploration, the discovery that one is capable of entering undreamedof realms of creativity, the knowledge that the search for selffulfilment is neverending and wondrous.

Beyond these issues the whole question of creating maturity had been pushed into the background. Old fashioned ways of "building character" do not work for the modern scene, and in some instances produced distorted adults. It cannot be dismissed because of that: we must strive to modernise our methods and create new kinds of mature characters who can handle both each other and the contemporary and future world. The challenge is by no means unknown. There are numerous studies which have the underlying theme: maturity is deficient in young people. Most of these relate to boys – are they men? The conclusion in

---

[35] How many school career counsellors even imagine the possibility of anthropology as a career, even if they know what the word means?

most of them is that maturity, if it arrives at all, usually comes well after schooling as young people face the real world and are confused by what they face. Some return to the family nest. The massive unemployment, especially among the young, in the first decade of the 21st century is devastating. In what follows we must bear this phenomenon clearly in mind.[36]

The emphasis on the mind and spirit implied in my last sentence does not reduce the significance of the biophysical.

The truism that healthy minds emerge from healthy bodies is only partly true. Many great minds belong to those who are or have been physically and emotionally warped. Touch a great philosopher and you will find a troubled soul. What *is* true, on the other hand, is that *all* thought and selfexpression arrives through the senses, is filtered internally as a result of sensory experience. Especially in the puritanical parts of the world, where the creative uses of some senses are denied, the ability of teachers to encourage sensory experience is strictly limited and rightly so, since maturing children are especially vulnerable to sensory abuse and dysfunctional influence. Yet a

---

[36] Among the publications note the revealing titles of the following: Cross, Gary. *Men to Boys: the making of modern immaturity.* New York, Columbia University Press; Coté, *Arrested Adulthood: the changing nature of maturity and identity.* New York, New York University Press, 2000.

balance can surely be attained in which sensory experience is valued, and individually encouraged, and the links between experience, creativity, and innovation are made known.

Furthermore, the world of physical activity intersects directly with the mind, its expression, and its choices. The physical and the mental are not opposites; they are part of one state. The choice of physical activity over desk activity is not a choice of body over mind. It is a choice in which body and mind unite to go in a specific direction. The application of thought and knowledge to sport and recreation makes this clear. Some children will make physical activity a greater part of their lives than others; almost all children should understand that this is not a separate, classified as different, part of life, but an integrated aspect. It will, like every other aspect, be used creatively by some and less by others, just as is music or scientific experimentation. But the biophysical and the mental are fundamental, part of every single one of us, in a way that music or scientific experimentation is not.

In parts of North America today some teachers are directly integrating exercise and thinking. They recognise that as high pulse rate gives energy to the mind and increases powers of concentration and perception. Exercise bicycles are installed directly in the classroom. Students work on them to get their pulse rate to say 120 per minute. They then go to their desks. Positive results, even on "problem" pupils is outstandingly high.

To start the process of knowing one's self, then, is a primary goal of school education. The search for that knowledge will never end if properly engendered.

At the same time, it is of utmost significance to limit that search for self. This will be done by placing it in context. Without balance and context an overemphasis on the ego is likely to be hurtful, to the child, and to others. It will engender the continuous lifelong question, the dominance of WhoamI? Anxiety because I do not know myself, perpetual introspection, inhibition from action because it might not be right for me. In this field, even more than in all others, it is of major necessity to indicate also that I will *never* fully know who I am; that *why* I am who I think I am doesn't matter so much   it can't be changed retrospectively   as *who* I am. I must learn when to think about it and when to stop thinking about it. The importance of the search is to find out what my values are, what I would like to do in living my life, how I can get on with others, how I can communicate myself to others, and how to make some reasonable choices for myself.

Education is replete with paradoxes, contradictions, and oppositions. Successful education does not allow one theme to dominate, balances the contradictions in ways that alert the child without creating improper anxiety, that make use of the paradoxes for creativity, and that meet the needs of different children in different ways.

Thus selfexpression is counterbalanced by awareness of and concern for others. I personally feel that *the primary underlying issue is courtesy, understanding and respect for others*. And I feel that somehow, all over the world, schools have limited success in conveying this message, and that very frequently the concern is treated as peripheral rather than fundamental. Indeed as we know only too well, schools in some places specifically engender distaste for the other, even to the point of preaching the merits of violence and martyrdom. If there is no courtesy and respect for others a school simply cannot function adequately in the ideal world. A functioning adult society cannot exist.[37] We will have more to say on this subject when we discuss terrorism and freedom. The issue links to so many other aspects of society violence, crime, autocracy, selfinterest pressure groups, attitudes to work are rather obvious. I shall identify others.

---

[37] Did – do schools in Rwanda teach knowledge of and respect for the two competing social groups? How much do northern Sudanese schools teach positively about their southern or their Darfur cocitizens? They don't and they are neither mandated nor equipped to do so. How many Christian schools fail to each Islam or Judaism positively, and vice versa?

Hence selfexpression should not be confused with selfishness and egotism.

In my elderly superficial observations I see small examples of the confusion. Young people at all times and places have difficulty in defining their personal space. Anyone who encounters young people on public transport, in shopping areas, in souks, anywhere where there is a strong possibility of physical contact, is bound to get an elbow in the ribs, toes stepped on, the sensation of being pushed aside as the energetic young, in groups, steam ahead. One remarks on the natural courtesy of a youth who gives his, or more usually her, seat to an elderly person of no matter what ethnic community. One often feels that in such a case it is parental, not school, influence that has been responsible; and that peer pressure is against it through derision, especially amongst boys.

Trivial. Not at all. Fundamental. Which is why I repeat the point.

If courtesy is not taught in little ways, the large ones, when there, are hypocritical.

Some schools, of course, do in fact stress courteous behaviour. All should. How?

I do not like the word "tolerance" in multiethic or crossreligion contexts.[38] It implies that

---

[38] Note the following by E. M. Foster: "Tolerance is a

there is something about another's behaviour that I don't particularly like, but will tolerate. Yes, indeed, we often do run across behaviour which we dislike and tolerate. Often when we run across behaviour that we dislike and should **not** tolerate; we should do something about it.

What I object to is the easy way in which we can think of tolerance of rather than respect for **or understanding** of others. It is not tolerance that should be emphasised in schools, but respect and understanding. Tolerance implies "Real weird he digs classical music. Who cares?" or "They have such weird customs. I don't mind, though, that's for them". Patronising.

On the contrary, respect for others implies "I wonder what he gets out of classical music? Makes him interesting." or "What they do makes considerable sense for them. Even though it's not for me, I'd like to know about it." And understanding means just that, figuring out the reasons behind the behaviour in question and placing them in cultural and "philosophical" context.

One of the results of the late 'sixties was the reemphasis of the idea that discipline, however

---

very dull virtue. It is boring. Unlike love, it has always had a bad press. It is negative. It merely means putting up with people, being able to stand things." Quoted in the *Globe and Mail* July 5th 2005.

valued in sports, was unnatural in mental activity, and that "failure" was an assault on the persona. On the contrary, both discipline and failure are essential experiences for a truly civilised person who wishes to be capable of the fullest selfexpression and the fullest contribution to total wellbeing. Blaming others, or circumstances, or upbringing, can too easily slide over into excuses for failures which should be faced up to and learned from, The "culture of complaint" as one writer perceptively put it, is very far from our global goals, fort both adults and children.

However much a creative person enjoys the outcome of his chosen activity, there will be costs involved. To commit to the chosen outcome requires the payment of those costs. They include not only the material, but the psychological. If you are not prepared to pay the costs, you do not value the activity as highly as you thought. To summon the resources, internal and objective, to pursue a goal, it is necessary to have the discipline to pay, in effort, in materiel, in mental concentration, and, quite often, in going through boring and seemingly pointless stages and bits of training. You may have to suffer through boring instructors. To get to the fullest enjoyment of achievement it is necessary to be prepared to go through times when you ask yourself, is this all worthwhile?

You do not simply get an answer out of the air. There has been groundwork laid for those flashes of insight, of intuition, of bodily achievement, of controlled logic.

As I have said, and will repeat, there is no greater betrayal of a child's capabilities that to pretend to him or her that whatever they think is objectively as good as what someone else thinks, just because it is thought. That any thought is as good as another. That what matters is to do the thinking, and that the skills of communicating that thinking are insignificant. This sort of betrayal is not to be confused with the genuine attempt to encourage the emergence of the child's thoughts and then to show, skilfully and gently, that those thoughts can be extended by the application of discipline   even by going through disliked procedures.

The betrayal I have mentioned is matched by another equal treachery, the denial of "failure", the belief that the term "failure" has to mean the denigration of the individual, that it is somehow shocking and should never occur. It is true that in the past, and still in the present, failure has been used as a punishing stick in that way; it has discouraged and destroyed individual talents.

The word "failure" should be brought back into current dialogue. It should be used with understanding as a positive element in life. To "fail" means that you have *tried*, that you have attempted something that is for some reason at this point beyond you. To fail gives you guidance. It tells you what to work on it may even be lassitude or lack of discipline, but it can also be lack of a technical mastery, of understanding. It may even tell you that the subject matter will not, eventually, be for you.

Placed in a positive context, failure should be a challenge. It should alert both teacher and child that something requires attention. As a child I failed in both mathematics and French. My teachers dealt with the other pupils who understood and were not so mentally lazy. My father bought me a French tutor and in a couple of months I was top in the city's schools. I wish he had thought to do that in mathematics, for in later life I found, without knowing any math, that symbolic logic has an extraordinary appeal and value that my laziness undermines.

In my case the teachers did not have the will or the interest to advise someone who, to them, was a bit of an idiot and lazy to boot. Literature recounts many tales of dedicated teachers whose avocation is to find and nurture the wandering child, to bring him or her through the tests of discipline and failure. It is also full of accounts of harsh disciplinarians who have little interest but to give vent to their own internal problems, and in doing so stifle the growth of others. For many talented men and women the suffering of school is something to eventually be put behind them, for adult life is their real school, the place where they find an outlet for their skills and even achieve fame. True. But many others fall by the wayside. And what a waste of school resources and energy to let the opportunity slip by.

Embrace failure. Let teachers resurrect it as a positive force. It will be there throughout life; it is a step on the path to achievement; it must be understood, not fled from. He who does not fail does not try; indeed is not alive.

The question of sex education is fraught and highly controversial. It needs serious addressing because, as I shall be arguing in connection with the family, and with health and the law, sexual ills are at the source of many or most of personal dysfunctions and interpersonal troubles. Far from being a subject addressed on tip toe it should be front and centre in the concerns of Youth Maturity Institutes which I advocate later to replace schools. We choose to downplay or hide such facts as that the relationship between mother and child at the breast is highly sexual; that babies are tactile; that young children are curious and interested in the body, experimenting with it and investigating. Add to that the perception, perhaps the fact, that sexual experiment is going on amongst teens and in preteen friendships.

Our attitudes to sex are cultural, and we need cultural adjustments to handle them. Except for some of the potential medical consequences and the psychological effects of repression, there is little biological about our thoughts about sex. What indeed is a sex act? Voyeurism? Playing with one's own genitals? Intimate caressing? On a small island in the southern Solomons I witnessed young girls below the age of ten dancing a hissing dance, in which the rhythms and hisses coincided – as did the rubbing of genitals on genitals and genitals on thighs. Sex act or fun? The licentious ribaldry of cross cousins of opposite genders in some parts o Fiji would get close to sexual harassment if performed in a Canadian bureaucracy – yet they are designed to say "no copulation allowed" and to emphasize the delightful but forbidden danger. A Western phenomenon emerging as I write is that of the daisy chain, in which young preteens of both sexes join their naked bodies in a circle and play with the one next in the chain.

Repression makes behaviour with sexual content seriously damaging. It often removes the highly desirable supportive and warm touching that should exist between appropriate adults and troubled children. And it turns sensuous or insecure children into dysfunctional adults in many psychological areas. And I will be asserting later that it is a prime mover in crime and hatred.

So Youth Maturity Institutes must do something about it. They will focus on parents (see Chapter IV on the family). But they will also investigate and innovate in sexual education.

Sex education today is primarily biological – how the reproductive system functions – medical – for example, the dangers of sexually transmitted diseases and unprotected sex – the moral, psychological and social implications, and how to get help. It is inescapable that the emphasis is on danger and discomfort rather than pleasure and joy. Is it any wonder that searching teens ignore the warning and take risks.[39]

The problem is that the truths about sex as joy are ignored, and young people are too often experiencing the rumblings, discomforts and ignorance of sexual pleasure as they try their hands at it. Guilt, fear and ignorance turn the experiences into distaste and repeated searching for something better. Pity the young girl faced with a would be lover who doesn't know how to stimulate her before he satisfies himself. And pity the selfconfidence of the young boy who discovers his inadequacy, or the arrogant young man who thinks that this is what it is about. And for that read, at least for a while, almost 100% of young intercourse.

What to do. Don't raise your eyebrows. I'm serious because the implications are serious. People engage in sex for enjoyment. That characteristic is given to us so that as we engage in sex we can also procreate.

---

[39] Fortunately I am not alone in my thinking. On 23rd May 2006 the Sex Education Forum associated with the Department of education in Britain issued a report asserting that the subject was treated overbiologically in schools.

It is not even certain that the evolutionary function of sex is limited to procreation. For example, various theories of female orgasm are rooted in the assumption that that is what sex is about. But studies have shown that the biological theorems underlying such a postulate are quite mistaken and that the female orgasm has no bearing on the power to conceive. And while male orgasm and ejaculation go, shall we say, hand in hand, once again there is little of any relationship between its physical manifestation and rate of conception.[40]

While sexual activity has a bearing on procreation it is also there, deeply embedded, for its own sake. It is an activity which can be, should be, joyous and wholesomely rewarding, engendering compassion, love, delight, and the renewal of the body and the senses. It can go seriously wrong, become nasty, evidence of sickness, fumbling and crude. To keep it in balance and to gain the most from it, young people *need to be coached in sex as an art form*, just as they are taught the essence of aesthetics in art or the beauties in mathematics. Vestal Virgins and other priestesses undertook this task for young men as a religious duty. In numerous cultures young men were and are initiated by engaging prostitutes. Neither of these institutions engenders more than

---

[40] Cf. Lloyd, Charlotte A., *The Case of the Female Orgasm: Bias in the Science of Evolution*, Cambridge, Harvard University Press, 2005 and also Margolis, Jonathan, *O: The Intimate History the Orgasm* London, Arrow Books, 2005

some technical knowledge for the satisfaction of the male. Rarely does it educate the male in the desires of the woman.

Girls are marginally better off. Self experimentation and playfulness with other girls can create considerable sensual satisfaction, so that lesbianism may be a pleasing outcome. But many grow into women who are overcome by guilt, dry dissatisfaction and "frigidity" so that even sex for procreation becomes an unpleasant chore.

So how can Youth Maturity Institutes undertake appropriate coaching and education? Get with it, pedagogues. The blackboard alone will not do. And it needs to completely avoid exploitation by and the perversion of instructors. It must be entirely sensitive to the individual child, yet skin to skin, body to body teaching of ways to satisfy the other partner and retain one's own integrity.

One must inset an obvious warning. If adults are to teach younger adults the arts of sex, is there not a risk of perversion and abuse? Most certainly there is. But remember we are dealing with such matters within the context of Youth Maturity Institutes which will have many more resources to deal with such matters than present day schools. And we are working with the expectation that there will, in time, be fundamental changes in the behavioural ethics of youths becoming in their turn adults.

Even then there are certain principles to be observed, rigorously and sensitively. Biologically, young people become pubescent at different ages. There are some who, for whatever reason, resist and dislike sensual touching. It would be disastrous if sexual education, in the sense in which I am using it, became a classroom exercise to be administered mechanically to a specific age group. At the very least, this has to be something in which the individual child's readiness is assessed accurately For some it may be almost from birth, for others not until the late teens or not at all.

Below I shall be opening the challenges for pedagogy. This is clearly one of them. Should instruction be given in clinical surroundings, as if it were an extension of hygiene? Should there be and to what degree, an enhancement of sensuous atmosphere – lighting, music, scent. How far should group instruction be desirable, effective? Is it possible that for some sexual activity will be repulsive, and for what reasons, and with what consequences? Should homosexuality be included and under what conditions if any? Should instructors/instructresses be given a special *cachet* and perhaps privileged and circumscribed status?

Whatever your, the reader's views, this is not a matter to be ignored. Give it deep, constructive thought.

For it is fundamental to many many aspects of a future world, well beyond the confines of the sex act itself – family life, equanimity, peace with one's self and the world, selfconfidence, anger control, even crime. We must face up to it, and follow through with determination.

At present we are going through what I hope is a blip on a hidden screen. We are, up to a point quite properly, tying education to social goals; but the blip on the screen tells us that the primary goal is to train young people for employment. Vocational and/or practical education is, will be, and should be of as much concern as the socalled academic, for this is the path that many will choose in life, and it is significant for the full life and recreation of many whose primary occupation will be less definable.

So here I address a problem of pedagogy. Let me illustrate. Many years ago I administered an educational programme for the United Nations which consisted of extending the horizons and knowledge of senior civil servants from developing countries, in almost all substantive fields, from social work to hydraulic engineering. The previous director of the centre, with great perspicacity, set in place a system in which he talked with each of the fellows to determine what, in their *theoretical* understanding they were lacking. At first the fellows resisted. What they wanted were the latest practical techniques and gimmicks. Each individually tailored programme, however, was designed to reinforce the *principles* from which the practical techniques emerged, to create professional ongoing contacts with the world of advanced knowledge, and to help the candidate to control, throughout hiser life, the flow of *new* information, techniques and ideas. He faced the issue that the "latest" today is the "outdated" tomorrow; that education in the "latest" will be démodé by the time the student returned home. In other words, he aimed instead at broadening capabilities for lifelong development, individually, instead of making the experience a oneshot, classroom kind of quickly outdated and ephemeral instruction. In that context the experiment, for that was what it was, was "too expensive" to last, yet it was in truth a most efficient and longlasting expenditure of resources.

Similar principles apply to "practical" instruction in high schools.

The reasoning is simple. If you train children with employment in mind, what precisely is that employment? You begin educating in that manner in the teens, but it will be four years (more if tertiary education follows) before the child is offering his or her services. In the present and future world, changes in the work place, in both technique and distribution of tasks, move so fast and unpredictably that you may be training for dead ends. Furthermore, unless there is a very close liaison with the *whole range* of employers, it will be inevitable that the skills represent only a portion of what is needed. How many schools train butchers in sushi techniques? (Some do.) How far behind were schools in adapting auto mechanics courses to the electronic age?

Furthermore, it is obvious that the work place itself will change many times during the career of the employee, and that an employee is likely to change jobs more frequently than at present. How can schools keep up with the fast changes and movements in occupation? They can't, unless they specialise as technical high schools, which is not always to be recommended, and also may not be what employment needs require.

What the school can best do is to educate, not train. Even for those whose major aptitude is practical, it is still the mind that counts. Skilled tradesmen and secretaries can adapt. They understand what lies behind the practice, they play with alternatives in their minds, they are not shocked but challenged if there is a technological revolution, and they have psychological command of what is needed to go through the adaptation. Schools that build programmes on the concept of a survey of employerspecific needs are doomed to fall short as out of date

This is not to say that school and the workplace should be separated. Children should *know* what the workplace entails not as a fixed static entity, but one that is always in fluctuation. Since time is limited, not all careers can be demonstrated by class activities. The notion of dynamics needs to be extended by indications that there are other worlds out there, other kinds of industry and commerce. And, especially for the more academically inclined, that boring subjects are sometimes of great advantage, from languages to abstract mathematics.

If the school is to combine practice and theory in generalizable ways, employers will still fret about the lack of trained applicants to do immediate tasks. As most Europeans have known but maybe are losing sight of that is the task for the employer himself. For that kind of training, there is no substitute for it being on the job, linked precisely to the issue of earning a living. A modernised concept of apprenticeships which will have to be followed time and again by refresher training still makes sense. Some large industries may be able to support class activities, either inhouse or in association with training or technical posthigh schools. It is their responsibility.

Don't dump this on secondary schools. They have too much to do to create the dynamic fundamentals and to nurture creative aptitudes and youth maturity.

One of the concomitants of undisciplined selfexpression is the inability to communicate effectively and to discriminate between incoming messages. Disturbingly, many adults take manipulatory advantage of this.

Before World War II ideology was linked to political propaganda. Both the left but especially the right honed the skills of communicating falsity and manipulating halftruth. Crowd behaviour, mass rallies, manipulation of mass theatrical devices, endless repetition, slogans instead of thought all these were common. Mostly, educators could see them for what they were. As a youth and young man I found that classes in logic and books which showed the nature of the techniques and the logical *legerdemain* quite fascinating of course using what I had learned to support my own prejudices!

It is difficult to find such classes and books today, especially for high schools.. States still manipulate with propaganda, but, save for those which are ideologically founded, their positions are more subtle. They make use of PR firms and techniques, with communication models derived from advertising, but now being cynically distrusted as "spin". In the industrialised world the techniques of propaganda have been taken over by a kaleidoscope of pressure groups. Pressure groups organised around particular points of view and philosophies are a natural outcome of democratic life. But it behoves the citizen to see clearly the relationship between argument and data, to know the empirical base of points of view, the logic and assumptions with which it is upheld. Youth is particularly vulnerable to the power of repeated assertions, the misuse of emotion, and loud slogans – yes, even when teachers use them.

And this applies, even more, to nurturing the ability to appraise critically the numerous ideologies and unsupported "scientific" and folk claims with which all of us are confronted today. Without sacrificing independence of thought and respect for mavericks, youth needs to be able to make judgements about balderdash, mumbojumbo, "obscurantist bunkum, swirling hogwash, mendacious codswallop" and to be guided to simple expressions in their own language, avoiding the obscure language which is nowadays typical of corporations, politicians and academics[41].

Ideally, a citizen society equipped to judge and think and appraise would, by its own standards and criticisms, reveal the strengths and weaknesses of arguments, and hence punish by scepticism those who try to win by playing tricks on the mind.

There is evidence that the public senses much of this. There is widespread cynicism about political statements, derision about the way the media fasten on a limited aspect of a "story" and repeat it *ad infinitum* until it goes away, neglecting the balancing data. While many fasten upon visual scenes of horror and distress, others know that this

---

[41] I am indebted to E. S. Turner's review of Francis Wheen, *How Mumbojumbo Conquered the World, a short history of modern delusions* Fourth Estate, 2004 in the *Times Literary Supplement* Feb 14th 2004 p. 36 for the choice of epithets.

is manipulative, replacing thought and balance with blood and tears.

A few recognise that, while it is proper for children to know what demonstrations are about, what lies behind them, it is exploitative to include very young children in those demonstrations; it is abusive and brainwashing, especially at primary school age. By the secondary level, lessons in logic and rhetoric become essential for the formation of critical citizens, and teachers must be prepared to have their values and perspectives openly challenged and debated..

I am disturbed about other phenomena. The movements of the late 'sixties in the "West" properly shook up received ideas in almost all public fields, from sex to the environment. In part they did so by affirming the significance of the emotions, of feelings, of the subjective, and did indeed provided a muchneeded corrective to the idea that logic is detached from the senses and is the only path to understanding[42]. Paradoxically, however, one result was to create group tyrannies, ideologies that built dogma and used emotion, particularly anxiety, alienation and anger, to bind adherents together.

---

[42]See my *Towers Besieged: The Dilemma of the Creative University*, Toronto, McClelland and Stewart, 1974 for a fuller discussion. To be republished by Webzines of Vancouver, distributed at Lulu.com in 2010.

Out of that came positions that held certain beliefs to be absolutely right, positions shared by some, not all, parents and teachers. Schools become the loci for the transmission of such beliefs, whether they were about the dangers of nuclear catastrophe, global warming, overpopulation, depletion of nonrenewable resources, crime, sexual harassment, and much more.

Here enters a matter of difficult judgement. Such issues are indeed a matter for study and education. They will not be understood in their complexity and balance at very young ages. They must be approached at later ages. By the end of high school, pupils should be in a position to approach such topics *independently* from the teacher and with an ability to work out their position after having looked at argument and data – they should be becoming adept at finding and thinking about both.

My problems are twofold.

Many of the issues are presented in a highly charged emotional context in which adults transmit their own fears, *creating* anxieties, fears and even emotional upset in personae who are not ready for it. If this matter is not dealt with, goes the message, the apocalypse will arrive. And it is going to be *your* task to deal with it. It will be on *your* consciences. Can anyone forget the strained faces of *primary school* children in the 'fifties and 'sixties as they expressed fears of nuclear catastrophe? Now the fear that strikes home most immediately is fear of sex=AIDS, of poverty; of violence on the street, of terrorism, of unemployment, even, in some parts of the world, of the possibility that the United States will destroy our religion and culture.. Fear permeates the schools. Somehow we must replace it, not with overconfidence, but with balance, thought, belief that we *can* and *will* make a difference, by playing thoughtful roles where our capabilities count.

The second problem is that even wellmeaning and just positions are frequently tainted by dogma; and slogans replace thought. Time and again I see high school students praised in public when they trot out the latest fashionable position on a complicated issue, repeating *ad nauseam* alreadytired clichés. We do not expect worldshattering innovation from high school students. But by the end of high school clear individual, even original, statements of position, which are not simply the regurgitation of a teacher's or parent's ideology, should be the norm. This is even more serious an issue in those parts of the world where the basis of learning is by rote, and based on fundamentalist religious beliefs.

My own statements here are condensed and hence somewhat simplistic. I must go further, although even then the legitimate debate will only be opened up, by no means concluded. I would like to see schools consciously and clearly organise their approach to teaching and engendering thought around the following kinds of ideas.

Children can be helped to comprehend that understanding can be achieved through two alternative but interlinked processes. The one is subjective, intuitional and aesthetic, making use of words *and other signs* (harmonies, shapes) characteristic of "the arts". The other is rational, logical and communicable through words or similar (mathematical) signs. In making judgements about the efficacy of what is revealed, ideally the nature of the mix of the modes should be assessed. In dealing with the more subjective, it is of course interesting to pursue the influence of the creator's history and personality. This, though, is a part of knowledge itself, as revealing how it came to be, *not* part of the judgement of the significance or otherwise of the ideas themselves. Youth must understand that *ad hominem* arguments are not arguments. Whatever the nature of the communicator, it is his or her statements that count, in themselves. (It is nevertheless legitimate to interpret the *meaning* of the statements, where they are ambiguous, in terms of other signals the communicator may have given by his or her other statements and behaviour. Behaviour is then identified as a part of the statement.)

Both methods deal with ideas which consist of logical relationships, though differing in how they go about presenting them. Music consists of types of sound, notes, tones, movement, rhythm, harmonies, volume, all knit together into relationships which are the obverse of chaotic. Natural science includes the teasing out of explanations, that is relationships between this and that variable. So do the social sciences. Painting and architecture involve form. So it goes on. The horror of Hiroshima or 711 can be approached through art, communicating through visual form, the connotations of music, poems which link the act to feeling and experience, statements that show the relationship between nuclear action and catastrophe. It can also be placed in the context of, that is it can be related to, total war, generalisations about the dynamics of war and international politics, the state of the world society at the time, the linkage between that and the present, the proximal and fundamental causes of the events. All these and many more relationships are there to be explored, and full understanding needs them all. Although it is a statement of a relationship, it is superficial indeed for children to be encouraged simply to say "I think it was horrible". They must know there are other relationships involved, other generalisations to think about, approached through well constructed modes of thought and expression which we call disciplines. Disciplines are tools, tools that the young need to learn to use.

Within that mastery they may learn to criticise, be dissatisfied, with what the disciplines can do. There may here be the seeds of creative endeavour. But most of us cannot create, cannot innovate, unless we have the kinds of building blocks that schools can provide. Remember that invention and creativity are based on reordering what is know, that is the building blocks.) (Yes, it is true that some creators and innovators find their building blocks away from school, even rejecting the institution. But disciplinary building blocks they do find, nevertheless.)

Even subjective assessments involve statements about more or less, that is about quantity, whether or not the quantities can be enumerated. There is more or less beauty, subjectively speaking. Ugliness is negative beauty.

When explanations are involved there is an inherent significance in the quantities. The arts deal with single representations, unique cases   the original painting is not more or less interesting because it is replicated in prints; it is *unique* in its statements. The same applies to a theatrical or musical performance, a sculpture, a book. That is, the single case has a certain validity, which is *dependent upon its success in communicating*. The communication may be contemporaneously ineffective, but received at some future time, which makes immediate judgement problematic. Popular approval may be ephemeral, yet the relationships involved, for example in "hard metal", are in communication, and are thus there to be teased out, examined, as part of "knowledge", both subjectively and objectively. Youth needs to know these things as part of the fundamental basis of what they are "learning".

In the critical examination of what is being communicated, teachers dealing with human affairs seem to place considerable emphasis on trying to reveal the hidden agendas, the unstated values, of what is there. Quite often I feel that such revelations sometimes come from teachers' own hidden agendas and political perspectives (in some parts of the world, not so hidden). Yet the validity of the principle is indisputable. My reservation can be dealt with by teachers inviting and respecting the same critical attention to their own presentations.

Matters of equal importance, however, are not so frequently addressed. We have already noticed the value of the single case, the unique and nonreplicated statement. It is important to relate this to and distinguish it from, *explanation* in the more formal sense, not because of the nature of the revealed assertions, but because of the demands of the methodology.

This morning I was reading a front page story in a well respected and carefully presented newspaper. It dealt with ozone thinning for the coming summer, a matter of great concern and certainly a matter for school discussion. The main space in the story was contained in a full column on the front page. That consisted of repeated statements of concern, linked to such phrases as "It has been shown that". The identification of who had done the showing and how it was done was not mentioned until a very short column concluding the story on an inside page. There was not the slightest attempt to communicate any reason for accepting or rejecting the findings by representing the pros and cons of the methodology and its locus in general scientific knowledge. The implication was that the results should be accepted because they came from a reputable scientific organisation – and because the newspaper presented them.. One assumes the results to be valid until someone comes along later with another story. This is unacceptable. It is as *ad hominem* as the dismissal of a politician's ideas because of his sexual peccadilloes.

Even where data *are* presented quite fully, citizenchildren need to learn how to evaluate them. This applies especially to anecdotal and statistical material. Is the anecdotal to be considered as a unique work of art? Quite possibly. No more and no less. Since it is unique one can draw legitimate conclusions *subjectively.* Within the media anecdotal evidence does not have the same seriousness or sincerity of purpose as a major work of art. Most frequently the portrayal of incident communicates to the emotions on subjects for example crime that are open to consideration from the other, more logical, more enumerative methods. A citizenyouth must be aware of the values and emotional impact of the unique instance; but also to be able to place that in the context of knowledge obtained by other methods.

Doubt. Uncertainty. Scepticism. Yet we must act on the basis of what we know now without waiting for the ultimate truth. These are major

319

conundrums that youth have to be prepared for, have to understand if they are to live with the huge changes in knowledge that are being thrust at them.

Youth need that understanding, *and the acceptance of it* more than ever for psychological reasons. The unknown has always been a threat. Deep within ourselves, in primitive, perhaps irrational, fear, we do not know how to deal with it. It impinges on our personal lives every day, it is thrust upon us as a characteristic of the world, indeed of the universe. We correctly discuss the possibility of annihilation by projectiles from outer space. What is troublesome is the serious anxiety and stress that comes from fear of the unknown. I am not concerned here with the modes of dealing with it, from religion to witchcraft, alternative therapies or fatalism, many of which at least have the possibility of relieving stress. What are more serious are the inhibiting features, the negative pessimism, inhibition of activity, chronic anxiety and depression, which flow. Suicide among youth. Alienation.

It is fundamental to serious education that children learn to deal with the unknown, especially before a personal crisis hits them. They must examine the validity and limitations of unique experience, learning from it but not turning it into dogma. A teacher who is sick may be ill because of the effects of a new detergent in the washroom.

That is a matter for investigation. But if it turns into a dogma it can dangerously deflect investigation from some other causative possibility even one that is at present not identified.

It is a primary responsibility of school education to engender clear individual judgements about the presentation of information, and to show how youths can get to the sources themselves and at least be sceptical about inadequate materials, however persuasive the cause. What I have argued for is complex. In its sources, like everything else taught in school, it is embedded in subject matter which belongs in universities and beyond, which high school students cannot normally be expected to fully master. That in itself is not a reason for dismissing it. The principles *can* be (and often have been) taught directly in high school. And, with good pedagogical attention, they can be communicated indirectly as an aspect of normal studies.

To move toward the informed citizenship that is necessary in our goals we must reemphasise, especially in high school, the arts of logic, discourse, debate and rhetoric; the relationship between data, theory and judgement; the ability to search for, assess, and use data; the positive force of constructive criticism, both logical and aesthetic;

the role of sensory experience in arriving at observations and judgements; and the ability both to speak and to write about wellmarshalled ideas. School children should be able to test the statements of teachers with confidence and skill, but on the basis of reasoned argument and data, and mutual respect.

We want our children (grandchildren) to be educated in such a way that they utterly reject slogans, false jargon, and improperly communicated data.

The social purpose of the school links, as I have said, with other objectives than the vocational. I will be discussing the distress of the elderly who find themselves unstimulated, bored, and alienated. We know of the unemployment of youth. We know that most countries have high steady rates of unemployment and that one of the major difficulties in developing countries is linked to chronic underemployment. In other words, perhaps fifty per cent of the world's population has *unwanted* time on its hands[43]. To the extent that this is true I ask you to suspend judgement on that issue for the

[43] I will be showing in Chapter **XI** that this is likely to continue, and that, *properly handled*, our new world should value it, not reject it.

meantime the primary institution for properly handling the situation is, once again, the school. To be stated bluntly, schools must be able to help children to find ways to stimulate their leisure time and to obviate *boredom*, one of the most depressing characteristics of old age, unemployment, and youthful crime.

For this reason the educational system has a major responsibility, at least equal to the others I have outlined, to assist children in the task of discovering their selfdirected creative and recreational capacities. Modern schools do some of this, by including courses in the arts, from music to theatre, and practical skills such as carpentry and metalworking. However, when such activities are simply slotted into the timetable problems arise. They inevitably compete with one another for rare time slots, which include what most consider to be the basics, and the artistic courses become the target of parents who see them as "frills". The "practical" courses are almost always justified by vocational rather than avocational considerations. Furthermore it is impossible for schools as they are now to bring students in touch with the whole variety of possible pursuits one of which may be precisely what the student finds stimulating.

To remedy this schools would have to be able to plan and justify the activities in terms of the principles I have outlined before. Most adults will have a hard time agreeing, since the underlying argument runs counter to the philosophy, which I shall continue to dispute throughout my theses, that Work is King. Hence those responsible for educational policy will have an uphill struggle to make those policies clear, consciously advocated, and fully planned. Creative Leisure is Queen. And here we have the beginning of the thought that school as known at present are inadequate. We need something better.

Lying behind the discovery of the creative self is the challenge to learn to occupy oneself when not being supervised. A number of cultures deliberately used isolation in stressful conditions as a rite of passage. Selfreliance, even in highly interdependent communities, was necessary to survival. Isolation forced the young candidate for adulthood to know his inner being, and to know that being in its relationship to a potentially threatening nature, a nature with which the candidate learned also to be at peace. It was an exercise in being, and in spirituality. Such procedures could well be studied. So too could modes of meditation, relaxation, and emotional control.

Similar exercises can expose the values and dangers of living with small groups, mutual dependencies under stress, the uselessness of making a habit of ascribing blame to others or giving dysfunctional expressions of aggression, and learning the ways of small group diplomacy. For some young people will find their creativity not in the private actions of solitude but in the cooperation of acting with others toward a common outcome or sharing resources and skills.

It will be for the pedagogues to work out such possibilities. The objective of drawing out selfreliance and unimposed creativity carries the additional benefit of improving selfknowledge and becoming sensitised to small group interactions which have implications for family life and the workplace as well as for unpaid positive activity.

The issues lead to the conclusion that the school courseridden day is insufficient. Good schools already intrude into family life through the demands of home study. Perhaps more of that should be done in current school class time, moving some of the avocational activities as is done with sports   outside the conventional ivesparental judgements about the possibilities, and permitting, for example, more inclusion of evening and weekend cultural activities in the youth's overall preoccupations.

Carrying this theme to its ultimate conclusion will require major changes in the organisation and operation of what we now call schools in our 21st century society.

Since the school has children in its care for such an enormous proportion of their time, and since those children are subjected to so many confusing, worrying and contradictory influences in their lives, the school cannot avoid being in a position of *nurturing*. It may not want to do so, it may not be mandated to do so, and it is almost certainly not equipped to do so. Yet in this responsibility it is almost equal to that of the family.

What I have written so far has dealt mostly with the mind. But the mind is inseparable from the body, the senses, the emotions, the influences, the interactions, and the memories. *Pace* some forms of psychoanalysis, the child is far from completely formed in infancy. What happens in school will be a major influence in creating the everdynamic or staticallyconfined persona.

A great deal of this cannot be *controlled* by the individual teacher, for it is a result of the complexities of the institutional *ambience*, peers and other teachers. Individual teachers do, frequently, detect problems of concern which range from attention disorders to malnutrition and the possibility of crime. They give of themselves through advice, discipline, listening and referral. By role definition they must give priority to the effects of what they detect to the operation of the classroom and the formal work of teaching itself. Very commonly the child's personal problems can show through surly indiscipline, avoidance of work, theft, obscenity, anger, nonchalant insolence, gang behaviour, bullying and violence all the problems, in fact, that are found in the adult world, but in more vulnerable forms.

Consultation with parents may, but mostly are unlikely to, help, since teachers are not in a position in to enter into family therapy. Teachers by themselves cannot create the remedies. Yet schools have to deal with concerns, just as they are now learning to deal with the "physically and mentally challenged" oh, what wonderful and inadequate jargon to obscure the reality that the child, deprived or contorted with respect to his or her capabilities may or may not feel "challenged" but certainly needs attention and help. It is an inescapable responsibility that has serious consequences for school mandates and organisation.

All of which intersects with the issue of behavioural discipline. There has been a school of socialisation that asserts that the only legitimate form of control is that of argument. The problem is that it doesn't always work.... And when it does it can sometimes breed conformity rather than courtesy.

Hit 'em and learn 'em in righteous anger and its sadistic extremes has gone by the board in many parts of the world. There, teachers must control their reactions, however provoked. On the other hand some parents encourage their children to express their angers, which can mean placing the self before others with insolence, refusal to heed, and rejection of what the school is trying to do just as disruptive reactions as the surly introversion of unexpressed problems. More frequently than not, minor irritants of these kinds move through the classroom, as peers delightedly cheer the culprit on. Then follows open defiance, the use of appeal procedures to undermine the teacher, and the intervention of angry parents convinced they are not themselves responsible, or frustrated ones who do not know how to deal with situations that are out of control.

Indeed, in some areas I know of the school in effect has no effective powers of discipline and control, and would be totally lost if it were not for the decency of the majority of the children. There are, it is true, possibilities of assigning extra work or detentions, which the hard core can simply refuse to honour. When that happens, when violence breaks out, when there is habitual absence from the classroom, when there are drugs or weapons, the ultimate threat is there. Exile, banishment from the school. What a game! A game that tempts others who are toying with the lure of dropping out. To be officially pronounced unwelcome in the school, no longer hassled by authority, officially able to roam the streets exactly what such delinquents want......

We do not want this in our world. Not only does it represent the loss of an individual to the common good, but it is an example to the halfalienated and is disruptive of those who have other ideals. It is an instance, potentially, of the spread of an antischool innovation. Since parental responsibility is either not there or is insufficient, the school itself must develop other tools, even though, without outside help, it cannot get at root problems such as dysfunctional family life.

There are two methods at least which might help. As I write this I read of an experiment in Toronto. Youths expelled for violence are identified as such and transferred to another specialist programme for them only. Instead of roaming the streets each student works (expensively) with a psychiatrist and a programme coordinator. In the pilot programme, fifty per cent of the students have been judged ready to return to regular schooling. At least for the others some education is achieved. My information does not reveal what happens if the youths refuse to cooperate, nor what kind of family involvement is in place. Nevertheless the thought behind such approaches deserves attention.

Another method, also being experimented with in various contexts, is to involve the children themselves in peer responsibility, and to give them some of the tools to do so. As in so many other cases, older methods which have gone out of psychological fashion (such as the use of prefects) have been ridiculed on the basis of extreme caricature. All methods, old or new, have their defects. Perhaps one should look again, and tease out the positive from the negative.

Many schools nowadays have some form of student council, a useful way of enabling, usually the better, pupils to voice difficulties and to organise events. There are also emergent studentteacher initiatives, such as plays and discussions, which aim at demonstrating such topics as the handling of violence when it occurs, the difficulties of sex, or the release of anger. Even in primary schools selected children are trained in mediation, intervening in quarrels to persuade quarrellers to look at each others' points of view, to find ways out of the situation before it explodes.

Experiments of these kinds are novel, welcome, and full of hope. But they cannot deal effectively with every situation, and cannot always be on top of day to day incidents. We shall see part of the remedy in the reorganisation of proposed Youth Maturity Institutes below.

It seems that the old idea of a "school spirit" based on identification with the school, pride in what it attempts to do, rivalry with others, and internal pupilbased discipline, is worth another look. As with any other type of cultural or subcultural identity, it can go too far, with autocracy emerging, too much interference in private acts, too much peer pressure, and, in extreme instances, schools becoming rivalrous gangs. What is different nowadays, and even more we hope in the future, is that in the developed world the teachers who have the ultimate responsibility are better informed about such dangers and are likely to be more sensitive to their emergence.

Let us then consider reinventing (where it has to be reinvented) the system of prefects for day schools. Let there be chosen leaders at various levels in the school, with responsibilities according to the degree of maturity that their age can handle. Senior prefects might very well act as disciplinary agents and interveners under policies formulated by, or with the assistance of, the student council. Let them have the authority to discipline for designated infractions   giving detentions for example; to maintain order and respect on school premises and at school functions; to report serious infractions; to present constructive ideas to council and staff; in short to supervise, *on behalf of the student body*, standards of good order and courtesy.

One of the primary tools that street gangs use to reinforce solidarity and identity, is dress and body decoration. They do so naturally, out of spontaneous recognition of principles that are as old as human groups. Schools in many parts of the world, and especially North America, deliberately gave away this reinforcing tool. In some form, whether through simple uniforms or badges, it needs to return. It is one way of enhancing pride. I am on my mettle because I can be seen to be a *member* of the school that has a great team, organises volunteers for a social cause, puts on an exciting art show, or perhaps, even, is the place where academic achievement gets us going. At least when I'm wearing that uniform outside of school I behave; I'm noticeable and proud of it. [I'm well aware that the wearing of uniforms at schools where state schools do *not* wear them is an identifier of difference that is often not acceptable and is even embarrassing to the wearers. Acceptance changes when the custom is *general*.]

The easiest part of this discussion is to write the words; the most difficult to interpret the principles in specific contexts, to give them pedagogical content and reality, to make them work. None of my statements can be considered as an absolute.

First and foremost it is the teachers who have the responsibility for method and content, for the specifics of classroom and school. They claim to be, and are, and should be, the professionals. It is what they have learned, their experience, their skills, that makes the difference. But those skills, as with any profession, must work in context, the context of societal aims, immediate culture, and changing knowledge.

One of the realities is that henceforth they will be working in a society that changes ever more rapidly, and that they must secondguess what the needs of the future may be. Is that to be toward some vision of Utopia, a world in which we wish ourselves to live, even though we may never see it in our lifetimes? Some vision of a better world? I hope so. But if so that kind of ultimate purpose needs discussion, needs teacher attention, needs definition, even though that definition is bound to change over the decades.

This is a area that lies beyond the horizons of teachers alone. Teachers are in a position to be arbiters of society, communicating (deliberately or without noticing it) their own values. But they do not have the mandate to *decide* where society should go. In that they are simply one set of citizens. Who then does? The interplay of parents, nonparent voters, political and community leaders, teachers, other professionals who, as we shall see, are involved with the same objectives.

Teachers then, as it were, interpret the objectives. The trouble is that the objectives, at this stage in our evolution, are not spelled out for society as a whole (except, for example, in fundamentalist religious schools or autocratic state systems), and can only be defined in simplistic and programmatic terms, tinged with political ideology. Just the same, some observations can be made.

One is that in a future world society and culture not only *will* consist of varying groups, cultures or subcultures, with nonuniform ideas, but *should* do so. The reality of the statement for contemporary societies is beyond dispute. Look within your country. It is there[44].

To the extent that this is so, it follows that schools *must* themselves vary. The concept that each State school must have an identical, centrally determined, philosophy, curriculum, and pedagogy is now revealed for what it is, an ideology based upon a false sociocultural premise, upon a false objective that we should all be the same, and upon an impractical establishment.

Ideally, varying schools should match variations in child response to varying methods, varying parental philosophies, and variations in cultural realities, at least. Such clear matching is seldom practicable, but close approximations are possible. Perhaps the following principle is worthy of thought: schools and teachers within schools should have the utmost flexibility to exercise their ideas in directions which link with a recognised dream and educational philosophy; but no child should be forced into a particular school. Choice

[44] This point is expanded in Chapter VI, Community and Diversity and has been foreshadowed in out discussion of innovation.

that is now available to some (the better off) should be available to all.

Such a principle implies that variation should not merely be between state schools and private schools, religious schools, schools for the rich and the not so rich. State systems themselves need to abandon the assignment of children to schools on the sole criterion of geographical proximity, a policy which derives from the false notion that equity and equality of opportunity imply pushing every child into the same cauldron. Equity and equality of opportunity imply the opposite, that every child should be in the school that suits him or her best. The identification of what is "best" will not be accurate. It involves parents' ideals and parents' knowledge both of the child and of the nature of each possible school, a knowledge that will undoubtedly change with time and experience.

Hence movement of pupils between schools must be possible. And schools must provide parents with information   documentation, for example, about its educational philosophy and goals, its methods, its achievements, what it is trying to do better. *Every school in the system should be required to formulate and enunciate its point of view.* Every piece of data that bears on the parents' potential evaluation of the school should be public.

One specious argument against the idea is that once it is known that one or two schools meet needs better than others they will become elite, based on restricted entry. Of course that is possible, but it reveals inflexibility in the school system. (It may also involve prejudice and lack of knowledge of the alternatives.) It may encourage some other schools to emulate. But in addition it will be the case that there will be no single definition of "better". Parents will not be like lemmings, moving in one single direction. Schools that meet children's varied educational needs best require replication; others require downsizing.

The two most difficult sources of inflexibility are teachers and buildings. If choice reveals that certain wanted types of teaching are not reflected in the distribution of teacher skills, then, at least in an adjustment period, some individual teachers will be in difficulty. The implications are that in the long run teacher education itself should teach less dogma and more adaptability; that there should be maximum support for teacher reeducation; and that unadaptable teachers will have to go or be assigned elsewhere to a school where their skills fit bretter.

At present the conditions under which teachers do their work are highly variable, country to country, sometimes responding to bargaining conditions, sometimes to social status, sometimes to poverty, sometimes to religious ideology. However I do not know of any countries in which the conditions of work and education, except in some of the most expensive private schools, correspond to the need. Sometimes good principles have been subverted by union action and bargaining into privileged "rights". This is not professional.

Days off for professional education, in which the school closes; long summer vacations, originally to permit children to undertake agricultural tasks such arrangements, fiercely union protected, become inflexible, inefficient, rulebound, subject to abuse, and archaic. The first, for example, are often boring, not observed by individual teachers, and, while sometimes useful, are not administered to face up to improving and updating the skills of *individual* teachers. That requires more than the occasional discussion or lecture, but weeks of analysis and education. Teaching, especially in high school, is an evermoving profession, in the roles required, and in the subject matter. Educational updating requires much more, witgh longer term refresher courses and opportunities for serious debate.

It is a normal fact of employment that teachers in most systems take their classes home with them, figuratively and also literally. Much of their work consists of outofclass paper work, including marking and preparation. When classes take place throughout the day, either teachers stay very late at school, or work at home, with effects not only on their own domestic arrangements but on overworked stresd. The short breaks between classes, or class time off, are seldom adequate to do serious work. Despite what the public regards as soft and privileged work time, teachers in most advanced systems are typically stressed out, under constant emotional and psychological pressure, especially when dealing with undermotivated, tumultuous children; to say nothing of those with severe personal problems. Moves in several systems to mix "special needs" children into conventional classes, while highly desirable in theory, add to teacher stress (especially when the teacher has no education in the specialty of the needs) and divert him or her from attention given to the ordinary, who, in their own ways, are just as needy. Unless very special measures are taken, such moves are typical of the ways in which principles can come to grief because the material and organisational resources are not adjusted sufficiently.

If to these present difficulties we add the requirements of striving for our ideal world, without other adjustments, mayhem and breakdown could destroy what little is left of the high school system. Any reforms must be built around the capacities, physical and mental, of the staff teachers *and others* whose task it is to deliver.

In many systems the school year is built around terms divided by short breaks one, two, or three weeks instead of a concentration of holidays on a long two month summer break typical of others, during which the dynamic of school progress can be threatened. A number of breaks of around two weeks enables the progression of teaching with little interruption of the dynamic, especially if some of the breaks are designated for projects, independent study, alternative creative activities. Such breaks provide an opportunity for teacher refresher courses as well.

Teachers are not only overworked but also inefficiently directed. Some systems provide teachers with, not just the occasional class off during the week, but up to an equivalent of classroom time for study and preparation. Initially, in systems where teachers are not accustomed to that, the provision of such time could be significantly abused. Many teachers are simply not used to the idea that handling the subject matter requires continual research and reading. Such teachers would not know what to do with their time, except paper work, until guided into its effective use. (Are there still teachers who have the time, the drive, the energy, the knowledge, to *contribute* to the growth of knowledge, to undertake research, however modest; even perhaps to involve their classes in that activity? Yes there are. They should be among the role models, though it is too much to make that a formal requirement until our brave new world is here.)

An efficient educational system requires a surplus of resources beyond those immediately used in the classroom. Contrary to the drives of budgetminded administrators, if you show me an educational institution of serious intent in which all classrooms are being used at every minute of the day, and in which there are no teachers outside the classroom, I will show you a static, unresponsive, bureaucratised, antieducational operation, unable to meet society's needs.

Why? When considering the distribution of teachers, it should be obvious that they should be pedagogically sound and know their subject matter. In secondary schools particularly, it is not good enough to say, as some have, "Give me a class and

I'll teach it anything." That is the sure way to superficiality. But teachers take ill, the ideal system would require them to take time off for formal reeducation, and they must have an opportunity to take real holidays that would involve being absent for terms. Redistribution among existing teachers, reposting, now often means assigning teachers to subject areas of which they know little or nothing. Short term replacements are often temporary substitute teachers, which may often be effective in individual cases. But as a *system* it cannot be efficient. Such substitutes usually have to have other sources of income and cannot afford to place themselves in a oneline teaching career position; their standards and updating cannot therefore be rigorously controlled. Both these situations *require a pool* of subjectoriented teachers in the career stream available for replacement allocation. Members of the pool would not be in the classroom until called upon, but would be salaried.

I have been referring to refresher education. The movement of school responsibilities into nonvocational and therapeutic fields, as I am about to propose, will increase the range of required specialties, of differing combinations of skills. School professionals, just like health professionals, will in some instances be stimulated to recombine their skills: a combination of language teaching and family therapy might be a case in point. And just like health professionals, or university professors in North America who are seeking promotion, they will require formal certification, from time to time, of their continued pedagogic and coexistent subject area skills.

As I write I am living in an urban area in which the distribution of the population is changing fast. Immigrants are arriving in substantial numbers, finding living space in new areas, and needing educational courses (such as language) which differ from those of the past. Some locations are no longer affordable for new growing families in the same numbers. Changing technology requires new subject matter which is unevenly developed and which requires altered forms of teaching and working space. New interactive multimedia teaching tools again require new forms of space to be effective even bringing the home into the classroom (especially with web based distance learning). Old school buildings are sometimes emptying, and some cannot be adapted easily to new teaching needs.

Demographic forecasts are notoriously affected by value and political judgements and are seldom reliable in detail. Educational authorities are thus reluctant to spend large capital sums on new buildings when the trend that demands them may be applicable only, say, for six or seven years. They meet the need by throwing up temporary portaclassrooms, which parents immediately identify as substandard and discriminatory.

Yet the flexibility afforded by mobile classrooms is clearly more desirable than the inflexibility of monuments hewed in stone. The unresolved problem suggests that the expenditure of money, efficiency of operation, and educational flexibility and quality will be best where buildings can respond to differing needs from decade to decade instead of dominating and freezing the delivery of service. If this is so, then there is a major architectural challenge to design school buildings which can easily be moved from one location to another, which consist of modules of differing functions which can be combined and recombined to fit changing educational needs, and which, probably, are less expensive than conventional structures. Paradoxically, this may be more easily achievable in developing tropical countries, making use of traditional structures which can be removed and rebuilt with less cost. Here is a field for UNESCO innovation.

Someone has to take decisions and to provide resources in an environment in which, at least in the short term, resources are getting scarcer. The desirable specifics will vary so much from one system to another that I can only write in generalities. But it should be clear by now that we need to rethink the structure and operation of what we now call schools, if they are to properly educate, nurture and create cohorts of welladjusted future citizens.

The initiative to establish and design variable schools will come mostly from parents, from some teachers, and from some citizens. Since it is the community providing the funds, it is likely that what I will call the Youth Maturity Institute management authority will be vested in an overall area board which allocates funds and authorises establishments. The board will need to represent the taxpayers and those who elect the political authority; it should also have representatives of parents and teachers (not in their selfseeking but in their professional capacities); and it might be beneficial to have representatives from senior high school classes. The danger in such a board is that each of these constituencies will provide members, elected or chosen, whose debates will result in some sort of majority opinion. The danger then is that the majority will be seen as having a political mandate to exercise that opinion throughout the system, giving no voice to alternative philosophies and styles. This is the opposite of what we are endeavouring to achieve. Hence it seems essential that the terms of reference for such a board require as a matter of law that the board recognises the principles of school, now Youth Maturity Institute, variation.[45]

As I have said, each individual Institute should be required to establish and publicise its philosophy and methods, paying special attention to its unique character. The initiative for doing this should come from both parents and teachers *and other professional contributors* acting in concert. Until our world becomes less confrontational there will undoubtedly be conflict between opposing philosophies; someone will lose out. The area supervisory board needs to ensure that the Institute management council losers will be accommodated,

---

[45] In late 2005 the press reported that the United Kingdom government is planning to remove schools from Local Council jurisdictions, giving them greater control over their curricula, philosophies and operations. It has been interpreted as moving the principles of the public = private schools into the state sector and giving more weight to independent religious schools. This is a step in the direction toward Youth Maturity Institutes but I have not seen reference to any required element of material such as risk taking, elimination of violence, or the integration of therapy professionals into the system. We do not expect the full implementation of Youth Maturity Institutes to be achieved over night.

that there is another school for them to join, or that one can be organised. Considerable initial adjustment is likely to take place, a necessary price for the achievement of the ultimate goals.

I deliberately placed the phrase "other professional contributors" in this context. There are now in fact examples not only of private schools in the conventional sense but of schools established by large industrial firms. Such schools are in response to two drives. One is the improvement in working conditions when working parents have onpremise schools (especially for younger children) with recreational as well as classroom space. Parents can visit in their breaks, and their children will be occupied instead of returning home to an empty house.

Another motivation, for upper year youth, is vocational training. It is very doubtful if adequate applied training for the workplace can be conducted effectively in conventional schools. It is often best done on site. Large firms can do this with either narrowly focused classes, in association with and supplementing Institutes, leading to apprenticeships or by actually locating and financing upper year broad education on their premises.

The feasibility of such schemes does not have to be limited to commerce and industry. The civil service, hospitals, universities, large public service and charitable organisations also have roles. Education affects us all; it percolates throughout; the barriers should be of malleable rubber.

A similar principle works in reverse. The objectives of the proposed Institutes run far beyond the capacity of conventional schools to honour. This implies not that the objectives are wrong but that school capabilities must be altered to meet them. The most ineffective way of doing this is to throw money at schools and teachers. For most teachers are not educated to carry out many of the tasks (such as therapy for a suicidal youth), and do not have the time or energy even if they were equipped to do so. And school management would have to undergo a revolution to assess and address the broadened role; managers notoriously find this difficult although there are many innovative school heads and principals trying new approaches which have to be dubbed "experimental".

We are dealing with the "whole" child. We are seeking a holistic education. The state of knowledge and professionalization of society create more and more specialists who are dealing with various parts of that whole. Their perspectives need to be brought together, and *the use of their manpower optimised*. There is dreadful duplication, waste, uncoordination, and confusion, not in the best interests of the child.

In order to achieve our vision, the concept of "school" as an institution with a narrow mandate needs to be jettisoned. They should be replaced by organisations which are mandated and equipped to nurture children and youths in a holistic manner toward the objectives of individual maturation.

As I have hinted, let us call these, until a better term is devised, "Youth Maturity Institutes."

First, each Youth Maturity Institute should have a management committee in which teachers, parents and representatives of youths from the final class should be represented. The task of the management committee should be to ensure that the teachers and staff in their day to day operation, act in accordance with the approved school philosophy, and to organise the operation of the Institute.

Second, each Youth Maturity Institute should have an advisory committee consisting of members appointed by the various bodies in the community concerned with the welfare of youth. To the extent that they bear upon the philosophy of the school and the needs of its operation, there could be included, for example, representatives of churches, youth organisations, social services, the media (not for "stories" but as being perceived as partly "responsible" for what goes on), police, medical services, employers, unions, and high school pupils. It would consider identified problems (such as drugs, violence, for example), the bearing of all of the services on each of those problems, possible coordination and changes of policy, not only in the Youth Maturity Institute but in the institutions which surround it.

Third, there would need to be a fundamental reappraisal of financing, the conception of "school hours", and personnel. We are dealing not only with the classroom where the teacher is paramount, but with recreation, and individual and family counselling (not in the vocational but in the psychological sense) with wide ramifications.

What has to come is the redirection of appropriate outside services into the Youth Maturity Institute itself. Social service youth and family counsellors should move their offices and operations into the Institute, be seconded into the Institute from their bureaucracies, and have their budgets identified as part of the Institute budget, subject to Institute management.

Other organisations which have a bearing on school programmes need to be brought more formally into the Institute budget and field of responsibility. For example, the Youth Maturity Institute, in the running of its theatre programmes, might contract with a theatre company or organisation to do part or all of it, to the benefit of both. Many organisations concerned with the culture of creativity, or the creativity of culture should be more intimately involved with Youth Maturity Institutes, both on premises and off. Such contact would have the additional advantage of introducing children to the hard reality of creation (without putting them off), giving the starry eyes something to focus upon[46].

Since we are proposing an institution which has a holistic view of youth development, it follows that therapeutic and judicial functions[47] should be removed from external organizations and integrated with the Youth Maturity Institutes. This gives the Institutes opportunities to adopt therapeutic and restitutional procedures in the case of violence and delinquency. It enables them, in each case, to focus on the troubled youth and to take as long as it takes, and by whatever means it takes, to reintegrate the youth into peer society. The use of therapy, even of medical knowledge, and of alternative ways of

---

[46] And it would have an effect on the role of and support for such groups

[47] This relates to the reform of the "justice" system in Chapter **V**

dealing with crime come together in one set of coordinated actions which in a formal judicial system is limited by professional bureaucracies and often stymied by the state of the law. Healing circles, psychotherapy, peer group and parental influences will all be part of the considerations as the youth is challenged to recognize the damage he or she has caused, and to make restitution to those who have been hurt. Incarceration or expulsion will not be part of the answer, although indigenous methods of spiritual isolation may well be in some instances. The issue is made more complex by the discovery that there is a gene which influences antisocial behaviour, though it can be overridden by appropriate environmental and therapeutic circumstances.[48] Restitution, recognition, reintegration are the three 'r's. Such an approach will relate to major reforms in the judicial and legal systems which I will be proposing.

Clearly parents are intimately involved. Frequently they react defensively, protecting the family boundary, or from the shame of guilt and

---

[48] There is a thirty year study of this matter by S.A. Mednick, W.F. Gabrielli and B. Hutchings "Genetic influences in Criminal Convictions: Evidence from an Adoption Court" in *Science* vol 224. no. 79, 1984 which traces the behaviour of those with the gene. Quoted in in Jane Walfogel, *What Children Need* Cambridge, Harvard University Press, 2006,

perplexity. If a child acts aggressively or criminally the cause may not be in the family. Or it may be. We need medical and therapeutic analysis. Parents should not be fingered immediately as the culprits. But they must be brought to understand, helped to deal with the issues and change their habits, and given support, together with the child. Not even "special needs" teachers can do this by themselves. There has to be team work in the Institutes, another reason for stressing the need to use them to replace schools.

Paradoxically, the more such methods succeed the more inner tensions may arise, unless another theme is addressed. For underlying a certain percentage of delinquency is the attraction and excitement of taking risks[49]. Street car racing, experimenting with drugs and sex, toting an hand gun or knife, using machetes in moments of hysteria. Logical argument will have only a small effect when such youth drives are paramount. Recognitions of consequences in dramatic form, the experience of devastation, will. But it requires a more widespread policy.

---

[49] For the attitude of legal authorities to "precautionary risk" see Sunstein, Cass R. *Laws of Fear*. Cambridge and New York, Cambridge University Press, , 2005

Bronislaw Malinowski's dictum "Let cricket replace warfare" has become a cliché, but deserves attention for all that. For the ills I am addressing it is far too soft. Many – not all – boys and an increasing number of girls want risky challenges, both mental and physical, without which they cannot move knowledgeably into adulthood. Show me a road racer and I will show you a school that is too bland in its challenges. This is an essential part of education, which cannot be completed in the classroom. Youth Maturity Institutes, as do a number of schools, for example in the Duke of Edinburgh's network, need to plan to encourage and support appropriate risk taking. Recently a Canadian private school decided to drop challenging winter skiing because of tragic deaths from an avalanche. On the assumption that all reasonable precautions were taken, the cancellation was a mistake. Risk taking implies just that, risk taking. Mollycoddling so that there are no risks defeats the purpose – and there will be accidents along the way, or the risk will not be there.

Schools are in fact better at devising intellectual risk taking tests mathematical or chess challenges and competitions for example. But these reach only the elite. Professionals must devise ways in which the youth at whatever level, feels challenged, excited by even small accomplishments, prompted to risk the next stage.

Fear and anxiety are the concomitants of risk taking. Both are normal states even when risk is not at the forefront. Over the decades there have been enormous fears, communicated to school children, about atomic bombs, nuclear war, ecological disaster, poisonous foods. These have been communicated by teachers, parents and the media. There is no justification for this. On the other hand fear and anxiety are a normal part of risk and should be accepted as a normal state. Youth must learn to deal with them constructively in order to reach maturity and the Institutes have a major role in developing ways for this to happen.

At the same time there are those for whom various forms of fears and anxieties, phobias, Invade ordinary life in circumstances which may be deemed unwarranted, leading to the serious inhibition of appropriate behaviour. Again, the Institutes will have a pivotal role, not so much through teachers, though they may draw attention to the issue, but for therapists and parents.

Youth Maturity Institutes would accumulate an immense amount of experience and knowledge of direct interest to those dealing with social issues outside the Institutes themselves. Schools in my part of the world seem to have an almost nil impact on the fatally growing use of methadone and other drugs. They are not equipped to do so. But Youth Maturity Institutes would be. I would find it very difficult to believe that such Institutes, operating effectively, would not know the sources of the drug. They could combine an attack on crystal methadone with risk taking – for example assigning young atrisk victims to accompany police on inner city drug beats. Show them what doctors and nurses have to go through to deal with extreme cases. Remember that therapists, doctors and police are involved directly in the Institutes. The synergy that comes from the juxtaposition of professionals with quite different perspectives will lead to many innovative ideas. And it is one thing to lecture and to show a documentary but quit another to visit the live scene, prisons and hospitals.

The needs of poor countries require special comment. In many of the poor countries' rural areas, despite the trauma of war, and migration disruptions, and the ever present threat of famine, floods, and the depredations of both nature and man, the absence of a sophisticated therapeutic and institutional structure need not hold back a movement to reform. In some societies there are already male agespecific initiation rituals which can be adapted to go the youth maturity route. This is seldom the case for girls, other than, say, the declaration of puberty. Closely knit communities and kinship bonds do not mean the absence of internal strife, and they are sometimes the very sources of dissatisfaction and emigration. Nevertheless, skilled attention to their positive elements can aid the process.

Despite this, poverty and a natural emphasis on the less personal processes of development create national priorities in which youth maturity may take a back seat. Thus the capability to establish functioning Youth Maturity Institutes will depend on the success of developing countries to gain reasonable levels of living – and hence upon other aspects of the globe which I approach in later Chapters.

Much the same concerns relate to possible resistances from conservative religions, such as, perhaps, forms of Islam. It is *not* the intention of my discussion to advocate the forcible imposition of a particular form of Youth Maturity Institutes on specific cultures, where a Western model may not be appropriate. It would however be demeaning to assume the contrary, that modern Islam is somehow contrary to the principles of such Institutes. There are many educational practices in some parts of Islam which are contrary to the precepts of the

Institutes – in some instances, for political reasons, violence is advocated; in others learning is by submission and rote. But no one can accuse reformist Turkey, preSaddam Iraq, or Iran, at least in the cities, of not having educational values and achievements which would be entirely compatible with their own variants on Youth Maturity Institutes.

There is no time to lose. We need the generations which Youth Maturity Institutes will create. Without those generations, the rest of the task of creating our desirable world by 2100 will be a rough ride. We expect the Institutes will minimize human tendencies to violence against and disrespect for others. This is needed to give us the risk taking courage to reform the totality of society. Fortunately, if we have the will, the replacement of schools with Youth Maturity Institutes need not be a long drawn out affair. It could be accomplished in many parts of the world by 2050. Globally, UNESCO (pending the United Nations changes I recommend later in this book) could take a lead role in nudging States to take action, and spreading the word and the message. In order to remove violence from the world and to create mature citizens there will need to be policies of an effective new kind of global government.

Education and global government depend directly upon each other.

That having been said, there are no quick automatic results. There will be trial, error, mistakes. After the introduction of Youth Maturity Institutes, critics and naysayers point out "But there has been no reduction in violence". Of course not, in the short term. It will take a minimum of twelve years for those entering the new system to mature out of it. It will take longer for them to parent new intakes and to find their roles in society. We must learn to be patient and not give in to short term desperation.

Social structure and cultural values as related to economic growth

First published in the *International Social Science Journal* vol. xvi no.2 pp. 21728 1964

The ways in which the anthropological notions of value and of social structure can be related to the process of economic growth are examined. Nine propositions which indicate the manner in which certain characteristics of value and social structure affect economic growth, including statements which imply a neutral effect, are then set out.

There will clearly be a variety of contexts in which economic growth can take place successfully. The institutions of Japan, the United States, the U.S.S.R. and China differ substantially, yet permit growth to take place, at differing rates and with variations in emphasis. One wonders whether it is possible to go beyond the particularities of specific institutions and cultural patterns to generalize in a useful way about the significance of relationships. Presumably, the analysis will not posit a direct relationship between one or more items of social structure or of values and income growth. The relation□ships will be indirect, and will influence the component parts of a system of production and distribution.

Among the significant elements **iii** such a system will be authority and decisiontaking, the availability and use of material resources and Qf skills, organization, a distributive mechanism, and *an* adaptive inte□gration. To some degree, values and social structure influence the nature of each ofthe~e elements, and their ability to perform adequately within the system.

II

The experience has often been noted that terminological and semantic confusions, together with differences in the type of analysis for which concepts have been developed, have tended to keep economists and anthro□pologists apart. The notion of 'value' is a case in point. Rather than argue for a proper or correct use of the term, I shall distinguish three important differences in usage and endeavour to relate each of them to the topic of economic growth.

The first is the group of ways in which the idea of value relates to the degree to which action will be exchanged for satisfaction or goalachieve□ment. A more usual way of stating this would be to say that values are wants, with the implication that preference schedules, opportunity costs, and similar frames of reference are related to them. However, I wish to use the less usual formulation for a number of reasons. One is that I wish to subsume within this group such ideas as 'the value of money' and 'the value of leisure', using the common denominator of action. It is then necessary to draw attention to the cost elements in action, such as the provision of resources, the sacrifice of time and foregone opportunities, the exercise or acquisition of skills, and the use of organization, and to assume that the relationship between value and cost will determine whether or not a partic□ular want or preference will become prepotent.

To do this in any sense which is acceptable to an anthropologist implies a serious return to some of the older positions taken in the theory of consump□tion, and to examine these in a manner which contemporary anthropology should make possible. For example, there is today a tendency in both economics and anthropology to treat such behaviour in rational terms, and to imply that such concepts are not relevant where irrationality rules. To a large degree, this is because anthropologists have been frightened off by the apparently *a priori* assumptions of rationality which dominate the logical abstractions of economic modelbuilding, and partly because economists assume that market behaviour, when dominated by firms, can be rational and tend to exclude the strange goals of alien cultures from their models. The assumption of rationality is not necessary, however, since all we are stating is that there is an empirical relationship between cost, value and effective demand.

To give reality to the equations is necessary to include nonmaterial as well as material wants and costs, and to relate them. In some writing, this is done in a halfhearted way. We speak of the 'preference for leisure', of 'psychic costs' and of 'immaterial benefits'. In order to create the sticks and carrots of an economic system, and to predict public reaction to their application, it is not enough merely to record that such preferences, costs and benefits exist. It is necessary to know, for example, at what point members of a society will decide that the preference for leisure is too costly, and begin to shift towards other goals; or the degree to which a society will use its consumption income for increased religious or ceremonial expen diture; or whether one can expect a greater demand for transistor radios than for books; or whether villagers, for whom a road and market have improved income, will spend on village amenities or be awakened to the delights of the town and migrate.

Clearly, there are difficulties in making this kind of analysis for any given situation. To deal in futures is always risky, to establish accurate elasticity functions without statistical series or monetary prices may be well nigh impossible. But to adopt the position at the opposite extreme by predicting demand and supply reactions on the Western model, and rele gating irregular responses to the category of inexplicable irrationalities is dangerous. This is particularly the case when the problem is to create a national dynamic economic system pretty well for the first time, for under such circumstances authorities are concerned with bringing about funda mental changes in value: cost ratios so that new patterns of action emerge. This is what the anthropologist calls cultural change.

In practical terms, the proposition emerges that national planning systems should pay fundamental attention to actual and potential cultural change,

translated as far as possible into a series of cost:
value ratios (in the above senses), in order to
predict possible directions for the economy.

A second approach to the idea of value is that of
cultural pattern or theme. Such approaches have a
number of variations of emphasis. They take the
ideational content of a culture and show that it
contains a corpus of consistencies, which may
relate to the world view or conceptual predilections
of the culture, or to the psychiatric implications of
the social structure, or to the effects of a particular
kind of resource base. Once the consistencies have
been identified, the analyst may show that action is
normally related to them, and may therefore be in a
position to predict whether behaviour changes will
be acceptable. In essence, these are at tempts to
create theoretical structures which shortcut value
analysis.

If the policy of economic growth is related to
the maintenance of the preexisting cultural system,
or if it is determined that the preexisting system
must be taken into account in assessing the costs or
desirability of change, the thematic analysis of
values can be highly useful. It may also be
extremely useful when it can point out that
elements in the thematic structure can be hitched to
a production or consumption dynamic, provided
that certain of the ethnocentric notions of the
planners can be modified. Thus, inflation of
ceremonial exchange, Ghandian philosophy, or the
demands of a harem, may, under appropriate
circumstances, he related to increased production
and circulation of wealth.

At the same time, it must be recognized that the
analysis deals in norms, and since it tends to neglect
aberrant features in a culture, may he static rather
than dynamic. I do not want this issue to be
confused with the question of mobility or

adaptability within a traditional social system, a question I shall refer to later. I am referring here to the frequent occurrence of cultural change when circumstances make it possible for ideas and behaviour to conflict with the currently established themes. The aberrant or abnormal or inconsistent person gains an opportunity to make his point or establish his mode of action.

It may well be that some economists and political figures have made too much of the apparent need for a revolutionary change in traditional mores in order to permit a breakthrough into continued economic growth. If so, I do not wish to appear to be on their side, for this can be the lazy way of avoiding the attempt to find, within traditional societies, the dynamic rnainsprings of change. But the opposite error is also possible, namely to concentrate so firmly upon the consistent themes of society that the poten￼tiality of the contribution of the non—conformist is overlooked.

A third method of approaching value is to consider it to he the enduring ethos *of* a culture, expressed primarily in moral judgcments or statements of desirability. This approach is of considerable significance in anthropology, since behind it lies the authority of Kluckhohn, and the influence of his work and that of his followers, particularly in the Rimrock project. When the word ~value' is used in anthropology at the present time, this is the sense that immediately comes to mind. Nevertheless, as I have explained iii another context,' I regard this as an approach which does not readily link with the notion of value in other disciplines. \While it constitutes part of the data which might be brought to bear in order to perform the exercises suggested in the paragraphs relating to the first two approaches to the idea of value, it is primarily an analysis of comparative world view and moral philosophy, and relates only indirectly to effective 01' potential demand as action.

Clearly, there may be highly significant moral issues which may affect the orientation of behaviour towards or away from economic growth. At one level, there is the Protestant ethic. At another, there are duties arid proscriptions such as the Muslim approach to interest, or the Hindu respect for cattle. However, as Kurt Samuelsson[2] has shown convincingly, it is not at all clear whether the Protestant ethic followed or preceded the rise of capitalism; it was contained within very different religious systems, and where stated explicitly it was against capitalism rather than for it. On a broad scale. Samuelsson[50] has shown the ethic to he largely neutral in its effects. In addition, even relatively rigid systems such as that of Muslim theology are capable of considerable amendment and modification, and specific taboos of the Hindu type which have an important effect on economic growth are limited both in number and significance. I would argue that, since human beings have a considerable capacity to rationalize, philosophical systems are seldom in themselves an impediment to economic growth, and that it is not necessary to assume a particular kind of philosophy as a pre]requisite. Such a position, it seems to me, is consistent with another anthropological view, namely that mythology consists in the manipulation of symbols to justify and legitimize action *and* interests.

---

[50] *Religion and Economic Action,* London, Heineman, 1957

III

To concern oneself with social structure is to analyse relationships between roles, and between institutions, associations, and groups as functioning entities. In this connexion I wish to draw attention to three sets of problems of general interest to economic grovth. These are the structural forms with respect to which economic *growth* may or may not take place, the degree to which adaptability is possible within relevant social structures, and the instrumental effectiveness of elements of a social structure.

Each society has its own range of principles which govern social relation□ships. Since many of these are deeply internalized, are habitual and intan□gible rather than consciously designed, and are not normally directly attacked by Western technicians or reformers who often do not understand their nature, they are relatively enduring. This is particularly the case, for example, in family structure, and in the structural arrangements of small groups which may be concerned with decision making. I am not arguing, of course, that such structural arrangements are unchanging in the face of pressure, hut merely that there is a conservative element. I then go on to ask: in so far as traditional social arrangements do retain their older forms, what can he said about their effect on economic growth?

The reason for putting the question in this way is that there still seems to be a considerable body of opinion which would hold that social structure must approximate Western forms before economic growth can be expected. This should be disputed on theoretical and on empirical grounds.

Positively, a social structure represents the

framework within which persons act and organize to get things done. To give some examples, when I appealed to individual acc₁uisitiveness iii Fiji to persuade villagers to build me a small jeep bridge, they performed a shoddy job because their individual interests were elsew3hcre. When I was able to relate the same requirement to a contract based on structural relations between my own social unit and theirs, with the appropriate symbolic manipulations of structured ceremonial exchange, a firstclass piece of work was done. Again, lineage principles of whatever form can be used for the mobilization of capital and labour; the family structure of China and Japan can he as significant in the formation of enterprises as was that of Europe in the early days of the industrial revolution.

My contention at this point is that social structure does not in itself either inhibit or promote economic growth. It does, however, have an important hearing upon the forms of organization for economic growth which are appropriate in given circumstances. Thus, if economic planners can identify the principles of cooperation and adaptation which are inherent iii their society, the)' should be in a position to mobilize these to provide vehicles for organization. To do otherwise would be to overlook an important creative potential, and perhaps to engage in unnecessary schism and controversy, diverting attention from the real issues. It is not necessary to turn a matrilieage into a patrilineage or to create a nuclear family before economic growth can take place, and to attempt to do so may delay the takeoff for a considerable period of time.

In adopting this position, I am emphatically not attempting to argue that traditional social structures in their pristine state contain within themselves all the forms of organization which are necessary for economic growth to take place with complexity. This point will be taken up below. Nor am I denying that changes in social structure will take place as a result of the forces unleashed during the process of economic growth. Again I do not deny that some 'societies" are so schismatic and pluralistic that integrated action is impossible.

Evidence has been consistently accumulating in anthropology that traditional social structures are highly adaptable and flexible mechanisms. This evidence has tended to be concealed or misinterpreted for a number of reasons. Within the timespans of direct anthropological investigation, the mount of indigenously stimulated change observed has been minimal, and there has been a tendency to stress conservatism, tradition and custom in delineating the characteristics of a society.

But, clearly, within a continuous system, adaptation between individuals and groups must be a characteristic feature. More and more anthropologists are stressing this. Dorothy Lee for example[51] in as remarkably imaginative *tour de force* has used ethnographies to show the ways in which individuals can act creatively and freely within apparently limited cultures. Raymond Firth[52] stresses the scope for preference and choice. Edmund Leach[53] demonstrates that the ideal description of a social structure can give too static an impression, for behind the tules lie interpretations of them, and their manipulation for

---

[51]*Freedom and Culture*, New Jersey, PrenticeHall, 1959

[52] *Elements of Social Organisation* London. Watts. 1951

[53] *Pul Eliya, s Village in Ceylon*, London, Cambridge University Press, 1961

personal and group interest.

Field studies of social change have also stressed that a common result of administrative order and similar pressures has been to reduce rather than to increase the adaptability of social systems. My own observation in Fiji, for example, indicates that the system of land registration in that colony did not take into account sufficiently the competitive and adaptive principles which underlay the relationships between families and lineages, and the modifying effects of influences which lay outside the lineage system but which nevertheless were part of the social order. The new system, intended to protect and to create order, did so at the cost of flexibilities which could have contributed to economic growth. Similarly, in many colonies, the position of chiefs has been stabilized and supported by alien sanctions, reducing the impact of traditional processes which made chiefs answerable in terms of results. We must be cautious in implying that ascription of roles is inconsistent with or contrary to achievement.

Admittedly, it cannot he assumed that the adaptabilities of traditional societies were oriented towards economic growth. My point is rather that, given an orientation towards economic growth derived from other aspects of the cultural reality. Adaptability is a necessary prerequisite to success. It is incumbent on those who guide policy to discover the adaptive forces in the society before them, and to use these rather than to ossify the society by the application of rules and methods which inhibit them.

The greatest and clearest defect in traditional social structures is that they do not provide sufficient forms of organization for instrumental effec□tiveness throughout the complex range of activities necessary for economic growth to take place. In this sense, certain functions, such as those of banking, credit supply or marketing, are either not performed or are inadequately developed. As discrete tribal and similar groups are brought within the bounds of colonies or new national States, such functions continue to be defective, or are concentrated in particular social groups or geogra☐phical areas. Some writers, such as Hirschman[54], would argue that differ☐entiation of economic systems within a rapidly developing country does not in fact hold back total economic growth, provided there is minimal integration so that some form at least of distribution of results takes place. Nevertheless, the absence of essential functions in an economy as a whole can hold it back, and the social structure must expand in scale and com☐plexity by the creation of new institutions.

As we have seen above, the new institutions do not have to be of Western or capitalist form, provided they meet the essential requirement of providing for decisiontaking and executive action. It may be simpler to copy Western forms, or to amend traditional forms towards a Western pattern, rather than innovate; but this can only be successful if the structure of new organ☐izations is consistent with the types of social relations, and the nature of decisionmaking and authority is such that the members of the organizations recognize it to be valid for them.

IV

[54]   A.O. Hirschmann, *The Strategy of Economic Development*, New Haven, Yale University Press, 1958

I wish now to set out a number of propositions which relate to the previous argument but are more specifically relevant to the theme of economic growth.

Any integrated social structure can become a basis for economic growth. Whether in fact it does or does not depends on whether innovation is directed towards expanding it in scale so that new functions can be performed, and whether its component parts are related to goals and objectives which are consistent with economic growth. That is, the keys to economic growth are to be found, not in the forms or principles of the social structure, but in the specifics of organization, and the nature of the value system.

In the field of values and of social structure there are few barriers to economic growth, and these can usually be clearly identified. The problem ~s not so much to destroy what might stand in the way, but to build on what is there, and to supplement existing arrangements where necessary.

The selection between values for entry into an effective demand schedule is not dependent merely upon their absolute relationship to one another. In the first place, there are. particularly in underdeveloped countries, limits to the range of possible cost variatio1~ because of limitations iii the use of resources and *of* technology, and because of the high nonmaterial costs which might be involved in cultural change. Thus there are limitations to the range of potential demand from which new values might be chosen, and this range is dependent upon the existing partial and practical possibilities of production and supply.

Iii terms of technology and the ingenuities of trade, underdeveloped countries have access to the total range of material goods, so that it is tempting to rely on the notion of insatiable expanding demand for consump□tion goods as the carrot for economic growth. This of course would not be valid, because of cost limitations referred to above. Thus selections must he made which can to some degree be influenced by planning policy, as to which preferences will be satisfied.

In so far as these selections arc made consciously by responsible author□ity, they will have varying effects upon economic growth. It is possible, for example, to select goals by reference to some standard of welfare (hospitals), or to an arbitrary concept of acculturated patterns (types of clothing), or to preferences revealed by earlier cash market hehaviour. None of these are, in themselves, adequate. since they do not posit an accurate relation□ship to growth. Each type of reference does, however, provide data about values which can he used iii further analysis.

In order to bring the analysis nearer to the relationships we are seeking, I suggest that it is desirable to introduce notions about the way in which values are linked with one another, and particularly to refine ideas about the differences in multiplying effect as between values. Far too frequently, productive effort is directed towards a specific point in demand which has no further ramifying consequences for other aspects of demand. Thus inadequate village schools do not increase the demand for learning or anything else. A change in agricultural practice may improve social conservation and improve leisure, without establishing further unsatiated wants. On the other hand a good school may increase the demand for further education, or a road the demand for city goods. In either case there is a multiplication of demand, with an alteration in the value pattern such that people are more prepared to meet new costs, and hence are motivated to further action. There is thus a case for concentrating supply to encourage such changes.

The point is reinforced by the consideration that disequilibria call forth rectifying action and generate change. This applies both in terms of social organization and values. This does not imply necessarily that there should be conflict, disruption, disorganization, or similar stresses which can inhibit action and discourage creativity. It implies a more or less systematic frame work—pattern of values or social structure—by reference to which adjust ments *can* he made.

Nevertheless it suggests. as Hirschmann has pointed out, that balanced growth as commonly used in developmental circles max' not in fact be a prerequisite to economic growth, and that undue stress upon it may in fact inhibit both growth arid welfare.

Balanced growth implies that planned action must see to it that each element in a productive others. Thus stresses. bottlenecks, undue emphasis system alters immediately and in harmony with on material things, or profit to the detriment of the culture or welfare will he avoided. In line with Ilirschmann's argument, I would hold that balanced growth can con1u~c emphasis upon the non—material, and upon welfare, with equilibrium. This ~s consistent with the previous position taken in this paper that the nonmaterial must he considered as an essential part of the costbenefit equations leading to relevant valuation and demand schedules. This is a different thing from saving that the system *must* he in equilibrium, for disequilibrium may appear at any point.

Balanced growth, equilibrium, perfect adjustment, are ideal states and abstractions seldom achieved in reality. One may validlv continue to argue that they represent ideals towards which to work. But one may also argue, as I understand Hirschmann to have done, that lack of balance will have a more stimulating effect than balance itself. In other words, if you have not yet achieved your ideal goal in terms of income levels, it is better to be out of balance, thus being selfstimulating and injecting alterations which will lead to further growth. Thus, it might be argued that it is better to create a good school at the village level rather than to use the same resources for a poor school and a poor dispensary, since the good school ould engender a demand for a good dispensary.

This kind of example, however, suggests a modification to the position. It will clearly not always be the case that desirable gaps will be filled, however critical they may he. Thus, notions about linkage are essential to the planning of success. The case for the good school receiving priority would depend on whether one could predict the linkage. Predictions of such a nature can sometimes be more accurate when attempted on a national scale. For example, a high educational standard may lead to a demand for medical services, whereas this would not necessarily apply to the activities of microcosmic communities. On the other hand, prediction can be more accurate on other occasions when intimacy of knowledge about local conditions and institutions can reveal the relationships more surely. This suggests that differing sets of propositions will be relevant at different levels of planning or decisiontaking, from that of the locality up to the state level.

The systematic exploration of linkages between small constellations of elements in the economic system derives from the importance of tracing the consequences of a proposed institutional or valuational change, so that **it** can be adjusted in the most appropriate way to bring about a desired objective. On a broader scale, it seems necessary to set out the necessary functional elements in an economic system undergoing the experience of growth, and to match these with values and institutional arrangement. The following rather random list indicates the kind of functional elements **I** have in mind.

Effective decisiontaking in productive and distributive units.

Patterns of exchange such that the units can obtain the goods and services necessary as factors of production.

Orientation of managers towards economizing and expansion.

Provision for the 'enskilling' of the managerial and labour force.

Availability of physical factors of production at suitable prices where increased consumption of them is indicated

.Provision of financial capital and credit facilities.

A system of physical and technical/commercial information communi□cations.

A system of marketing products.

A system of pricing or evaluating transactions.

Elementary though such broad categories may seem to be, they are often lacking in effective form, and they can provide a check list for assessing the adequacy of institutional arrangements. Thus adequate agricultural credit facilities are lacking in Fiji, and I am sure that the system of communications is defective in most parts of Africa. Yet unless all the above prerequisites (and most probably several others) are reflected in a country's institutions, one cannot expect economic growth to take place with maximum effec□tiveness.

One further dimension needs to be added. The institutions fulfilling these functions must be interlocking in a mutually adaptive manner. In other words, there must be reaction mechanisms so that institutions can respond to changing conditions.

Economic growth implies a dynamism in society. At various points in the preceding argument I have referred to such matters as 'orientation towards expansion' or 'stimulation of change'. The underlying point of view needs to be brought out into the open more fully. Some societies, particularly traditional ones, seem to have been in a state of static equilibrium, such that adjustments were entirely within a selfperpetuating system, save for cat aclysm or critical pressures from outside the system. Many of the inno vations introduced from the Western world, including some brought hy government, have been incorporated in such a way that they have not produced a permanent dynamic, but have merely changed one form of static into another.

It is no longer possible for such conditions to be characteristic of nation States, except in highly atypical circumstances, for forces of change are now linked on a worldwide scale. Nevertheless, the problem still remains when we consider alternatives of policy, because it is possible for governments to concentrate too high a proportion of their efforts on activities which do not introduce or support a dynamic. This is very clearly the case where intervention is based on the introduction of a physical facility or technical innovation, without consideration of the implications for values and social organization. Since the analysis of values and social organization is in many respects more difficult than that of technological deficiency, because more technicians are available than social analysts and because false assumptions are too readily made, government intervention in, for example, rural areas, tends to be nondynamic. It is one thing to introduce a new agricul☐tural method, to build a road, or provide a dispensary. It is a totally different thing to stimulate the values and organization that permit communities and institutions to expand their activities and horizons through their own initiative.

Such a task is a primary objective of such movements as community development. Even in this kind of context, however, the community development organization tends to concentrate on enabling specific tasks to be achieved, rather than on creating dynamism. There are very few recorded examples in which a community development team has with☐drawn, leaving behind a securely established organization for growth.

While it is true that economic growth began in European and American countries with very little assistance from persons able to carry out systematic analysis in the social sciences, the situation is quite different today. Under contemporary conditions there is an expectation that the process can be speeded by the application of knowledge about methods. There is recognition that questions to be solved are not merely commercial or technical. It ought to follow that governments would regard socioeconomic advice as valuable, and would make provision in their organizational plans for its application as a resource.

That this is not done as a matter of course is partly, though not wholly, a reflection of the lack of success in the social sciences to date in putting together their knowledge in such a way that individual specialist officials can be trained to analyse complex situations from th~ point of view of growth, bearing in mind that growth is not merely a form of economic adaptation, but involves processes analysed in political science, sociology. and anthropology, and techniques considered in such disciplines as commu□nity and regional planning, social work and adult education. I would hold that the provision and use of professionals of this character for association with all levels of government would have an important impact on economic growth in those countries where the public sector looms large.

Because many social structures are oriented towards limited traditional functions and do not make provision for institutions specializing in the total range of functions of the kind listed above, it is necessary to identify a source of authority which will concern itself with the creation and stimu□lation of relevant institutions. If this central task is not fulfilled, the appro□priate amendment of institutions will perforce be left to the slow and painful trial and error methods associated with social evolution. Clearly, under such circumstances the source of authority will be government.

This means that government is a most significant force affecting the foundations upon which economic growth will be built, and that success or failure, particularly in the early stages of growth, can be attributed closely to the efficacy *or* ineffectiveness of government in handling the institutional problems involved.

A further implication is that the relationship between organs of govern□ment *at* all levels and economic growth functions ought to be a direct one in many cases where iii established economies the relationship is indirect. For example, it may be necessary for central government to stimulate the development of local farms, transport arid marketing services, in such a manner that they grow out of the interests and needs of local communities. For many reasons such as limited supply of suitable managers or the difficulty of relating stock company organization to local methods and initiatives, or the des~rabi1itv of tapping local ideas in terms of evaluating possible projects it *may* he desirable that the analysis, planning and exe☐cution of such projects he made a local re~ponsibi1itv and that this be done most appropriately through a governmental institution.

Thus, economic wealth can be affected by the types of responsibilities allocated to junior levels of government, such as local authorities. Con☐versely, an analysis of the institutional requirements of economic growth will suggest amendments in the conception and organization of local govern☐ment. In many respects, this may prove to be one of the most significant points for creative thought and action in designing more viable economic systems to meet the challenge of growth in newly developing countries.

The Significance of Modern Cults in Melanesian Development

The title may indicate that this is an essay in applied anthropology and in one sense it is. But to do so it examines a variety of cults throughout Melanesia and attempts to construct a theory which both explains their occurrence and thus guide policy. The theory itself was examined in a symposium on millennial movements throughout the world organised by Sylvia Thrupp, the social historian at Chicago. First published in the journal *Australian Outlook* vo. 4 1950 pp 116125 it was condensed and reprinted in Lesser and Vogt, *Reader in Comparative Religion* Harper and Row, 1958, 1965, 1972. This is the version reprinted here. In that reader it was followed by a paper at the same symposium by David Abele, entitled *Relative Deprivation Theory as applied to Millennial and other Cult Movements.* The two sets of ideas were very similar and were discussed later in such studies as Ian Jarvie *The Revolution in Anthropology* which was summarised in the journal *Oceania* and in Peter Worsley *The Trumpet Shall Sound.* The deprivation theory, coupled with the influence of ideas from Judeo ChristianMuslim concepts turned out to be capable of explaining sociopolitical movements of many kinds from peasant revolts to *intifada,* each with the addition of an appropriate variable to the model. – and, dare we say it, the 2011 movements in the Arabic world.

Although we know that in New Caledonia and Fiji the Melanesian people have shown themselves capable of considerable political development, many of us who know the Melanesian in the New Hebrides, British Solomon Islands, and New Guinea are in☐clined to doubt the possibility, at least in the near future, of Melanesians organizing their own political movements. The "Fuzzy Wuzzy Angels" of the war, emerging from the bush with hardlycomeby garden produce, resist☐ing many forms of agricultural innovation, chewing betel nut, wearing castoff clothing, speaking seemingly mutilated forms of Eng☐lish, appear to be far removed from any form of modern organization. The British Solomon Island experiments in Native Courts and Councils, though a tremendously promising innovation, have been temporarily arrested by a strange native cult. The suggestion that there might before long be a panMelanesian nationalist movement would evoke incredu☐lous smiles from most European Island resi☐dents, who point to the impossibility of persuading laborers from different communi☐ties to work together in harmony, to the multifarious languages and cultures, and to the absence of anything approaching a cen☐tralized organization in traditional life.

It is the purpose of this article to suggest, however, that this is far too simple an inter☐pretation of Melanesian possibilities. An analysis of certain apparently isolated Mela☐nesian cults, which have grown up in Euro☐pean times, will give an indication of some of these possibilities. We may begin by a brief summary of their features.

THE TUKA CULT OF FIJI

About 1885 a prophet arose among the hill tribes of Fiji. He claimed that it had been revealed to him that before long the whole world would be turned upside down, particu☐larly that the whites would serve the natives, the chiefs would serve the common people, and his followers would have eternal life. Jehovah was subordinated to local gods, and through the use of supernatural powers deriv☐ed from the gods, the prophet was enabled to secure the obedience of a large following. This following drilled in European style to repulse the expected advance of the Adminis☐tration. The prophet was banished, but the belief in the *tuka* cult continued.

THE BAIGONA CULT OF PAPUA

The *Baigona* Snake Cult of the Northern Division of Papua operated for many years from 1911. The prophet had the secrets of sorcery and prophecy revealed to him by the *Baigona Snake,* and cultivated its goodwill by special rites. He sold the secrets of the cult to those who wished to be initiated. The movement was characterized by trances. Its rise coincided with the attempt to bring the area under administrative control. An ad☐ministrative patrol was endangered and ad☐ministrative pressure to reduce the trances and abolish the sale of initiation in accordance with antisorcery policy was not completely successful.

THE LONTIS CULT OF BUKA

I have not been able to find details of this cult, which occurred in 1913 during the German administration. Numerous arrests were made.

THE GERMAN WISLIN

OF THE TORRES STRAITS

This is the first clear specimen of the genus now known as "Cargo Cult." It occurred in 1913 on the island of Saibai, Torres Straits. The prophet declared that his followers would see the *markai,* the spirits of the dead, who would come to them in a steamer, bringing all kinds of manufactured cargo, and who would kill all the whites. Those who disobeyed the prophet would lose all their money and would be unable to earn any more.

THE TARO CULT AND

ITS RELATIVES IN PAPUA

This cult, very much akin to the *Baigona,* but in which the native vegetable taro took the place of the *baigona* snake, was more vigorous in its proselytism and lasted from 1914 into the late twenties. Dreams, ritual, and shaking fits played a prominent part in it. Offshoots were the *Kava Kava* and *Kekesi* cults in the same area (Northern Division).

THE VAILALA MADNESS OF PAPUA

The *Vailala Madness,* which swept the Gulf Division of Papua from 1919 to 1923, was in the hands of sorcerers who had the power of divination during trances, and who encourag□ed their followers to take part in orgies of shaking fits. The great bullroarer ceremonies of the kinship groups were abandoned, and new ceremonies were created to take their place. A steamer was expected, bringing the deceased relatives who were to have white skins. The new ceremonies contained a Chris□tian element, flagpoles were given names and treated as the media through whom messages from the dead were received, there was a cer□tain element of military drill, and women were given equality. Public confessionals took place.

THE MURDER OF CLAPCOTT,

NEW HEBRIDES

In 1923 the inland people of Espiritu Santo, New Hebrides, were influenced by rumors of deathraising. The prophet concerned claimed that if all the Europeans were killed the dead would arise, with white skins. They would bring European goods with them, and a house was built to receive these. To join the move☐ment, it was necessary to pay a pig, or a fee of 5/ to one pound. During a great feast the prophet's wife died, and a European, Clap☐cott, was immediately killed. It is stated that the same people killed some Europeans called Greig in 1908, but details do not seem to have been published. These are the only occasions in which Europeans have been assaulted during these movements, though resistance and threats have been offered on several occasions.

THE CARGO CULTS OF BUKA

In 1932 and 1933 a cargo cult arose which appeared to be related to the previously men☐tioned *Lontis* cult. The prophet claimed that a steamer would arrive, laden with good things, and that all Buka would be ruled from their village. A store was to be built to receive these goods, and the police to be resisted if they interfered. But the ship would not come while food was available, and hence gardens were abandoned for some time. The leaders were imprisoned, but the cult continued.

THE MARKHAM CARGO CULT, NEW GUINEA

In 1933 a prophet arose in this area who claimed that Jehovah was subordinate to Satan. Once again the spirits of the dead were expected to return, bringing goods; gardens lapsed; and séances took place. Villages were destroyed and community houses built, and it was erroneously believed that the Adminis tration would be passive.

THE CHAIR AND RULE

MOVEMENT OF THE SOLOMONS

About 1939 a European missionary en couraged the Melanesians of Santa Ysabel, Gela, and Savo to agitate for a seat on the nominated Advisory Council. He emphasized the need for a chairman and rules of proce dure. The movement got out of hand and was misinterpreted. The Melanesians elevated a flag, a wooden chair, and a wooden rule into positions of ritual importance. They wrote to friends in San Cristoval and agitated for higher wages. Those involved were punished and the missionary asked to leave the Protec torate. His memory was still revered in 1945 among some people. The Administration was prompted into plans for Native Courts and Councils by this movement.

THE JOHN FRUM MOVEMENT, NEW HEBRIDES

In 1940 a native of the island of Tanna declared himself to be the prophet of John Frum, a spirit which evidently took the place of the ancient spirit of Karaperamun, for merly of great power. John Frum declared that the whole island was shortly to change in natureits volcanic cone to be replaced by fertile plains, its people to be eternally young and healthy, and to have everything that they could ever desire. In order to achieve this end, it was necessary to hunt and kill all Euro peans, to rid themselves of the taint of Euro pean money, to rid themselves of immigrant natives, and to return to the old customs of polygyny, dancing, kava drinking, and so forth, which had been rigidly proscribed by the theocratic Presbyterian Church. Money was taken to the stores and a great spending spree indulged in. The Administration took action; arrests were made.

The movement continued, however, espe cially in 1942, 1943, and 1947, encouraged by letters from the former leaders, who had been banished to Malekula. A modern touch was added by the construction of an aerodrome for American Liberators. The imprisoned leaders succeeded in converting neighboring villages on Malekula. A similar movement arose on Ambryn, in which a house was built to receive goods from the Messageries Mari□times steamer "Le Polynesien."

THE NAKED CULT, ESPIRITU SANTO

This cult, seen from 1944 to 1948, appears to be connected with the Clapcott murder case mentioned previously. It has, however, rather different features. The followers of the pro□phet are to go naked and are to cohabit in public. Villages are to be destroyed and replaced by two communal houses, one for the men and one for the women. All animals and property received from the Europeans are to be destroyed. Old customs such as exogamy and marriage payments are to be scrapped. The people are no longer to work for the Europeans, but to wait for the arrival of the Americans, when they will receive

THE MASINGA RULE MOVEMENT OF THE SOLOMONS

The *Masinga* rule movement first made its appearance at the end of 1945 and in 1946 and is the most political of any of the movements that have yet appeared. In its early stages it appeared to have connections with the earlier Chair and Rule movement, and with dis☐affection which was rife on Guadalcanal, following the presence of Allied troops. It soon took on its own form, however, with Malaita the center. Buildings were erected to warehouse the expected free gifts from Amer☐ican liberators; monetary contributions were exacted from the adherents of the movement; the leaders were reputed to have boundless wealth in dollars and to pay their followers twelve pounds a month; Melanesians were for☐bidden to work for Europeans unless a wage of twelve pounds a month was paid; mission☐ary and administrative work was resist☐ed; demonstrations of several thousand natives took place on Government stations demanding education, higher wages, political independence, and the removal of Europeans; "soldiers" were drilled; the central organiza☐tion on Malaita established connections with Ulawa and San Cristoval and the movement was eventually copied in the Santa Cruz group and the Western Solomons. At first the Administration was prepared to tolerate the movement and wait for it to die out, but as resistance, and particularly drilling, grew in scale, several score of arrests were made. The movement still continues, and so do the arrests.

OTHER CONTEMPORARY MOVEMENS

At the close of the recent war, Melanesia was left with three described movements, *Masinga* Rule, John Frum, and the Naked Cult. There appears, however, to have been a general revival of similar movements all over Melane□sia, with the possible exception of New Caledonia, though we still await published details of them. There is the Apolisi prophet movement of Fiji, a cargo cult in the Loyalty Islands (the first reported) and in New Guinea, and a similar movement in the Purari Delta of Papua. This latter appears to have interesting possibilities, for it is reported that for the first time the Administration, while watching it carefully, is encouraging it and aiding it in its development programinclud□ing rebuilding of villages and reorganization neither Melanesian leadership nor Adminis□tration pursued them vigorously.)

These then are the principal details of about thirteen movements that have been described over the past fifty years. What is their signifi□cance?

The first point to notice is that the move ments are widely separated in time and place, from the Torres Straits to Fiji, and that this effectively rules out the possibility that they are copies of each other. Their similarities must be due to similarities in local conditions which produce them.

The movements fall into two main groups, with borderline cases in between. The first of these is seen in its purest form in the *Baigona* and Taro cults in Papua. There is no hint here of conflict with the European until the Euro pean Administrator, from the Melanesian point of view, "butts in." In their essentials, the cults are similar to those found everywhere in Melanesia at the time of the arrival of the Europeans. They express the indigenous Melanesian animist interpretation of the world and his centuriesold traditional delight in ceremonial and cult practices. They are novel only in that their origins have been observed and not speculated about, and from this point of view they are of considerable interest to the sociologist.

The other cults are a modern modification of this phenomenon. But before we make this clear, a number of alternative hypotheses may be disposed of.

First, there is the understandable Adminis☐trative view that these are dangerous move☐ments, interrupting Melanesian life, threaten☐ing good order, and evidencing the unhealthy despotic powers of sorcerers who, by trickery, have bullied the local people, and who make their fortune by the sale of their tricks. Of the political aspects of this view, I will speak later. But as a theory of origins it is most defective. No leader, it must be emphasized, in the absence of mechanical instruments or a police state, can force people to follow him or accept his doctrines. The traditional Mela☐nesian method of avoiding unwanted leaders is simply to move somewhere else, found a new village, grow new gardens, or retaliate by countersorcery or murder. It must be accept☐ed that the religious element in these cults is sufficiently near the Melanesian pattern to enable us to believe that their following is by and large popular. As for the sale of the tricks forms of Melanesian sorcery, and even the passing on of dance movements and songs. It is, as it were, payment for copyright.

Second, there is the view that the cults express a reaction to a particular event or organization. It is superficially possible, for instance, to blame the John Frum movement on to the rather rigid and narrow interpreta☐tions of recent Presbyterian proselytizing. Similarly, one could blame the Espiritu Santo movement on to the sale of liquor and to other abuses by the traders. And the *Masinga* Rule movement has been blamed on "Marxist elements" among American troops.

All these views possess an element of truth, but all lack conviction. Why should such diverse historical facts give rise to such unified movements? On the other hand, if we describe the position of these Melanesian communi ties in the modern world we can see that there is indeed a common element.

None of these communities is untouched by European influence; and none of them has been able to take full advantage of living under that influence. Moving roughly west to east, the Torres Straits have been the happy hunt ing grounds of pearl fishers and labor recruiters, but at the beginning of the century the island of Saibai was subject to no perma nent European influences; the Gulf of Papua is not a favorite area of European exploita tion, though there have been European planters there; Buka again is on the fringe of European activity; Gela it is true is very close to the prewar Solomon Island capital of Tulagibut here the movement was more definitely political rather than religious and it was stronger in the less developed north than in the more developed south; Malaita is a classic example, for here there was practically no European activity, while the almost over□populated communities sent their sons to other islands for plantation work; inland Espiritu Santo has hardly been visited by Europeans, though there is a thriving com□munity on the coast; Tanna is a small island well off the beaten track, again exporting a few of its people as seamen; and the Loyalty Islands, unattractive to European settlers, live by exporting produce to Noumea, the New Caledonian capital. Inland Fiji, at the time of the Tuka Cult, was quite primitive.

These people, then, have all been in contact with thriving European communities, but none of them have been able to participate in vigorous activity leading to a higher standard of life. I think it is most significant that two extremes of Melanesian life do not appear so far to have succumbed to these cults, though they have problems of their own. On the one hand, we have the thriving native settlements in or near such towns as Port Moresby, Rabaul, Vila, and in New Cale□donia, and areas of intensive missionary in□dustrial work. Here the people are in the grip of modern lifeand have little time or incli□nation to organize into cults. On the other hand, we have areas such as the interior of New Guinea and

Malekula, where cults con⊔tinue in their native form, unmodified by European intrusion.

If we accept this thesis, it is easy to under⊔stand that the similarities in the cults are due to the position of the communities halfway between the old and the new way of living; and that the differences are due almost solely to particular historical circumstances. The universals seem to be these. The "halfway" Melanesian sees other people who possess a way of living that he tends to envy. He has to find some explanation of European power in holding sway over multitudes; of the miracu⊔lous arrival of manufactured goods in ships and aeroplanes; of strange European behavior which sends away piles of raw materials; of the peculiar distaste with which Europeans treat him. On the one hand, this gives him an end of activityhe must strive to attain a similar power. On the other hand, it sets him an intellectual problem and gives him an emotional experience. His emotional exper⊔ience is jealousy, sometimes hatred, of the European who neither gives him these things as a friend not initiates him into the mysteries of the process of sale and production – indeed tries to gob him off with Biblical education. His intellectual problem is first to explain European success, and second to achieve a method of parallel success.

This problem must be solved in terms of Melanesian experience. There is behind him the great tradition of cults such as the *Baigona,* and animism. It is natural that he should turn to find a superior cult. At first, it was Chris tianity in many parts, which was conceived as a superior, sometimes as a supplementary, animism. This fails, or is not understood, and is molded on to something new. The new cult endeavors to copy significant European activi ties. There is the belief in shipping, that is, in the origin of cargoesfor remember, most Melanesians have not seen or experienced the manufacturing process. There is a mystical significance in the revolting white skin of Europeans, and in money, which circulates so strangely ; in flags and flagpoles, which the European treats with peculiar reverence; **in** towns and houses rather than villages; in soldiers and drillingwhich *must* be mystical, for what use is there in it? And in later years, of course, there is the myth of American arrival, so obviously based upon the big handedness and freedom of American troops. These things supplied the modern elements in the cargo myth, the myth which explained European successes and indicated the correct road to follow.

Trends in Motives and Organisation in Solomon Islands Agriculture

This paper was written for the Australian and New Zealand Association for the Advancement of Science meeting in Auckland in 1952 incorporating a model of cultural change.

The object of this paper is to outline the changes that have occurred in Solomon Island Melanesian agriculture since the arrival of the Europeans and to see whether some of the concepts of economics may be used to this end, supplementing the current anthropological approach.

At the outset I must make it clear that the paper is not based upon any deep understanding of native society such is would be expected to come from n intensive and prolonged anthropological field study. My observations as to the war and postwar periods were undertaken haphazardly during administrative duties and before I had grasped their full implications or I learnt the possibilities of observing more thoroughly. For the rest, I have drawn extensively upon published materials, especially those given in the bibliography[55]. The facts of the

[55] The data upon which this paper is based d are being more extensively set out among others, in A thesis under preparation in the University of London on economic aspects of Culture Change in Western Melanesia With special reference to the influence

paper are hardly new but it 1s
necessary to reexamine them in the
light of modern problems.

Early native agriculture

With regard to the early
literature on the Solomon Islands,,
two facts stand put. The first is
that there has been no systematic
attempt at study of agriculture *qua*
agriculture or as a problem in
agricultural economics, although
Guppy (²) and Ivens (9) (10) have short
sections on gardening, and though
Hogbin in his later work (13) (14)
gives   a
very clear and forceful picture of
the dynamic way in which men attain
egricultural wealth, there are, as we
shall see, many lacunae.

---

of the monetary economy, with the financial
support of the Emslie Hornian Trustees.

The second point is that Solomon Island society has changed a great deal in the pest hundred years It is true that observations by Mendana (5) by and large present a picture which is recognisable today. The view is very superficial, however, and if we examine later writings we must alter this opinion. The most striking example to me h c been the comparison of the writing of Verguet (1) (published in 1885 on observations he made in 1841,, with those of Fox (8) in 124 for San Cristovnl, and with my own memories of my own stay there in 1946. The illustrations given in Verguet are quite different from those given by Fox, and the descriptions of both, especially with regard to themeterial paraphernalia of ritual is unrecognisable today.

This raises the question of the validity of reconstructions of early native agriculture,, since we have no other early observers of the calibre of Verguet, and even such excellent later writers as Codrington pay practically no attention to agriculture (4). The answer is that we cannot hope to provide a completely full account of agriculture, and it is not necessary that we do so. The general principles of native agricultural activity are fairly clear, and even observations of the cultivation of traditional plants made today are reasonably useful for many descriptive purposes. We run cer tin risks of overlooking some changes, of giving some activity traditional status which in fact it should not have, but the degree of error is not likely to be large nor to affect the general conclusions that we draw. Nor is it indeed necessary to postulate a preEuropean agriculture as a starting point of study. All we need is a state of agriculture which preceded a later state of agriculture, in that way obtaining in that way obtaining the tie dimension essential to my study of change. The best way of doing this in the present circumstances is to postulate a "subsistence" or "primitive" agriculture which ca n be compared with a "cashcrop" or "monetary" agriculture[56].

---

[56] It may be pointed out, for instance, that if we are concerned with general principle or types rather than detailed ethnographic data, then many of the general definitions of Professor Firth (15) hold good for Melanesia

As will be apparent to any anthropologist, subsistence agriculture does not mean that every one produced exactly as much agricultural produce as he wanted for his own direct consumption. It is a purely relative term indicating that the standard of technology and of demand was such that men could if they so wished produce what they required for themselves, that the quantity of trade was relatively low, and, in particular, that produce was not exported to an impersonal speculative market. These points will be mentioned later, but it is as well to emphasise them at the outset.

Agsricultural activity, like any other activity, is organised to meet specific ends, which are present in the minds of the actors as a medley of conscious purpose, unconscious desire, and hhabitual drive. It is beyond our present task to examine the ways in which patterns of agricultural activity arise the

---

just as for Polynesia – the social effects of the standard of technology, and the significance of the ceremonial distribution of food, for instance. Institutional details, of course, vary considerably.

interplay of upbringing, of education, to the activity of the family, fellowvillagers and circumstances, of limitations and possibilities imposed by the environment, of the influence of developments in nearby communities. It is however relevant to note the ends which were in fact present in Melanesian society in the Solomons.

In the first place, of course, ngricultural activity provided food. Panna, yam, and taro were the commonest cultivated staples, varying in importance with soil conditions. It is interesting to note the influence of environment here upon the acquisition of taste. In areas where yam grew well if alwᵃys took pride of place: but in some areas, such as Gela, it was difficult to cultivate, and hence panna replaced it. Gela people became accustomed to panna preference, which they retained even when visiting ymgrowing areas or working away from home. Other foods cultivated included the plantain, and, since they required planting and a certain amount of care, one could al so include the breadfruit, coconut, and number of shrubs which provided edible leaves. Except in limited areas of the Western Solomons, the sago palm was not cultivated for its food value by Melanesians, but for its leaf, though in times of shortage the pith was occasionally eaten.

The direct consumption of food is not necessarily a simple phenomenon. Anthropologists have drawn sufficient attention to sociological factors which modify and accompany it such factors as ritual abstentions, proscriptions applying to clan members, abstentions during childbirth, and sO forth **(7)** **(8)** (9) (10). Indeed, we might draw together all such food habits, together with traditionallydeveloped tastes, under one heading, such as customary or hrabitual behaviour. By such a phrase we imply that for sociological reasons men, when confronted with specific situations, act in certain ways and adopt certin values which may be predicted for their society. Demand, in the economist's sense, is socially determined.

At the slime time there are two other concepts which may be applied to the same behaviour, the concepts of competition and complementarily. By competition I mean that a choice h s to be made as between ends or between means. A man m y choose his ends according to customary rule, by considering advantages or disadvantages rationally in terms of more ultimate ends, or by an emotional decision, or by a combination of all three. But whatever end he adopts for his activity, however unconsciously realised, principles of choice are involved, implying the sacrifice or postponement of some other ends not so important at the moment, whether they be leisure, alternative ritual forms, warfare, or what you will.

Competition is quite evident, for instance, in the provision of food. If we take a year's activity, most Solomon Island communities will eat both fish and tubers. But at any particular time they may eat fish alone or tubers alone or fish (of different kinds) in combination with tubers (of different kinds). In other words, even limited resources permit a wide variety in consumption. Moreover the biplane will he decided not solely by reference to some ideal st^{a}ndard of preference, but in weighing up, rationally or irrationally, the advantages and disadvantages to be attained in acting to achieve particular ends.   Any single activity involves a number of considerations inland   San Cristoval people, for instance, when deciding whether to eat fish, have to consider whether it can be bought from coastal dwellers and at what price, whether they are in a position to fish for it themselves by individual effort, whether the journey to get it is worth while, how much alternative food is available, whether the time used to get it could be better employed in gardening or taking part in a memorial 1 feast for   a departed   elder, and so on. Of course, not all these considerations will apply at one particular moment – men are   not   completely rational, sometimes certain things weigh more heavily on the mind than others. Nevertheless I feel that anthropologists have tended to overlook to some degree the play of competition in native life.

Sociological and environmental determinism plays large part in establishing the range of ends in a community, and even in establishing habitual responses, but it does not destroy the great variety of life and the numerous competing ways of employing time arid resources.

By the second concept, complementarily, I mean that in order to achieve certain ends particular resources or particular kinds of activity must be combined. Insofar as they may be substituted one for another, they are said to be in competition; insofar as an increase in one involves an increase in another they are said to be complementary. Thus if we take the end broadly as the provision of food, the cultivation of panna may be conceived as being in competition with t he cultivation of yams.

If however we take a specific occasion, the provision of food for marriage feast, it may be customᵃry to provide specific kinds ☐ of food in which several resources are mixed. Thus coconut flesh, tubers, and forest nuts ne combined into may pudding recipes, pounded and fermented or baked, and for this purpose may be considered to be complementary. The activity of gardening. involves clearing, burning, digging holes, planting, weeding, gathering, and considerable ritual in many stages ,all of which may be considered as complementary activities.

Comparison of the two examples shoes a further distinction. Not only are resources or activity complementary, but they are complementary to different degrees. The complementary nature of the resources in the first case is based upon their power to combine to produce a tasty or ritually required dish. But if one of them is lacking or difficult to procure,   substitution may be possible, although there will be a loss in subjective value satisfied. In the second case, it is true that different activities may be combined in different proportions   one family may take greater care over burning, while another may be painstaking over clearing   but the variations possible re no greet, and it is not practicable to do away altogether with one activity, at least in the native's view, without complete loss of the end result. The food is complementary in a less essential sense than the item of technical activity; we may say, to introduce another term, that the elasticity of demand is greater in the case of food than in the case of the item of technical activity. Such variations of degree introduce the possibility of measurement, but we have not the space to go into this complicated question at the moment.

The reason I have paid particular attention to these concepts is th^{a}t I believe that they and others developed with some precision in economics can be of considerable use in describing culture change. Their use m.es one ask such questions as, if value A is introduced as an end of activity, how will it compete for resources and time with value Bu If value C disappears as an end of activity, will it mean that the demand for D a.nd E lessens bee use they are complements, or increases because they are in competition? If resources increase, can we regard the demand for F as being elastic or inelastic that is, will it increase more than in proportion to the increase in resources or less? We .re accustomed to thinking of such terms as applicable to materiel goods

in a money economy. But, surely, even
if we cannot measure the quantities involved with
accuracy, the sme concepts apply in
relation to values and nonmonetary
activity. If ritual activity is held onto
tenaciously, demand for ritual is inelastic, and its
inelasticity may be compared with the elasticity
of demⁱnd for food or art forms or
whatever is relevant. The functional
interrelations of behaviour may be
observed through the degree of competition or
complementarily which applies. If
ritual decreases it will permit
totemic objects to enter into competition
as food. If Churchgoing or labour supply
or court cases increase, time available
for other activities (including leisure) must
decrease, and we can query how the adjusᵗment is
made, what rearrangements are necessary.

Let us now note as briefly as possible
the salient features of Melanesian

agriculture that are relevant for our present discussion. Apart from food, there were numerous other agricultural ends. Cultivated)1 nuts provided numerous items of raw mterial, such as that from sego palm and coconut, spoons and bowls from the coconut, weaving material from coconut and pandanus, wood from coconut and breadfruit. There is no need to enlarge upon the list.

The food used was not simply for direct consumption the prevention of hunger. In particular it ws used for ceremonial purposes and the ostentatious display and exchange of goods the!, accompanied most socially important occasions. Certain foods, particularly the firstfruits, were sacrificed to the spirits when occasion demanded. Stores of food, either gathered or left to ripen in the gardens, were important capital resources, for they could be used to maintain craftsmen while working to order, to supply the feasts which called forth the labour required for cooperative activity such as housebuilding or garden clearing, to feed visitors. In most cases such uses were deliberately planned for, thus maintaining the direct relationship between production and use, but a margin for emergencies had to he maintained thus introducing a speculative element.

To fulfil these ends, agriculture as a whole was sometimes in competition with and sometimes complementary to fishing and animalhusbandry (of pigs), and selfsufficient agriculture was in competition with acquisition by exchange. As with the fishmarkets of Malaita, the problems of choice were often decided by reference to limitations of resources in particular areas. Trade between

Gela and Malaita for instance altered as the balance of resources changed – as Malaita became richer in coconuts so the export of coconuts from Gela declined. The pattern of trade has not been investigated authoritatively, but it is quite extensive (18). Agriculture also competed with forest gathering – of nuts, roots, edible leaves, fibres and the like.

Given the desire for agriculture, organisation of activity was required. Here again we may observe the operation of competition end complementarity within a socially and environmentally determined framework. Techniques were simple but effective, permitting the use of lend on the almost universal steeplysloping hillsides. Large trees were felled by chipping and burning to prevent undue shade, but habits of shifting cultivation had reduced the stands of mature trees so that the task though lengthy, was not as great as might be thought. Roots were left in the ground to hold the soil together many of these quickly started to grow again. The main implements were shells for weeding and the well:mown digging stick for making holes. Certain signs, such as the budding of particular trees, provided indications of times for various operations to commence. Ritual incantations, prayers, end s orifices were made at every stage. Most of these factors are an expression of technical knowledge and the interpretation of the unseen forces controlling or having n effect upon agricultural fortune. Such knowledge and interpretation was passed on from generation to generation by upbringing, continual association with such activity, and by the lack of environmental factors which could indicate the possibility of anything else. Given these factors, the people could conceive of no substitute for these methods, which, so far as we know, were varied in direct proportion to the quantity of endproduct desired[57].

Agriculture was organised with reference to numerous soci^{a}l groups, of which we may distinguish groups of kin, local groups, and groups of friends. Working parties were seldom institutionalised though Ivens (9) reports named cooperting groups on Ulawa but the individuals cooperated

---

[57] An economist might object that diminishing returns would be expected. Diminishing returns are however largely a function of scarcity of the best resources, and except in limited areas I doubt if this principle applied in any great degree in the Solomon Islands.

very much according to circumstances.
Clan members, village members, and
friends would gather to help families
prepare the garden ground, build houses,
paddle canoes or go fishing. This often
involved the leadership and direction
of a village heed. People were
attracted to such cooperative work by
the preference they h ad for group
activity rather than isolated
activity (though there
were a few semihermits and
introverts), by the joy of the feasts
that accompanied such work, but the
sense of achievement that resulted from
the rapid progress made, and by
affection for the family for whom they
worked. An allied principle of great
importance was that of reciprocity.
Those who cooperated were often
working off debt they owed to the
family for similar service rendered

to them in the past or else they were creating a moral obligation for aid some time in the, future – a truly n^{a}tive form of interest. Hogbin (13)(14) has given very clear accounts of the operation of reciprocity and the calculation of obligations as a factor governing advancement in materiel wealth and social prestige.

The principles governing the use of land have been given hardly any attention by investigators in the Solomons. There is no satisfactory account of the systems o f land rights, although it would 'dear the t overall rights were held by clans, where such groups existed, and immediate rights of usufruct by individuals. The importance of inheritance in transmitting wealth was diminished by the quantity of lend available, for those with lees land could relatively easily extend the areas of cultivation, either in unclaimed l•nd, or in land claimed only by the clan and not by individuals. Nevertheless, the fertility of land varies and costs of production vary even more when the density of bush,, distance from the village, steepness of slope, and availability of water are taken into account. Certain property such as sago palms, coconut trees and nut groves could be on or after the death of the owner, and this, together with the special character of the soil required for their growth, resulted in a certain inequality of wealth. This tendency was limited, at least in the case of coconut resources, by the destruction of some trees on death, but it must be admitted we have very little concrete evidence of the distribution of wealth.

Let us now sum arise the main characteristics of selfsufficient agriculture and the place of agriculture in social life. Techniques were limited, but adequate to sustain tradition 1 standards of demand on a relatively egalitarian basis. Production and consumption were relatively directly related, at least when concerned with the speculative and round about character of production in our own society. Nevertheless, food was used for a variety of ends. In particular, it entered into ceremonial end was used in exchange designed to call forth labour. The low standard of technique, the relive lack of capital resources, and the relative abundance of lend prevented any gross inequalities of wealth, though some specific shortages and differences of individual capacity and will to work prevented society from being completely egalitarian. Indeed the close relation between standrd of wealth and standard of work was reflected in the high prestige given to men of wealth, who tee me men of power. Agriculture was related to other soclial activities in several ways. It competed wiith them in satisfying ends, and it was undertaken as a complement to them: in one sense other activities and values limited and controlled agriculture (as with religious conceptions and preferences of organisation), and in another sense agriculture exercised controlling influence on them (as with political structure, or conceptions of material wealth).

Before going further we may see if we can discern any elements of change existing in native society before its stimulation by Europeans. This is rather difficult because I cannot look back at things in a Melanesian manner and because no chroniclers of change existed before the arrival of the Europeans. We can only make assumptions on a priori grounds. There are however a number of theoretical hypotheses that can be made and applied to both the preEuropean and the postEuropean situation; and certain deductions can be drawn from them regarding the subsistence economy.

Let us define a state of secial equilibrium as a state of society in which patterns of activity (involving the means taken to satisfy ends and the statistical weight of various types of activity) is maintained. For a state of social equilibrium to exist, there must be present four factors: the ends adopted by individuals must appear to them to be mutually ;compatible; resources and knowledge of means, including their distribution, must be unchaining; given current resources and knowledge of means, potential ends (i.e. unsatisfied hopes and desires) must be brought as near as c n be managed to satisfaction; and effective ends (i.e. those actually satisfied) must he achieved with the maximum apparent efficiency (i.e. least sacrifice of alternative ends, resources and time). The greeter the lack of adjustment in these factors the greater the state of disequilibrium. Further, men will tend to adjust all factors except tee rate of change of resources and knowledge of means in such way that a state of equilibrium will be reestablished. [58]

---

[58] We must recognise here, as do economists

In Melanesian society we can discern a number of factors which, if the above hypotheses are true, must have resulted in disequilibrium 'and therefore change. We may regard knowledge of means as relatively static, and, speaking for small community units, we can infer that ends were relatively compatible. We can say this on the assumption that pure invention is a rare occurrence[59], that the communities were sufficiently old for behaviour to become adjusted, and that there was relatively little contact with communities of radically different culture which would have increased the range of perception end new ideas[60].

---

when using an allied concept of equilibrium, that in our own society actual equilibrium is never achieved though we can discern tendencies towards it. No sooner does one action result in adjustments by other people than new conditions intervene to cause disturbance in other directions, in particular, knowledge.

[59] See my publications *The Conditions of Social Performance* and *Fixing the World* for a later extended theory of innovation.

This was only relatively so, however. The prevalence of warfare indicated that, at log as outside the smallest community units, ends were sometimes regarded as incompatible. Resources, being beyond the control of man in large degree must have changed from time to time, resulting in alteration of behaviour. Such changes would have included population trends, and the influence of weather in drought or times of excessive rain. Warfare itself must have resulted from time to time in changes in the relation of man to resources the land available to them, the size of the political unit or social group, and so forth. Contact with other groups must have resulted in the perception of hitherto unknown ends, which

---

[60] I now doubt this. One of the great sectors of innovation was almost certainly religion and supernatural beliefs.

were then available for adoption, becoming potential and perhaps effective, resulting in diffusion. Such alteration in ends, and alteration in resources, must have resulted in further changes in means, as the pattern of means and ends, considered in terms of efficiency, would require new balances.

These considerations must not be unduly laboured, but they should draw attention to the dynamic aspects of primitive society, so often mistakenly described as totally static..

The effects of European activity

We are now in r position to describe and interpret changes in agriculture which resulted from the presence of Europeans. European activity affected each of the four factors in equilibrium both directly and indirectly the indirect effect being

trrcer.ble through the operation of
competitive and complement☐ary principles.
We may consider these from the
agricultural point of view.

Ends, since they control activity, may
first be examined. Observation in this field
tends to support the view that the concrete
form of ends changes, that the meaning given
to ends changes as connotations alter in the
new society, but that function, in the sense
of subjective purpose, of a new form is
similar to that of the form replaced. They
do not support the view that function, in the
sense of interrelations with other ends and
activities (through competition or
complementarity), does not alter.

To exemplify, in agriculture there was
considerable ritual activity, in particular
prayers and offering's to the spirits during
operations, and the sacrifice of firstfruits.
Today, Christian. communities pray to God

for the success of gardens, and conduct harvest festivals. The concrete form of this activity has altered and so has its meaning in terms of a synthesis of the new theology with old conceptions. The subjective purpose has not altered. But the interrelations of the activity with other activity has altered pari passu with its form it' calls into play a different religious organisation, with different sanctions and methods of reward; it involves Churchbuilding; it sometimes caste doubt upon the efficacy of certain spells in agriculture with which it is in competition, and therefore in a complementary way upon certain spells in other activities; it places ritual power In the hands of r priest, thus partly removing it from those of the sorcerer and removing part of the religious sanction supporting the secular authority of the headman, and so on.

This does not, however, justify us in
reaching the conclusion that the general ends
of agricultural activity are the same, though
the form may have changed, and the effects
be different. Let us trace each of the four
factors in equilibrium in its direct and
indirect effects at first limiting the argument
to the period preceding the war.

European activity was not directly incompatible
with Melanesian agriculture, and thus no
direct conflict arose in 'this field, and
information is too vague to permit any precise
description of any indirect effects. We may note,
however that a large number of incompatible ends in
other fields were solved by the use of political
force on the part of the Europeans and by secrecy
and reserve on the part of the Melanesians thus
headhunting was gut down, and men of the
status o f headman or chief hid themselves
from. European eyes by means of puppet
gobetweens. Though we have no dir.ect descriptive

evidence, this must have had indirect effects on agriculture. For instance, the allocation of time must have altered when the. cessation of headhunting or the administrative enforcement of the maintenance of paths is considered. This competitive effect is matched by complementary effects such as the decline in feasts required for headhinting, and therefore in agricultural demand.

The effect of European activity upon resources and the knowledge of means will mainly be considered in relation to techniques and organization, t but we m y record here the way in which connections with the great outside world opened up new choices, and broadened the range of agricultural goods possessed by the natives fruits, such as pineapple, and improved strains of pigs, dogs, and so on. Apart from this, however, we can assume that native resources in particular the availability of land and labour on balance remained very such the same, though we will have more to say in connection with techniques and organization.

European activity had a very marked effect
upon the range of ends and therefore upon the
relation of potential ends to effective ends, and the
efficient achievement of ends, Natives could choose
activity not only by reference to former Melanesian
patterns, but, added to these, there were ends
interpreted from the actions of planters, traders,
officials, and missionaries. These first took on the
form of hopes and desires, and then ns;
they became satisfied became effective demand.
Sometimes activity was directly copied, as when
Queensland labourers adopted clothing; sometimes it
was inculcated, as when missionaries exacted the wearing of
clothing, or when plantation labourers
carried the taste for rice into the villages. The most
significant thing about this, from our present
point of view, is that agriculture became
directly concerned with the achievement of
such ends, in addition to those already existing
through the use of barter and money exchange with the
traders. I think, however, that it is true to say that
before the war there was a fairly steady equilibrium

achieved in this field. European living standards were not particularly high, and hence the range possible desires presented to the natives was limited. It was also limited by the smll range of goods kept in the stores, which hardly altered over fifty or sixty years. This conclusion may have to be modified if we find that the depression and consequent decline in purchasing power caused any frustration.

At the same time we must take note of a number of indirect effects. Thu essential feature of this ne range of ends was that it could be purchased for money, and although agriculture was an important earner of money, it was not the only one. The collection of copra and ivory nuts was rivaled by fishing for trochus shell and bechelemer, and above all by the sale of labour to Europeans, particularly for European agriculture which was in competition with the cash crop element of native agriculture. Since the organization available – minimally small Chinese traders – was not able to pay a goof price for village produce natives preferred on the whole to sell their labour to Europeans than produce themselves. This was in contrast to the New Hebrides where there was about an equal balance between plantation labour and peasant agriculture and New Caledonia where few native labourers needed to work away from villages.

We must also bear in mind the role of agricultural as a complement to and in competition with other ends. In contrast to labourselling agricultural ends were complementary to the satisfaction of those ends connected with village life. The sale of labour competed not only in the market with the sale of peasant copra, but also involved a temporary break with the subsistence element of agriculture and all that went with it even if he remained in

the village men had to adjust his activity
between cash producing and subsistence
agriculture, house building, church
attendance, festivals and the like.

Given this new range of preferences,
certain adjustments were necessary in the
techniques and organization of agriculture.
In connection with resources there has
been an increased tendency for
competition for the ownership of different
kinds of resources and increased
competition of this kind is very largely a
function of scarcity however and since
pressure upon resources has not been great
in the Solomons in relation to their
availability, competition has not been
great enough to involve any radical
departure from old methods. One can
however observe a number of tendencies.
There is thus a tendency for individuals to
extend their concepts of ownership of

land. Not only do they require more land for cashcrops, but land not now in use may have a potential value if Europeans require it for plantations. Individuals are beginning to claim rights over virgin forest, while the rights of the clan decrease as it becomes less organized. Men must now decide whether they will use land for subsistence crops, cattle or coconuts – since pressure on resources is still slight however such questions may be decided by reference to the quality of the land rather than the returns to be expected. Virgin resources are so great that the decision whether to use coconuts for food or for copra is not yet of serious moment.

By the time war had broken out, knowledge of appropriate techniques had not changed much either due to the fact that for most individuals there were other ways of earning cash than by agriculture.

Melanesians were not hard pressed to it;
traditional techniques – almost haphazard
growth of coconuts, smokedrying, and
digging stick for gardens – were quite well
adapted to securing the returns they
required in relation to the effort. It is true
that some individuals impressed not only
by monetary wealth but by the prestige of
doing as the Europeans did, maintained
their own neatly planted plantations and
pastured cattle. But such individuals were
rare. They gave an indication of the way
activity might shape if motives intensified,
but sere otherwise not significant.

Nor have we any reason to believe that
the organization of agriculture change in
any of its essentials. Labour teams
continued to operate in the same manner,
and the role of reciprocity was still
important, even in connections with those
natives who had copied European estates

in their techniques. It is sometimes said that the introduction of money which could be earned by plantation labour altered the balance of wealth from the older people to the younger people; and therefore the structure of authority and leadership, involving agriculture among other things, must have altered. It is true that there must have been some institutional disturbance of g\the equilibrium, but it is also true that by the outbreak of war there had been ample time for a return to the former structure, though based upon money rather than garden produce. Even in early days the accumulation of wealth depended on the energy of the young men, who could obtain wealth and therefore more wives and therefore more wealth. Today the young man works for money, but this gain only provides the initial impetus in a dynamic situation. The young men of 1900 and 1910 have had time to

acquire wealth and the present status of
elders – it will be interesting to note if
their children tend to inherit cash wealth
in addition to other forms of capital, such
as shell string ornaments, and whether the
former egalitarian structure of society
gives way to greater difference in
inherited wealth.

It might be thought that preoccupation
with wage labour must have some effect
upon agriculture, if not through effects
upon resources and organization, then at
least through the altered balance of
available time, If other things had been
equal this certainly would have been the
case; men could have offered labour
services only by sacrificing time spent on
other things including agriculture,
However when we view native life as a
whole it is evident that time can be
diverted from many other things. In

agriculture itself it is now no longer necessary to protect women from armed forays by enemies, and the felling of bush with iron axes is a much shorter operation than heretofore. These savings are probably a little more than balanced by the loss of women and children's work in monogamous households though to decide on this point we would have to now more about the degree to which friends and relatives respond. It is certain that for reasons unconnected with the supply of labour to plantations; the need for time has declined had permitted this supply without serious dislocation. In part this may be due to the moderate number of labourers recruited – about one in thirty population – to the reduction in warfare, fishing, canoe building (in some parts), handicrafts, some ritual activity (perhaps more than balanced by church activity), and the like. It is a pity however that we cannot measure time spent on these activities and the quantity of agricultural produce obtained over a long period of time.

To sum up, the pattern of agricultural activity changed, but not in any great degree. Subsistence agriculture was retained for, in terms of local organization, income, and prices [sic!], it was the most efficient method of achieving the ends for which it was designed. Cash crops were produced mainly as a byproduct product of subsistence labour, fore the demand for money could be satisfied more easily by plantation labour. It is incorrect to say that native agriculture was unprogressive and not competitive considered in relation to possible alternatives. It served its purpose very well. We have no reason to suppose that given an intensity of purpose for which it was not designed it would not have changed. Indeed we can observe something like this happening now, as a result of wartime experience.

Effects of the War

The broad outlines of wartime activity are clear. The Japanese advanced as far south as Tulagi and Guadalcanal and the main body of Europeans evacuated. Cash production came to a standstill. The Japanese remained for only a few months (except for some isolated pockets which were left until the surrender) and did not have any positive influence on the natives who quickly learned to distrust them. After the American counterattack some fled into the bush where they looted gardens and killed most of the livestock in such areas as Gela. The American and New Zealand occupation by scores of thousands of troops lasted for three years and had much more lasting effects. Although the main occupation was concentrated on Guadalcanal, Tulagi, the Russell Islands and New Georgia, troops frequently visited even the most outlying parts while natives from these parts flocked to military areas whenever opportunity arose. Thus effects of the occupation permeated the whole group.

This contact did not originate without mixed feelings.

PAGE MISSING from the original copy

For this are numerous. They had sometimes been told this by a few of the troops with antiimperial ideas. The British exacted prices through the trade stores which were not only contrasted with American and New Zealand generosity but with prewar prices which were much lower. The trade stores only supplied goods which pandered to the bodily tastes of the natives whereas many of them wanted substantial capital goods. In fairness to the administration we must record that these conditions were largely outside their control, being governed by the supply policy of the United States corporation. Finally the administration, with an eye to postwar conditions, refused to increase wages which, though slightly higher than prewar, did not correspond to price levels and were not nearly competitive with prices offered by troops on the black market or by private individuals in the New Hebrides.

The most spectacular result of these and other factors was the organization of a political movement expressing native frustrations which I have described elsewhere.(20) (23) But there are special implications for agriculture and lessons to be learned for its postwar organization. We may now turn to the examination of these.

Implications for the postwas situation

The present situation[61] has the following chief characteristics. Except for a small survey party on Guadalcanal and occasional naval visits, troops have left the area. European planting companies have returned but not on the prewar scale. They are however interested in obtaining labour on the basis of one pound per month plus keep. The price to be obtained for copra f.o.b. is forty to fifty pounds per ton, higher than ever before[62], There are

---

[61] This is 1949.

[62] The Solomons figures however compare unfavourably with the New Hebrides where wages are four to five pounds per month and copra reached a peak last year of

considerable internal and external transport difficulties, partly met by occasional mail shipping from overseas under the control of one of the large trading firms operating widely in the Pacific and by unscheduled interisland trips by small government vessels although there are signs that copra production has been increasing in recent months, recent figures show a serious collapse by comparison with prewar years. Before the war the Solomons constituted one of the chief copra producing areas of the Pacific, exporting about 20.000 tons annually. During the war no copra was produced but employment more than doubled. Since the war copra is produced at a rate of 1,500 tons annually, about $1/13^{th}$ the prewar figure. This does not mean that employment has fallen to $1/13^{th}$ the prewas figure because presumably numbers will

---

seventy pounds.

still be engaged in rehabilitation work, while government services have increased considerably. But it does indicate a considerable loss of income to the Protectorate.

This tremendous slump, following upon such a stimulating boom, is bound to have significance for the future of the economy. Even if we neglect the obvious political danger signals we can deduce the nature of this from our general hypotheses. We can begin by putting on one side direct effects upon resources: since there is no activity of any moment there is no significant pressure upon them. On the other hand there has been advance in technical knowledge among some natives, who have elements of driving, vehicle maintenance, carpentry and the like. This advance has not been thorough enough or widespread enough to involve a real understanding of mechanical techniques but it has, in conjunction with the sight and handling of mechanical contrivances, whetted the appetite for more. It is not safe to assume that techniques have been properly inculcated, but it is clear that the ground has been prepared for their teaching of manufactures. Hitherto during the war these had been obtained at a cost of next to nothing. This will not happen again, even though the Malaita people have built warehouses in expectation of the arrival of the millennium and it will be interesting to see just how elastic is the demand of the native people for these things.

This raises the problem of economic efficiency. We have noted from time to time the great diversity of competing ends in Solomon Islands society, many derived from ancient times, others originating in recent times. Agriculture and its different forms must be judged by the degree to which it satisfies some among these ends and at what sacrifice of alternatives. Only upon such a judgment can successful policy be based.

It is my contention that native village agriculture will satisfy native ends far more fully and at less social cost than most forms of plantation agriculture; though this might not be true if the processing of secondary products became more of a reality. Peasant agriculture enables full participation in village life, the adjustment of the calendar to local needs, the adjustment of economic organization in native patterns, and the desired balance between subsistence and cash crop agriculture. It may be contended that this was true in prewar years but that natives chose to work on plantations instead. But now the balance has moved in the opposite direction. Village life was sacrificed enough during the war. Standards of purchasing power are higher – people will not work except for higher income The question is can peasant copra production be organized to provide higher returns, and can rather more expensive capital goods be introduced to provide the required rewards? The questions I have discussed elsewhere and I will be content here with drawing attention to the problem.

The question of efficiency is also very relevant in considering crops alternative to copra. An instance of this is the rice growing scheme recently introduced by the Agricultural Department. Rice stands high in native estimation, Melanesians have been willing to pay high prices for it, and have been accustomed to it as a choice of food on plantations. It was not grown in native agriculture largely because most were ignorant that it could be grown, and one or two attempts had failed for technical reasons. During the war a large scale rice growing scheme was started by the Agricultural Department on Guadalcanal, which impressed the natives with its possibilities, and in several areas, with administrative encouragement, native plots have been started This however involves a radical departure from old techniques. Not only does rice use some of the best land, but it involves painstaking gathering and intricate methods of dispatch to government stations for husking, while returns vary considerably.

I have not heard whether the scheme is in fact a success. But we can predict a number of problems that are bound to occur. If rice is still available in stores and if natives have the income to pay for it, the purchase of rice will compete with its growing, and, especially since purchase is easy, growing may not become the habit. This possibility may be countered by the presentation of a wider range of goods in the stores, providing competition for the limited amount of money available. Again it is quite possible that if copra production becomes more profitable in the villages through government organization natives will abandon rice cultivation for copra making since presumably they would have to sacrifice leisure.

This is not in the least to suggest that the introduction of rice has been a mistake. On the contrary the above questions of balance are likely to be decided differently in different areas and success in some can be anticipated. The availability of copra producing and rice growing land (and subsistence crop land), the relative efficiency of the organizations set up to buy and process copra and rice, on the communications between stores and villages, on the time available for agricultural pursuits. But these questions do indicate that successful production is an econ, though technical considerations play their part in deciding the economic balance. Moreover the successful production of new crops on an experimental farm is no indication of its possible adoption by the native community: one must consider social and financial costs and the availability of resources locally.

Conclusions

The description of social change in the Solomons had necessarily been brief and lacking in detail. This is largely because anthropological field workers have not been particularly interested in problems of economic choice. It has not been my purpose however to present finely worked out and incontrovertible conclusions. Rather, I hope, I have indicated that economics, which is something very different from technological description, had its part to play in the study of culture change; that socioeconomic problems are of primary importance both in field work and for administrative action; that present day, and even early, Solomon Island society is and has been a competitive one within its sociological framework; and that the present problems of these islands are of considerable significance for anthropology.

Bibliography

(a) References to Solomon Islands

agriculture

(1) L. Verguet Arosi ou San Cristoval et ses habitants, Revue d'ethnographie, 1885.

(2) H.P.Guppy, The Solomon Islands and their natives, Swan Sonnenschein, 1997.

(3) A Penny, Ten years in Melanesia, Wells Gardner Darton, 1887.

(4) H,R. Coidrington, The Melanesians, 1890

(5) Lord Hackney, Discovery of the Solomon Islands in 1568, Hakluyt Society 1901.

(6) Handbook of the British Solomon Islands, Tulagi, 1911.

(7) W.H.R. Rivers,, A History of Melanesian society, Cambridge, 1914.

(8) C.E.Fox, Threshold of the Pacific, Kegan Paul, 1924.

(9) W.G. Ivens, Melanesians of the south Solomons, 1927.

(10) Island Builders of the Pacific, Seeley, 1930

(11) H. I. Hogbin, Culture Change in the Solomons, Oceania, 1934.

(12) The Hill People of North Eastern Guadalcanal, Oceania, 1937.

(13) Social Advancement on

Guadalcanal, Oceania, 1938.
(14) bExperiments in Civilisation, Routledge, 1939
(15) R. Firth, Primitive Polynesian Economy, Routledge, 1939.
(16) J.S. Philips, Coconut Quest, Jarrolds, 1940
(17) C.Y. Shepherd, Report on Agricultural Policy, Fiji, 1944.
(18) C.S. Belsgaw, Economic Development of Gela, (typescript thesis) 1945.
(19) C.Y. Shepherd, Solomon Islands, Tropical Agriculture, 1945.
(20) C.S. Belshaw, Native politics in the Solomon Islands, Pacific affairs, 1957.
(21) C.M.Dzvis, Coconuts in the Russell Islands, Geographical Review, 1947.
(22) E. Ojala, Grassland plains soil of Guadalcanal, New Zealand Journal of Science and technology, 1947.
(23) C.S.Belshaw, The postwar Solomon Islands, Far Eastern Survey, 1948.

(b) Relevant general Works.

(24)   Smith and Pape, Coconuts, Consuls of the East, Tropical Life Publishers, 1913

(25)   F.M. Keesing, Standards of living among native peoples of the Pacific,   1913Pacific Affairs,

(26)   South seas in the Modern world, Institute of Pacific Relations and John Day, 1941

(27)   M.Mead, Role of Small South sea cultures in the postwar world. American Anthropologist, 1943.

(28)   R.G. Brown, Army farms and agricultural development in the south west Pacific, Geographical Review, 1946.

J.W.Coulter, Impact of war on the South Sea islands, Geographical Review, 1946.

The Effects of Limited Anthropological Theory on Problems of Fijian Administration.

First published in Roland Force, ed., *Induced Political Change in the Pacific: a symposium* Bishop Museum Press. 1965.

IN DEALING WITH FIJIAN MATERIALS, it is apparent to any serious research worker that for a colony of its size Fiji has not only been richly endowed with natural resources, but that it has been unusually fortunate in the research interests of its administrative and technical staff. The natural fauna and flora are well known and have been described in considerable scientific detail. Map ping has reached an advanced stage, and exhaustive material has been recorded on such matters as soil types, land tenure, and forest resources. When the Burns Commission on Population and Natural Resources took up its task, it could use as data voluminous studies dealing with a wide range of agricultural material. The census data at its disposal went back to the early years of the colony and reached a high standard of effectiveness in the portrayal of demo graphic trends.

The interest in systematic gathering of data began

early and extended into several social fields. It is not my intention to present a highly documented historical account of the ways in which administrators and others assembled social data, and of the development of the ideas which formed the framework for research, although strictly speaking my thesis would demand such a study. It is my hope, however, that there can be tentative agreement on the main outlines of these developments, sufficient at least to demonstrate that there is a significant hypothesis to be tested by a future social historian.

It is indeed remarkable that the accepted knowledge of Fijian anthro□pology and society has been obtained largely through the work of longterm professional residents, notably administrators and missionaries. One of the most perceptive accounts of land ownership was published by Fison (1880), a mis□sionary, and this itself was largely a protest against interpretations current in the administration of that early time. Men like Henry Balfour (1904), A. B. Brewster (1922), R. H. Lester (1940), G. K. Roth (1953), Basil H. Thom□son (1908) administrators all published scholarly works which provided a more or less consistent view of Fijian society. This view was also reflected in official minutes, surveys, and policy documents. Indeed, one might say that the view began with observations made during official work, which became extended through additional contacts and refined by scholarly ambitions. In□terestingly enough, many of these men were not averse to counting, crude though some of their methods of assessing affinal relationships may seem to presentday theorists.

It would be interesting to know the influence of Hocart (1929, 1931, 1952) in all this. Some of the inquiries, of course, preceded him, and it is at least possible that his interest in anthropology (he was a schoolteacher) was encouraged by his contact with missionaries and administrators of similar broad interests. There is also little doubt that his view of anthropology, and of the nature of societies such as the Fijian, was very similar to that of his colleagues. It was part of the Cambridge tradition of the early century, rein forced by contact between likeminded persons, by formal training during periods of leave, and by discussions with members of the Royal Anthropo logical Institute.

The first nonresident professional anthropologists to spend lengthy peri ods in Fiji were American. Laura Thompson (1940) and Dorothy Spencer (1941) made important contributions, but they were young, the significance of new approaches to field work were still only in the making, and they had to contend with an image of Fijian society which had already become firmly established in the minds of administrators, missionaries, and even Fijians. Only Buell Quain (1948) broke through the limitations the image imposed, but he was fortunate enough to be dealing with a clearly distinct variant of Fijian society and to have a theoretical perspective which forced him to ask new questions.'

It is a little difficult to be sure which came first as a factor influencing the formation of the image of Fiji, the "chicken" of administrative convenience or the "egg" of anthropological theory. The data were certainly scrambled, and many of the questions were posed in ways which could lead only to unsatis factory answers. Yet it is important to realizeand central to my thesisthat whatever the motivations, the questions and answers were consistent with a respectable body of anthropological theory. What is more, when they were related to practice, they worked and could be seen to work. Anthropological ideas and administrative policies were meshed together. Both were posited on the notion that a society described in ideal theoretical terms could and should work in practice; that variations from the ideal represented social impurities which administrative practice should treat with suspicion.

Where anthropology recognized social movement, as it did by implication when it recorded the distribution of variants of custom, it thought of movement toward or away from some stated ideal. Fijian society, in theory as well as by administrative reference, became the society of Bau. If the administrators had succeeded in making Bau the model for all Fijian society, as in effect they tried to do, there would have been little protest from the anthropologists. (As a matter of fact Fison did protest vigorously, which is perhaps why he is little quoted in the later literature.) Even before the advent of formal functionalism, stability was the theoretical norm of society and the ideal of administration. Unfortunately, stability became confused to some degree with stasis.

I shall now set out some of the typical formulations of the static view□point, contrasted with a point of view which incorporates my own personal bias.

There was, for example, the use of myth as social evidence. The relevant myths in this context were those which bore upon the exploits and migrations of social groups. The figures occurring in such myths were sometimes recent ancestors, although they often went back to the days of religious heroes whose descendants populated the islands. The anthropologists used such material to obtain data about social structure as well as migrations. Most of Hocart's work, *Northern States of Fiji* (1952) (note the implications of that choice of title) was of this kind.

There was a tendency to see myth as reflecting actual events of the past, and since there could be only one true description of an event, there could be only one true myth. One task of the anthropologist in dealing with the evidence was to sort out the accepted or valid versions from the peripheral or false ones. The approach had direct relationships with procedures used in the ad□ministration. It became evident very early, for example, that analysis of land ownership depended upon (a) views about the relationship between types of social groups and property, and (b) the validation of the claims of social groups which were based upon settlement and landuse patterns, and thus upon his□torical events which linked the groups to the land. One clearly had to know something about the history of the social groups. To the administrator and juristindeed, to the Western mindthere could be only one history, and the job of the administrator was to unearth it. This was done by a series of highly systematic and wellorganized commissions of inquiry, which used myth as evidence. By public hearing, the commissioners elicited evidence; they assumed that any counterevidence would be forthcoming through the lips of rival witnesses. But supposing there were two versions from two witnesses? There were no clear rules laid down as to how the commissioners should judge between them. But judge they did, for in the interests of administration there could only be one story, one claim to title, recognized. It seems fairly clear that the judgment was based on the social status of the witness, insofar as it could be identified. If one witness were identified as an elder of a senior *mataqali,* his story would prevail over the mythological interpretation of a junior. Lands commissioners in effect decided upon the prevailing social order and recorded a mythology which supported that order.

My own inquiries indicated a very complicated and confused situation. It is clear that the social orderby which I mean in this context the status relations of families and groups, as reflected in claims to propertywas not in fact "fixed" at any time that we know of. Those who had rival stories to tell either lost out in the judicial inquiry because they were temporarily eclipsed, or did not turn up to give evidence because they could foretell the outcome. The inquiries resulted in the recording of land claims, and hence came down on the side of stasis; but behind all these records there have been numerous adjustments based upon social processes which the myth reflected as an out□come, but which were not adequately stated in the text of the myth. Of even greater significance is the fact that the recorded proceedings in most cases merely state the bare bones of the decisions, without indicating the reasons for them or the nature of conflicting evidence. Today many Fijians do not recall myth, believing that it has been recorded for them in the documents of the Native Lands Commission. But here we now find decisions, not mythology, and hence the function of myth as a manipulable social charter has all but disappeared.

Fison was one of the few observers who raised his voice against the aris□tocratic and static interpretations of Fijian society which even in 1880 were beginning to dominate administrative thinking. The *family mataqaliyavusa*□ *– vanua matanitua* hierarchy of social groups was used as a universal interpreta□tion of social structure, and the *mataqali,* somewhat arbitrarily, identified as the landholding unit. Hocart's choice of the term "state" to describe the largest social units reflected somewhat the Westerner's desire to see and interpret permanence for such units, or at least to make them stable. The hereditary element in the acquisition of title and status was emphasized in social analysis to the detriment of the achievement element. The use of Bauan words to describe positions and processes spread through Fiji as administrators exerted their influence on the side of conformity. Sir Ratu Sukuna even compared Fijian society with an emergent feudalism (Mander, 1954). In his analysis of Fijian custom the patrilineal linkages of family were allimportant. Affinal proc☐esses were of course recognized, but their political and propertytransmission implications were almost ignored.

This kind of analysis enabled the administration to achieve particular goals. From the first days of Sir John Thurston's administration,[2] it allied itself with the chiefly families and reinforced their status and powers. It emphasized the communal elements in Fijian society and denigrated the powers of demo☐cratic decision. Building upon the notion of communal duties, it created a whole new superstructure of such obligations. Building upon the notion of dutiful allegiance to one's status superiors, it created an authoritarian Fijian adminis☐tration related to the elite families of traditional position. It was able to impose a uniform and static system of land administration, which regularized jural relationships, although it contributed nothing to economic growth. Through the system of land rents and the stabilization of customary payments, it enabled (in certain areas at least) recognized families to accumulate wealth in the name of tradition. It established a Council of Chiefs which became the aristocratic voice of the Fijian people (although much modified in later years), and it could comfortably rely on the idea that by custom and tradition the people religiously accepted authority. The idea seemed all the more valid because of the absence of any welldefined or organized movement to the contrary. The static, authori☐tarian, aristocratic view of Fijian society thus had profound consequences for the structure and operation of the Fijian administration. But was it a correct view?

This is not the place to present a detailed analysis of my views about Fijian society. But I can at least indicate a number of issues in which my con☐clusions differ radically from those set out about. 1n particular, I shall select those issues in which my data support my bias toward flexibility and adjust☐ment within society rather than stasis. Even here, 1 shall have to content myself with a summary statement.

Firstly, relationships between social groups were highly uncertain and mobile, and the status of family representatives within social groups could be altered by achievement. Despite the static effects of administrative policy, these factors can still be observed in operation today as families and social groups vie with each other for titles, social position, and property. Statements about the nature of social bonds vary according to the position of the person who is speaking. In general, those who have become dependent upon administrative recognition for their family position lean toward a hereditary explanation of that position and an authoritarian interpretation of its power.

Representatives of groups in a somewhat junior position stress the voluntary nature of alliances and of the support of family groups. Thus the Tui Serua, for example, who is himself regarded as a highranking chief, is quite emphatic in his interpretation of his relationship with the Tui Bau as being one not of junior vassal, but of ally. Furthermore, if at any time the Tui Bau wishes to make use of the Tui Serua's forces, the Tui Serua would consider the approach on its own merits. It is likely that the request would be met, but the response would by no means be automatic. Similarly, each of the component groups which at a given point in history provided support for the Tui Serua could withhold its support and even transfer its alliance.

Similar considerations apply to the makeup of the smaller groups such as *mnataqali, yavusa,* and *vanua.* Fijian villages are a patchwork of varying com binations of such units, and they combine in almost every possible permutation for purposes of ceremonial, political, and economic alliance. The nature of such combinations does not derive from the ideal structure set out in the clas sical articles, a structure which is in the minds of most Fijians and easily recognized by them. It depends upon the answers to immediate problems of selfinterest, seen within the context of certain recognized processes. Fison *(1880)* made what at first sight seems to be an unpardonable error. He states that a number of *yavusa* make up *a mataqali.* Normally this is the other way around, and in fact I do not personally know today of any instance in which the *mataqali* do not make up the *yavusa.* Fison's statement can be explained in one of two ways. Perhaps he was confused by the muddled combinations of village residence indicated above, which I must admit is the more likely ex planation. Or else he observed one or more *yavusa* which had shrunk in size without losing *yavusa* status, and alongside of them some *mataqali* which had grown in size and political importance, even perhaps sheltering a former *yavusa,* but which had not yet been accorded the full ceremonial status of a *yavusa. 1* have come across many instances today of similar flexibilities.

In this kind of rapidly adjusting context, myth and

471

ceremony are used to symbolize position. It is necessary and useful to define the relative position of families and groups. A leader wishes to know which of his allies are still with him. An ambitious man gains in status if he can be invested with the ceremonies attendant on rank; such ceremony pays handsome political and economic divi□dends. Thus every ceremony, every myth, is capable of infinite manipulation.

After I had partaken of several scores of the *yaqona* or *kava* ceremonies, early in my field work, and had observed the exchange of hundreds of whale's teeth, to say nothing of the other items of ceremonial exchange, I became quite disillusioned about the treatment of these matters in the literature. I now know, for example, that a man in the position of the late G. K. Roth, a respected and admired colonial administrator who became Secretary for Fijian Affairs, could never in his later career participate in ceremonies other than those he describes in his book *Fijian Way of Life* (1953). Here they are with all their complexity of ceremonial honor, elaborate ritual and pomp, color and sym□bolism. By the same token, I, as a humble field worker without a position in the Fijian hierarchy, could see such ceremonies only as an observer, never as a participant. Yet I, and all my Fijian village acquaintances, took part in so many ceremonies as sometimes to drive me to despair. There was an infinite variety of them, but each variety was carefully manipulated to honor, to em□barrass, to give support to, to jibe at, to reach a policy decision or to prevent in history provided support for the Tui Serua could withhold its support and even transfer its alliance.

Similar considerations apply to the makeup of the smaller groups such as m*alaqali, yavusa,* and *vanua.* Fijian villages are a patchwork of varying com□binations of such units, and they combine in almost every possible permutation for purposes of ceremonial, political, and economic alliance. The nature of such combinations does not derive from the ideal structure set out in the clas□sical articles, a structure which is in the minds of most Fijians and easily recognized by them. It depends upon the answers to immediate problems of selfinterest, seen within the context of certain recognized processes. Fison *(1880)* made what at first sight seems to be an unpardonable error. He states that a number of *yavusa* make up *a mataqali.* Normally this is the other way around, and in fact I do not personally know today of any instance in which the *mataqali* do not make up the *yavusa.* Fison's statement can be explained in one of two ways. Perhaps he was confused by the muddled combinations of village residence indicated above, which I must admit is the more likely ex□planation. Or else he observed one or more *yavusa* which had shrunk in size without losing *yavusa* status, and alongside of them some m*ataqali* which had grown in size and political importance, even perhaps sheltering a former *yavusa,* but which had not yet been accorded the full ceremonial status of a *yavusa. I* have come across many instances today of similar flexibilities.

In this kind of rapidly adjusting context, myth and ceremony are used to symbolize position. It is necessary and useful to define the relative position of families and groups. A leader wishes to know which of his allies are still with him. An ambitious man gains in status if he can be invested with the ceremonies attendant on rank; such ceremony pays handsome political and economic divi□dends. Thus every ceremony, every myth, is capable of infinite manipulation.

After I had partaken of several scores of the *yaqona* or

kava ceremonies, early in my field work, and had observed the exchange of hundreds of whale's teeth, to say nothing of the other items of ceremonial exchange, I became quite disillusioned about the treatment of these matters in the literature. I now know, for example, that a man in the position of the late G. K. Roth, a respected and admired colonial administrator who became Secretary for Fijian Affairs, could never in his later career participate in ceremonies other than those he describes in his book *Fijian Way of Life* (1953). Here they are with all their complexity of ceremonial honour, elaborate ritual and pomp, color and sym□bolism. By the same token, I, as a humble field worker without a position in the Fijian hierarchy, could see such ceremonies only as an observer, never as a participant. Yet I, and all my Fijian village acquaintances, took part in so many ceremonies as sometimes to drive me to despair. There was an infinite variety of them, but each variety was carefully manipulated to honor, to em□barrass, to give support to, to jibe at, to reach a policy decision or to prevent one from being taken, to emphasize that this was an intimate domestic occa□sion, to indicate that the event was in some sense of historical noteone could go on through every type of social relationship and every kind of social situa□tion that called for recognition. The voice of conformist authorityand you hear it speaking time and again in defense of Fijian purismcharacterizes variants as being unworthy of Fijian culture. Yet in my interpretation they are a fundamental part of the living, vital processes which enable Fijian men and women to achieve what they want to achieve by their own subtle, yet incisive, methods.

Consider now land use, land tenure, and the succession of landed prop□erty. The decision to recognize the *mataqali* as the exclusive landholding unit carried with it the recognition of patrilineal succession as paramount. A few of the qualifications of *mataqali* ownership were admitted by the form of rent division which allowed larger groups to exercise a relationship through their leaders. The important rights of individuals and individual families were all but ignored in the formal law, although they are still observed as paramount in Fijian practice. Again, the relationship between ihe groups in respect to a given piece of land is highly variable, depending upon the interplay of selfinterest, sentiment, power, and political ambition, to name a few factors. More sig□nificant is that land use gives a kind of title, and that an individual who gains the use of land without reference to any of the officially recognized procedures nevertheless, in Fijian eyes, cannot be dispossessed except by ingenuity or agreementcertainly not by law or force. Thus the unrecognized principles become important, and these include use of land by agreement following the performance of appropriate ceremonies, and the use of one's wife's or one's mother's land.

Indeed, the manipulation of affinal ties for personal or family advantage is one of the major preoccupations of Fijian life. It has been recognized to some extent in the literature by references to the vasuright principle, in which a man has access to the property of his mother's brother. This, however, is an extreme and not often used principle which can be extended over a much wider variety of relatives and a much greater number of uses. We have so emphasized the patrilineal (political and succession) elements in Fijian society that we have all but ignored the paramount importance and concern of affinal relation□ships. These predominate in the intimate and emotively charged arrangements which accompany the rites of passage. They influence a great deal of dayto□day behavior, including the composition of production teams, visiting, and recreation. And they provide a highly flexible series of links with other com☐munities which cut across the hierarchical patrilineal pyramid. I calculated, for example, that for one small village of 24 households, links established through wives and married sisters provided opportunities for the manipulation of social and property relationships with some 61 other villages scattered throughout Fiji. These did not include other links created through mothers and the secondary relationship of *vasu vata*. Many of these opportunities were fully used.

It is very tempting to argue from these kinds of data that my own type of approach represents an accurate and useful method of building up a more adequate kind of Fijian administration. I suppose that to some extent this is what 1, being human, am trying to say. But this is not the point I wish to make.

An emphasis on processes rather than on structure gives a different kind of a model for social analysis, and I happen to prefer it. I also believe that Fijian society has been limited by an unduly conservative administration, and I am delighted when my analysis and data uncover what seem to me to be principles within the Fijian society which permit a more malleable and flexible approach to administration.

But to say this is not to say that my own analysis is the only accurate analysis. Hocart, Roth, and Sukuna each thought that his own was accurate, and they were able men, at least as well trained for their day as I am for mine. The judgments will be made for tomorrow, not today, and the viewpoint of anthropology will again change and its methods become more refined.•

Let me emphasize the inherent limitation by yet

another example. The most sophisticated anthropological theory today is undoubtedly that which deals with social structure viewed from the basis of kinship organization. The ap☐proaches associated with this interest have had highly significant predictive

value. Writers have been able to uncover new and unsuspected elements in field descriptions, and theorists have been able to make coherent sense out of what seemed to be patchy and untidy field reporting. I have a great deal of faith in these approaches as contributions to theory and regard them as among the most significant achievements of contemporary anthropology.

Certain aspects of Fijian kinship organization have been extremely well reported (see Nayacakalou, 19551957). Scholars such as Rivers (1914, 1924), Hocart (1929, 1931), and Cap ell and Lester (1941, 19451946) have pointed up many details of regional variants, and in so doing have recorded a great many useful data. Indeed, we have more than enough data for theorists to offer some predictions as to the basic model of Fijian society.

We already have some moves in this direction. It is largely accepted, for example, that patrilateral crosscousin marriage is a common if not a modal occurrence. Claude LéviStrauss goes further: he writes

Le systeme fidjien apporte, en tout cas, une indication precieuse. On l'a longtemps consider6 comme un exemple caracteristique du mariage entre cousins croises bilateraux; des etudes recentes limitent et precisent cette interpretation. Les relations entre groupes patrilineaires *mbito,* dans la partie occidentale de Viti Levu, suggereraient assez l'echange generalise; pourtant, et d'une fagon genrale, le mariage des cousins croises serait plus rare qu'il n'a paru jadis,

et il se produirait surtout avec la cousine patrilat6rale. .
. . Comme un patrilateralisme croissant accompagne le
declin de l'echange generalise dans I'Inde, il se
pourrait que la meme manifestation, a Fidji, marquat
la frontiere orientale de l'aire occupee, d'une faqon
predominante, par cette forme d'echange (1949, p.
572).

Again, there is a notion circulating, based on
interpretations inferred from field reports, that Fijian
kinship could be described on the model of a twosection
system. One could argue endlessly about the slender facts
upon which these stories are based, and I shall in another
context introduce field material which would hardly support
the facts or the theories indicated here. But this is not my
major point.

What is essentially at issue here is that theory at the
moment demands that various discrete models be drawn up
for Fijian society. The hope would be that one model would
do, but if regional variants refuse to be consistent with the
model, modifications of the basic model will apply to
various parts of the country.

My own review of the literature and my field
experience lead me to feel that such an approach will be too
limited to be regarded as the most adequate way of dealing
with a society such as that of Fiji. The *takolavi* age grades,
which are among the bases for the idea of a twosection
system, do not, in the area with which I am familiar (the
Baravi coast line), have any effect whatso☐ever on
marriage. They may well do so, however,, in other areas. In
Ruwailevu, despite Capell and Lester (19451946), the
practice and theory of marriage put emphasis today on
bilateral, not patrilateral, crosscousin marriage. Against this
statement, note (1) in other areas patrilateral crosscousin

marriage does seem to exist; and (2) it is probable that a kinship model with crosscousin marriage at its center does violence to the functioning realities of the system of linkage between affinal and patrilineal relatives, which is highly mobile and political in its implications. Again, in certain parts of Nadroga, there is a clearly symbolized and structured system of formal communication between residential and political units, which in this form is quite absent in other parts of Nadroga. And so we could go on, for almost every element in the social system.

If we approach these questions with the views that seem typical of theory at the moment, we do violence to certain issues which are central to the interestsor ought to beof administrators and applied anthropologists. The model of Fijian society must be capable of considering all these things together. This is by no means merely a question of saying that if a man is brought up in Bau he behaves in ways which are different from those which apply in Navosa. Marriage preference is for women from outside the village. The villages con□cerned are from many variants of Fijian culture. In each village, therefore, there is a microcosm of Fijian society. It is a fact of daily importance to a Ruwailevu villager that he can behave with due accuracy and sensitivity toward Bauans, or people from Sigatoka or Serua. Any Fijian has kinship links of importance with people who do not share his model of kinship, if it is inter□preted in puristic terms. This is the reality with which the administrator and the Fijian must deal.

My conclusion, then, is this. Progress in anthropological theory consists in replacing one approximation with another, more useful to answer new ques□tions more adequately. Modern theories are approximations, just as were the older ones, and their limitations will seem strange to us in 20 years. Older theorists helped to lead administrators into policies which, from the vantage point of hindsight, were inadequate and perhaps even damaging. Modern theories may do precisely the same.

Does this mean that the anthropologist and the administrator must each go his own separate way? This certainly is not part of my conclusion. A more refined approximation is surely more useful than a less refined one. But in addi□tion it might well be argued that we should use the test of application a little more in judging the comparative value of theories.

'Acting British Consul, 18671869; Chief Secretary to Cakobau, 1872; Colonial Secretary, 1874; Governor, 18861897. This view is presented in a paper he wrote in 1874. Cf. discussion in Legge, 1958, Ch. VIII.

LITERATURE CITED

BALFOUR, HENRY
   1904. Address to the Anthropological Section.
      British Association for the Ad□vancement of Science (Cambridge). London: Spottiswoode.
BREWSTER, A. B.
   1922. The Hill Tribes of Fiji.
Philadelphia: Lippincott. CAPELL, A., and R. H. LESTER
   1941. "Local Divisions and Movements in Fiji." *Oceania 11:313341; 12:2148. 19451946.* "Kinship in Fiji." *Oceania 15:171200; 16:109143, 234253,*

297318.
FISON, LORIMER
   1880. "Land Tenure in Fiji." *I. Anthropological Inst. Great Britain and Ireland 10:332352.*
HOCART, A. M.
   1929. Lau Islands, Fiji. B. P. Bishop Mus. Bull. 62. Honolulu.
   1931. "Alternate Generations in Fiji." *Man 31(214):222224.*
   1952. Northern States of Fiji. Royal Anthropological Inst. Occ. Pub. No. 11.
LEGGE, J. D.
   1958. Britain in Fiji,
18581880. London: Macmillan.
LESTER, R. H.
   1940. "Betrothal and Marriage Customs of Mbau, Fiji." *Oceania 10:273285.*
LEVIS'I'RAUSS, CLAUDE
   1949. Les Structures L'lementaires de la Parente'. Paris: Presses Univ. de France.
MANDER, LINDEN A.
   1954. Some Dependent Peoples of the South Pacific. New York: Macmillan.
NAYACAKALOU, RUSIATE
   19551957. "The Fijian System of Kinship and Marriage." *J. Polynesian Soc. 64 (1) :4455; 66 (1) :4459.*
QUAIN, BUELL
   1948. Fijian Village.
Chicago: Univ. Chicago Press.
RIVERS, W H. R.
   1914. History of Melanesian Society.

Cambridge. *1924. Social Organization.* London:
Kegan Paul.
ROTH, G. K.
1953. Fijian Way of Life. London: Oxford Univ.
Press.
SAHLINS, MARSHALL
1962. Moala: Culture and Nature on a Fijian Island. Ann Arbor: Univ. Michigan Press.
SPENCER, DOROTHY
1941. Disease, Religion and Society in the Fijian Islands. American Ethnological Soc.
Monogr. *2.*
THOMPSON, LAURA
1940. Southern Lau, Fiji: An Ethnography. B. P.
Bishop Mus. Bull. 162. Honolulu.
THOMSON, BASIL H.
1908. The Fijians. London: Heinemann.

www.ingramcontent.com/pod-product-compliance
Lightning Source LLC
Chambersburg PA
CBHW020330270326
41926CB00007B/117